RAF Bomber Command Profiles

576 Squadron

RAF Bomber Command Profiles

576 Squadron

Chris Ward

www.aviationbooks.org

This edition first published 2025 by Aviation Books Ltd., 25 Cromwell Street, Merthyr Tydfil, CF47 8RY.

Copyright 2025 © Chris Ward.

The right of Chris Ward to be identified as Author of this work is asserted by him in accordance with the Copyright, Designs and Patents Act 1988.

The original Operational Record Book of 576 Squadron RAF and the Bomber Command Night Raid Reports are Crown Copyright and stored in microfiche and digital format by the National Archives. Material is reproduced under Open Licence v. 3.0.

All rights reserved. No part of this publication may be reproduced, stored in a retrieval system, transmitted in any form or by any means, electronic, mechanical, or photocopied, recorded or otherwise, without the written permission of the copyright owners.

This squadron profile has been researched, compiled and written by its author, who has made every effort to ensure the accuracy of the information contained in it. The author will not be liable for any damages caused, or alleged to be caused, by any information contained in this book. E. and O.E.

Every effort is made to trace the copyright holders of photographs and we apologise in advance for any unintentional omissions. These and other errors brought to our attention will be corrected in subsequent editions of this Profile.

Cover design: Topics - The Creative Partnership www.topicsdesign.co.uk

Photos and captions: Clare Bennett

A CIP catalogue reference for this book is available from the British Library.

ISBN 9781915335708

Also by Chris Ward from Bomber Command Books:

Casualty of War: Letters Home from Flight Lieutenant Bill Astell DFC
Dambuster Deering: The Life and Death of an Unsung Hero
Dambusters : The Complete WWII History of 617 Squadron
(with Andy Lee and Andreas Wachtel)
Time Link

Other RAF Bomber Command Profiles:

IX Squadron
10 Squadron (with Ian MacMillan)
12 Squadron (with Pete Colley)
35 (Madras Presidency) Squadron
44 (Rhodesia) Squadron
49 Squadron
50 Squadron
57 Squadron
61 Squadron
75(NZ) Squadron (with Chris Newey)
83 Squadron
90 Squadron (with Shannon Taylor)
101 Squadron
102 (Ceylon) Squadron
103 Squadron (with David Fell)
106 Squadron (with Herman Bijlard)
115 Squadron
138 Squadron (with Piotr Hodyra)
207 Squadron (with Raymond Glynne-Owen)
300 Squadron (with Grzegorz Korcz)
301, 304 and 305 Squadrons (with Grzegorz Korcz)
405 (Vancouver) Squadron RCAF
408 (Goose) Squadron RCAF
455, 458, 462,464 Squadrons RAAF
460 Squadron RAAF
467 Squadron RAAF
514 Squadron (with Simon Hepworth)
550 Squadron
619 Squadron
625 Squadron
626 Squadron (with Pete Colley)
630 Squadron

Contents

Introduction	8
Dedication	10
Narrative History	10
November 1943	11
December 1943	14
January 1944	24
February 1944	32
March 1944	36
April 1944	62
May 1944	68
June 1944	77
July 1944	85
August 1944	127
September 1944	137
October 1944	145
November 1944	154
December 1944	191
January 1945	198
February 1945	204
March 1945	211
April 1945	220
Roll Of Honour	227
Stations	235
Commanding Officers	235
Aircraft	235
Operational Record	235
Aircraft Histories	236

Introduction

RAF Bomber Command Squadron Profiles first appeared in the late nineties and proved to be very popular with enthusiasts of RAF Bomber Command during the Second World War. They became a useful research tool, particularly for those whose family members had served and were no longer around. The original purpose was to provide a point of reference for all of the gallant men and women who had fought the war, either in the air, or on the ground in a support capacity, and for whom no written history of their unit or station existed. I wanted to provide them with something they could hold up, point to and say, "this was my unit, this is what I did in the war". Many veterans were reticent to talk about their time on bombers, partly because of modesty, but perhaps mostly because the majority of those with whom they came into contact had no notion of what it was to be a "Bomber Boy", to face the prospect of death every time they took to the air, whether during training or on operations. Only those who shared the experience really understood what it was to go to war in bombers, which is why reunions were so important. As they approached the end of their lives, many veterans began to speak openly for the first time about their life in wartime Bomber Command, and most were hurt by the callous treatment they received at the hands of successive governments with regard to the lack of recognition of their contribution to victory. It is sad that this recognition in the form of a national memorial and the granting of a campaign medal came too late for the majority. Now this inspirational, noble generation, the like of which will probably never grace this earth again, has all but departed from us, and the world will be a poorer place as a result.

RAF Bomber Command Squadron Profiles are back. The basic format remains, but, where needed, additional information has been provided. Squadron Profiles do not claim to be comprehensive histories, but rather detailed overviews of the activities of the squadron. There is insufficient space to mention as many names as one would like, but all aircraft losses are accompanied by the name of the pilot. Fundamentally, the narrative section is an account of Bomber Command's war from the perspective of the bomber group under which the individual squadron served, and the deeds of the squadron are interwoven into this story. Information has been drawn from official records, such as group, squadron and station ORBs, and from the many, like myself, amateur enthusiasts, who dedicate much of their time to researching individual units, and become unrivalled authorities on them. I am grateful for their generous contributions, and their names will appear in the appropriate Profiles. The statistics quoted in this series are taken from The Bomber Command War Diaries, that indispensable tome written by Martin Middlebrook and Chris Everitt, and I am indebted to Martin for his kind permission to use them.

Finally, let me apologise in advance for the inevitable errors, for no matter how hard I and other authors try to write "nothing but the truth", there is no such thing as a definitive account of history, and there will always be room for disagreement and debate. Official records are notoriously unreliable tools, and yet we have little choice but to put our faith in them. It is not my intention to misrepresent any person or RAF unit, and I ask my readers to understand the enormity of the task I have undertaken. It is relatively easy to become an authority on single units or even a bomber group, but I chose to write about them all, idiot that I am, which means 128 squadrons serving operationally in Bomber Command at some time between the 3rd of September 1939 and the 8th of May 1945. I am dealing with eight bomber groups, in which some 120,000 airmen served, and I am juggling around 28,000 aircraft serial numbers, code letters and details of provenance and fate.

I ask not for your sympathy, it was, after all, my choice, but rather your understanding if you should find something with which you disagree. My thanks to you, my readers, for making the original series of RAF Bomber Command Squadron Profiles so popular, and I hope you receive this new incarnation equally enthusiastically.

My thanks are due, as always, to my other gang member/friends, Andreas Wachtel, photo editor Clare Bennett, Steve Smith and Greg Korcz for their additional support. Finally, my appreciation to my publisher, Simon Hepworth of Aviation Books Ltd for his belief in my work and untiring efforts to promote it.

Chris Ward. Skegness. July 2025.

Dedication

This WWII history of 576 Squadron is dedicated to the memory of Flight Lieutenant William Strachan, who undertook four sorties with the squadron as a pilot in April 1945 before ill health ended his operational career.

Born in Jamaica in 1921, he completed a tour as a gunner on Wellingtons with 156 Squadron, before undergoing pilot training and returning to operations for the final month of the bombing war. His name stands as representative of all who served 576 Squadron in the air or on the ground, particularly those in Bomber Command of non-white ethnicity.

May he and they rest in peace in the knowledge that they served with honour and distinction.

Narrative History

November 1943

At the time of 576 Squadron's formation, 1 Group had been undergoing an expansion programme involving the formation of four new Lancaster squadrons, which would make their presence felt during the newly-launched winter campaign. The long, dark, cloudy nights now enabled Commander-in-Chief, ACM Sir Arthur Harris, to return to his main theme, the destruction of Berlin, Germany's capital city and the seat and symbol of Nazi power. The next four months would bring the bloodiest and hardest-fought air battles between Bomber Command and the Luftwaffe Nachtjagd and test the hard-pressed crews to the limit of their endurance. In a minute to Churchill on the 3rd, Harris had stated, that with the participation of the American 8th Air Force, he could "wreck Berlin from end to end". He estimated that the campaign would cost the two forces between four and five hundred aircraft, but that it would cost Germany the war. This would remove the need for the kind of bloody, expensive and protracted land campaigns, which he had personally witnessed during the Great War, and had prompted him to "get into the air" at the earliest opportunity. It should be remembered that this was the first time in the history of air warfare, that the means existed to prove the theory, that an enemy could be defeated by bombing alone. It is only in the light of more recent experiences, that we have learned of the need, in a conventional conflict at least, to occupy the enemy's territory to secure submission. The Americans, however, were committed to victory on land, where film cameras could capture the glory, and would not accompany Harris to Berlin.

1 Group's new squadrons were 625, which had been formed at Kelstern on the 1st of October, 626 at Wickenby on the 7th of November and 550 and 576 at Grimsby (Waltham) and Elsham Wolds respectively on the 25th of November. Each was spawned by an existing squadron, 100 Squadron at Grimsby responsible for 625 and 550, 12 Squadron for 626, and 103 Squadron for 576. The intention was that the new squadrons would hit the ground running with their experienced crews, 576 Squadron benefitting from thirteen, along with nine Lancasters, which would be posted across the tarmac from 103 Squadron's C Flight on the 27th to become the new squadron's B Flight under the command of S/L Mervyn Attwater. S/L Attwater had joined 100 Squadron in the rank of flight lieutenant in August 1943, before being posted as a founder member of 625 Squadron and serving very briefly as a flight commander, undertaking a single operation before moving on again to 103 Squadron.

A Flight, commanded by S/L Dilworth, consisted initially of four crews posted in from 101 Squadron at Ludford Magna, the numbers to be made up of largely inexperienced crews from the conversion units, with, perhaps, one or two pilots and crew members embarking on a second tour. S/L Dilworth was an Australian, whose operational career had begun at 101 Squadron during its Wellington days in October 1942. When 460 Squadron's commanding officer was forced to undergo hospital treatment in December 1942, S/L Dilworth had been parachuted in on promotion to acting wing commander rank to succeed him and remained in post until February 1943, when reverting to acting squadron leader rank on posting to 1662 Conversion Unit. In August he re-joined 101 Squadron as a flight commander, until finding himself on the move again to 576 Squadron, for what would be another brief period of service.

In overall command was W/C Gareth Clayton DFC, who had begun the war as a flight commander at 107 Squadron, flying Blenheims under the command of the legendary W/C Basil Embry until June 1940. In May 1943 he learned to fly the Lancaster, before serving briefly as a flight commander at 100 Squadron, and arrived for duty at Elsham Wolds from his post as commanding officer of the Aircrew Pool at Hemswell.

In March, Bomber Command had introduced a Base system, in which a main station controlled two or three satellites for the purpose of greater efficiency. 11 Base was home to the stations occupied by the conversion units and Lancaster Finishing schools, 12 Base encompassed the main station at Binbrook (460 Squadron RAAF), and the satellites at Grimsby (100 Squadron) and Kelstern (625 Squadron), 13 Base comprised Elsham Wolds (103 and 576 Squadrons), Kirmington (166 Squadron) and North Killingholme (550 Squadron), while the 14 Base main station was Ludford Magna (101 Squadron), with Faldingworth (300 Polish Squadron) and Wickenby (12 and 626 Squadrons) as the satellites. 15 Base would be formed in October 1944 on former 5 Group stations at Fiskerton, Hemswell and Scampton.

Harris's assault on Berlin had begun in earnest with two major operations in late August and a third in early September, none of which achieved the hoped-for destruction and cost a combined total of 125 aircraft. During an autumn break from Berlin, probably prompted by the scale of the losses, greater success had been achieved against the twin cities of Mannheim and Ludwigshafen, and at Hannover and Kassel, but now the time was right to resume the Berlin offensive, and by the time of 576 Squadron's formation, three operations against Germany's capital city had already taken place, on the nights of the 18/19th, 22/23rd and 23/24th. The two latter attacks had been outstandingly successful and resulted in massive destruction but had also led to the withdrawal of the Short Stirling from operations over Germany. For the second-mentioned raid, the long-standing practice of allocating aircraft types to specific waves had been abandoned, allowing aircraft of all types to be spread throughout the bomber stream, which by the very nature of its short-wing design, exposed the lower-flying Stirling to the risk of being hit by bombs from the Lancaster and Halifax elements. Harris had never liked the Stirling anyway because of its lack of development potential and weak undercarriage, and a segmented bomb bay that prevented it from carrying a calibre of bomb larger than a 2,000-pounder. The Stirling was operated only by 3 Group, and Harris had already restricted the type's proliferation by posting out of 3 Group the Wellington units, 9, 57 and 101 Squadrons at the point when they were due to convert, sending them to the Lancaster-equipped 1 and 5 Groups.

On the night of 576 Squadron's formation and while 1, 3 and 5 Groups enjoyed a night off, 216 Halifaxes of 4 and 6 Groups and forty-six 8 Group Halifaxes and Lancasters carried out an operation against Frankfurt, where the blind markers established a firm H2S (ground-mapping radar) fix and delivered yellow target indicators (TIs) and red flares with green stars to coincide with the estimated time of arrival of the main force crews. Local reports described a modest amount of housing damage and 3,500 people bombed out of their homes, in return for which, eleven Halifaxes and a single Lancaster failed to return.

After a three-night rest for most of the Lancaster crews, 443 of them were briefed on the 26th for a return to the "Big City", Berlin, for the fourth attack since the resumption of the campaign. 1 Group detailing 153 Lancasters for the main event. Included in that number were eight representing 550

Squadron at Grimsby, just a day after its formation, while six ABC (Airborne Cigar) Lancasters of 101 Squadron joined a diversionary raid on Stuttgart to provide radio countermeasures cover (RCM) for a predominantly Halifax force of 178 aircraft. The plan called for the two forces to follow the same route, which involved an outward leg across the French coast and Belgium to a point north of Frankfurt, where they would diverge to their respective targets. 103 Squadron made ready a record thirty Lancasters, which the operations record book (ORB) suggested, as far as could be ascertained, was also a Bomber Command record and loaded those in the first phase with a cookie (4,000lb blockbuster) and six 1,000-pounders and the remainder with a cookie, twelve small bomb containers (SBCs) of 4lb incendiaries and seven of 30lbs. They departed Elsham Wolds between 16.57 and 17.31 with S/Ls Attwater, Scragg and Whittet the senior pilots on duty and set course for Beachy Head to begin the Channel crossing in what was a most unusual detour for an operation to north-eastern Germany.

An indication of the beneficial effects of the three-day lay-off was a 40% reduction in early returns compared with the previous Berlin raid, but there would still be fourteen among the 1 Group participants, including three of the 103 Squadron contingent. The others were spread among the first three waves in the bomber stream and found Berlin under clear skies, but despite the favourable conditions, the Path Finders overshot the city centre aiming point by six or seven miles and by a stroke of luck marked the Siemensstadt and Tegel areas well to the north-west, which happened to contain many war-industry factories. The Elsham Wolds crews bombed on red and green TIs from 16,000 (S/L Scragg) and 23,000 feet between 21.13 and 21.44 and on return spoke of a mass of fires and thick smoke rising to 15,000 feet. Night-fighters got amongst the bombers on the way home, and twenty-eight Lancasters failed to return, including three from 103 Squadron. It would be learned later that thirty-eight war-industry factories had been destroyed and many others damaged in the Siemensstadt and Tegel districts.

On the 27th, S/L Attwater led C Flight across Elsham Wolds' tarmac to the 576 Squadron site, and the new squadron would spend the next three days gathering equipment and welcoming air and ground personnel in preparation for going to war. There had been an airfield close to the current site since the Great war, but the new one opened in July 1941 with 103 Squadron as its first resident unit. It boasted three runways, the largest of two thousand yards, two T2 hangars and one J-Type and thirty-six concrete dispersal pans. Its location high on an escarpment within ten miles of the Humber estuary exposed it to bracing winds off the North Sea and sometimes sea fog, which, during the winter, chilled the bones of the many Australians who called it home at a time when back in Australia, their countrymen were basking in heat and enjoying Christmas on the beach. An Australian navigator, F/L Don Charlwood, serving with 103 Squadron during 1942 and 1943, described the highs and lows of life at Elsham Wolds in his book, No Moon Tonight, a classic of wartime literature.

The new squadron was alerted to the possibility of launching its operational career on the 30th, when Munich was posted as the target, but the weather caused a cancellation, and both squadrons were stood down. Having now spawned two new Lancaster squadrons, 103 Squadron reverted to a standard two-flight unit and the two squadrons would now live and operate side-by-side until October 1944.

December 1943

Berlin would continue to be the dominant theme during December, and as November had ended, so December began. A heavy force of 443 aircraft stood ready to take off in the late afternoon of the 2nd, all but fifteen of them Lancasters, after the main Halifax element had been withdrawn because of fog over their Yorkshire stations. 1 Group contributed 144 Lancasters and would benefit on this night from the operational debut of 576 Squadron, which loaded each of its seven Lancasters with a cookie and eighteen SBCs of 4lb and 30lb incendiaries. They departed Elsham Wolds between 16.49 and 17.10 with F/O Richards the only commissioned pilot on duty and after climbing out, left Mablethorpe behind them to rendezvous over the North Sea with the rest of the force for a straight-in-straight-out route across Holland and northern Germany with no feints or diversions. First, however, the crews had to negotiate a towering front of ice-bearing cloud over the North Sea, which would contribute to a 10% rate of early returns, eighteen alone from 1 Group, 576 Squadron represented by the crews of W/O Bassett and Sgt Whalley, both of whom suffered an engine failure. Having pushed through the challenging conditions, those making it to the target area found themselves mostly south of track after variable winds had thrown them off course and dispersed the bomber stream. They also had to contend with large numbers of enemy night-fighters that would harass the bombers all the way to the target, after the controller had been able correctly to predict it. The Path Finders employed H2S to establish their position at Stendal, but had strayed some fifteen miles south of track and mistakenly used the town of Genthin as their reference for the run-in. The 576 Squadron Lancasters were spread among the three waves and found good visibility as they were guided by release-point flares to the aiming point, where they encountered a thin layer of two to three-tenths cloud at around 5,000 feet but up to nine-tenths at between 10,000 and 12,000 feet, which the searchlights were able to pierce. They bombed on skymarkers and red and green TIs and where possible ground detail, like burning streets, from 20,000 feet and above, based on the 103 Squadron ORB, at sometime between 20.10 and 20.45, and reported scattered fires and a number of large explosions. Some claimed the glow was still visible on the horizon from 120 miles into the homeward leg.

It was a bad night for the bomber force, which lost forty aircraft, mostly in the target area and on the way home, and among them were four from Elsham Wolds, three representing 103 Squadron, and W4337 belonging to 576 Squadron. With the exception of the RAF flight engineer, F/Sgt Booth and his crew were all members of the RAAF, and none survived the crash near Mönchengladbach. Some returning crews made reference to the amount of light flak and "scarecrows", the latter a myth, belief in which was encouraged by higher authority in the interests of maintaining morale, claiming them to be special anti-aircraft shells designed by the Germans to simulate a bomber exploding to cause maximum disquiet among the rest of the force. No such shells existed, and each "scarecrow" was in reality a bomber torn asunder as its bomb load went up, but at a time when authority was rarely questioned, the belief flourished and many a veteran went to his grave convinced in the voracity of the story and the existence of the device. Bombing photographs suggested that the raid was only partially successful, causing useful damage in industrial districts in the west and east, but scattering the main weight of bombs over the southern districts and outlying communities to the south.

Having been spared by the weather from experiencing an effective visitation from the Command in October and exploiting the enemy expectation that Berlin would be the target again, Leipzig found itself at the end of the red tape on briefing-room wall-maps from County Durham to Cambridgeshire on the 3rd. A force of 527 aircraft was made ready, which included ninety-six Lancasters of 1 Group, six of them belonging to 576 Squadron, each receiving a bomb load of a cookie and eighteen SBCs of incendiaries before departing Elsham Wolds between midnight and 00.10 with F/O Leeder the only commissioned pilot on duty. On the previous night, a number of Australian war correspondents had lost their lives in aircraft belonging to 460 Squadron RAAF, and on this night the well-known American broadcaster, Ed Murrow, bravely hitched a lift in a 619 Squadron Lancaster at Woodhall Spa. The 576 Squadron element set course for the Dutch coast near Haarlem, rendezvousing with the bomber stream over the North Sea and losing the services of W/O Graham and crew to engine failure on the way. The bomber force was routed north of Hannover and Braunschweig (Brunswick) as if heading for Berlin, with an hour's journey to Leipzig still ahead, and as it turned towards the south-east with ten-tenths cloud beneath, the Mosquito element continued on to carry out a diversion at the capital.

Night-fighters had already infiltrated the stream at the Dutch coast, but the feint appeared to have the desired effect as few night-fighters were encountered in the target area, where two layers of ten-tenths cloud prevailed with tops at around 7,000 and 15,000 feet. Meanwhile, the Path Finders had marked by H2S with green skymarkers (parachute flares coded "Wanganui"), and the 576 Squadron crews bombed on these from 20,000 and above sometime between 04.00 and 04.15, observing explosions and a strong glow beneath the clouds. The emergence through the cloud tops of black smoke suggested that an accurate and concentrated attack had taken place, and the smoke and glow remained visible for 150 miles into the return journey on a south-easterly track towards the French frontier. Had many aircraft not then strayed into the Frankfurt defence zone, the losses may have been fewer, but twenty-four aircraft failed to return, fifteen of them Halifaxes. At debriefings, there were reports that around twenty cookies had been dumped in the North Sea just beyond the convoy lanes at 01.22, and these were 1 Group crews, who were shedding their largest bomb in protest at their A-O-C's policy of loading each Lancaster to its maximum all-up weight at the expense of altitude. AVM Rice had conducted tests to ascertain the maximum weight of bombs before the undercarriage began to buckle while taxiing, and it proved to be a counter-productive move, particularly when the slogan "H-E-I-G-H-T spells safety" could be found on the walls of most bomber station briefing rooms. Among twenty-four missing aircraft were just three from the ranks of 1 Group, including 576 Squadron's JB550, which crashed some ten miles south-east of the city of Jena with no survivors from the crew of F/Sgt Matthews. Local reports confirmed this as a highly successful operation, which had hit residential and industrial areas, and was the most destructive raid visited upon this eastern city during the war. Sadly, for the Command, it would take its revenge in time.

On the 5th, S/L Attwater found himself in hospital having his fractured jaw attended to, the ORB failing to elaborate on the cause of the injury but noting that F/O Richards had stepped temporarily into the breach to perform the role of B Flight commander.

Thereafter, adverse weather conditions kept most aircraft on the ground and minor operations carried the Command through to the 16th, when the Lancaster stations were roused to prepare 483 aircraft for that night's operation to Berlin for the sixth time since the resumption of the campaign. 1 Group put up 167 Lancasters, nine of them representing 576 Squadron, each loaded with a cookie and the usual quantity and mix of 4lb and 30lb incendiaries. They departed Elsham Wolds between

16.20 and 16.55 with no senior pilots on duty, and as they climbed into cloud, F/Sgt Scott's LM322 collided with JB670 of 103 Squadron and both Lancasters crashed at Ulceby, some three miles east-north-east of the airfield without survivors. *(There are two villages called Ulceby in Lincolnshire, one near Kirmington in the north and the other near Horncastle. The reference in Bill Chorley's Bomber Command Losses to the latter is incorrect.)* What would become known as "Black Thursday" had already begun badly and would end even more tragically. Probably unaware of the incident, the others set course via Mablethorpe for the Dutch coast near Castricum-aan-Zee, joining up with the bomber stream on the way across the North Sea and losing the services of F/Sgt Marsden and crew to an oil-pressure issue in one of the port engines.

Once over enemy territory the bomber stream headed due east all the way to the target with no deviations, knowing that a three-quarter moon would rise during the long return leg over the Baltic and Denmark, and that the very early take-off and the expectation of fog to keep the enemy night-fighters on the ground would reduce the risk of interception. Night-fighters were sent to meet the bomber stream at the Dutch coast, but the 576 Squadron element remained unmolested and pressed on to find Berlin obscured by ten-tenths cloud with tops at around 5,000 feet. The squadron ORB is scant on detail, but we know from other sources that the target was identified by red and green skymarkers, which were bombed by the 576 Squadron participants from 20,000 to 23,000 feet sometime between 20.00 and 20.10, after which the return over Denmark passed largely without major incident. Unfortunately, the greatest difficulties awaited the 1, 6 and 8 Group crews as they arrived home to find their airfields covered by a blanket of dense fog. With little reserves of fuel, the tired crews began a frantic search for somewhere to land, stumbling blindly through the murk to catch a glimpse of the ground, which for many proved fatal, while others gave up any hope of landing and abandoned their aircraft.

It was a bad night for 1 Group, which, in addition to the tragic collision between the Elsham Wolds Lancasters, had twenty others return early and sixteen crash on return, 100 and 101 Squadrons each losing four with heavy loss of life and 460 Squadron RAAF three. 576 Squadron's W/O Bassett and crew managed to get down at Wickenby, where JA957 crashed without injury to the occupants but sustained category B damage, which required its removal to a maintenance unit. These casualties were on top of the twenty-five Lancasters failing to make it back from Berlin, many of them accounted for by night-fighters over Holland and Germany while outbound, but 576 Squadron's DV342 crashed at Lichtenberg, five miles east-north-east from the centre of Berlin with no survivors from the crew of F/O McAra. In all, twenty-nine Lancasters and a mine-laying Stirling were lost in crashes at home, and more than 150 airmen killed in these most tragic of circumstances. Local sources in Berlin reported that a moderately effective raid had taken place, which had fallen principally onto central and eastern districts, where housing suffered most.

A three-day stand-down allowed the crews to recover from the Berlin operation, and it was the 20th when all stations were notified of a raid that night on Frankfurt, for which a force of 390 Lancasters and 257 Halifaxes was assembled. It was becoming routine for the enemy night-fighter controllers to plot Berlin as the destination for large bomber fleets, and perhaps that is why Harris selected an alternative target. A southerly approach to Berlin would take the force past Frankfurt to the north, as had been the case with the recent operation, when Stuttgart had been used as a diversion. The intention was to keep the enemy guessing as to the final destination, Stuttgart, Munich, Mannheim or Frankfurt in the south, or Kassel, Hannover, Braunschweig, Magdeburg or

Berlin to the north. If not deceiving the enemy entirely, the ploy might dilute the strength of the night-fighter numbers brought to bear, and on this night a small 8 Group diversionary raid was to take place at Mannheim.

1 Group made ready 107 Lancasters for the main event and thirty to assist the Path Finders in the diversionary raid by forty-four Lancasters and ten Mosquitos on Mannheim forty miles to the south. At Elsham Wolds, seven 576 Squadron Lancasters were loaded with the standard cookie and incendiary mix and dispatched between 16.50 and 17.05 again with no senior pilot on duty. W/O Frost and crew suffered an electrical failure during the climb-out and proceeded directly to the jettison area, and they would be joined on the ground by the crews of P/Os Jones and Young, who had also been let down by electrical and engine issues. The others set course for Sheringham on the Norfolk coast and the North Sea-crossing to the Scheldt estuary, before passing north of Antwerp and flying the length of Belgium to the German frontier north of Luxembourg. W/O Rollins and crew were over Belgium when an engine issue persuaded them to turn back and they bombed what appeared to be an aerodrome south-east of Mechelen as a last-resort target. The German night-fighter controller had picked up transmissions from the bomber stream as soon as it left the English coast and was able to track it all the way to the target and vector his fighters into position, many combats taking place during the outward flight, and the diversion failing to draw fighters away from the main action. The problems continued at the primary target, where the forecast clear skies failed to materialise, and the crews were greeted by four to nine-tenths cloud at between 5,000 and 10,000 feet. This allowed some of them to pick out ground features, while others fixed their positions by H2S, if so equipped, and the main force Lancaster crews simply waited for TIs on e.t.a.

The Path Finders had prepared a ground-marking plan in expectation of good vertical visibility and dropped red, green and yellow TIs, while the Germans lit a decoy fire-site five miles to the south-east of the city. Some crews described the marking as late and erratic, but those representing 576 Squadron found red and green TIs to aim at from 20,500 to 23,000 feet either side of 19.45 and 19.51. Most thought the attack to be scattered in the early stages, becoming more concentrated as it progressed, and many commented on the new cookies detonating with a brighter flash than the old ones and the glow of fires remaining visible for 150 miles into the return journey. Any success was achieved largely as the result of the creep-back from the decoy site falling across the suburbs of Offenbach and Sachsenhausen, situated on the southern bank of the River Main. Creep-back was a feature of most large raids, in which main force crews bombed the first fires they came upon, rather than press on to the briefed aiming point, and this resulted in bombs falling progressively further from the target on the line of approach. On this night, 466 houses were destroyed and more than nineteen hundred seriously damaged, rendering 23,000 thousand people homeless. Many cultural, historical and public buildings were also hit, despite which, the operation fell well short of its aims, and the loss of forty-one aircraft was a high price to pay. The Halifaxes suffered heavily, losing twenty-seven of their number, a loss-rate of 10.5%, compared with 3.6% for the Lancaster. The return of 576 Squadron's W4123 was awaited in vain, and it was learned eventually via the Red Cross that it had been shot down over Belgium with no survivors from the crew of Sgt Ball.

Just two more operations remained before the year ended and both were to be directed against Germany's capital city. The first was posted on the 23rd and involved an all-Lancaster heavy force with seven Halifaxes among the Path Finder element and eight Mosquitos to provide a diversion. The 128 Lancasters of 1 Group included eight representing 576 Squadron, each of which received a bomb load of a cookie and eighteen assorted SBCs of 4lb, 30lb and 40lb incendiaries, before lifting into the cold night air between 23.50 and 00.32 with F/L Smith the senior pilot on duty and a Sgt Benjamin Frazier, a US Army war correspondent, flying as a guest with F/O Morgan and crew. They exited the English coast at Sheringham and adopted a somewhat circuitous route that took the bomber stream in a south-easterly direction to the Scheldt estuary, before hugging the Belgian/Dutch frontier to cross into Germany south of Aachen, as if threatening Frankfurt. When a point was reached south of Leipzig, the route turned sharply towards the north and Berlin, while the Mosquito feint threatened Leipzig. The vanguard of the bomber stream reached the target to find it enveloped in up to eight-tenths cloud at between 5,000 and 10,000 feet, which might not have been critical had the Path Finders not suffered an unusually high failure rate of their H2S equipment. This resulted in scattered and sparse marking with red and green skymarker flares at which the 576 Squadron crews aimed their bombs from 20,000 to 23,000 feet, based on the 103 Squadron timings between 04.03 and 04.18. Well-concentrated fires were observed and at least four large explosions, one described as orange and red and lasting for thirty seconds.

A relatively modest sixteen Lancasters failed to return, but among them were 576 Squadron's ED713 and ED913, the former, captained by P/O Hughes, crashing in deep snow in a heavily wooded area near Hannover with three survivors, who were taken into captivity. The latter was brought down in the Berlin defence zone, killing F/O Richards and six others, while the bomb-aimer survived to become another guest of the Reich. A local report named the south-eastern suburbs of Köpenick and Treptow as sustaining the most damage, with 287 houses and other buildings suffering complete destruction. The above-mentioned Sgt Frazier wrote the following account of the raid, which was published in "Yank" magazine.

"Night plane to Berlin". By Sgt Ben Frazier, "Yank" staff correspondent.
England – A small village lay tucked away in the fold of a valley, just below the high, windswept, bleak plateau where a Lancaster bomber station was situated. Housewives were busy in the kitchen preparing food, and the men had left their ploughing to come in for the noon-day meal. In the lichen-covered Gothic church, the minister's wife was arranging decorations and placing on the altar freshly-cut chrysanthemums that had managed to escape the north winds and were still blooming in December.
The placidness of the village life was in sharp contrast to the bustling activity at the airfield. It seemed as remote from war as any hamlet could possibly be, although the provident farmers, living so close to an obvious military target, had wisely provided themselves with shelter trenches at the edge of each ploughed field. Nevertheless, the name of this quiet, lovely village had spread far. By borrowing it, the bomber station had made it one to strike terror into the heart of the Nazi High Command.
At the airfield V for Victor's crew lounged around B Flight office waiting to see if operations were on. They kept looking up into the sky as if trying to guess what the weather was going to be like. Some of the men chuckled, "Papa Harris is so set on writing off the big city that he hardly even notices the weather," one of them said, "the last time, there were kites stooging around all over the place. The met boobed that one." It was a strange new language. What the airman was saying was that the last time out, the meteorological men had given a wrong steer on the weather, and

the planes had been all over, looking for the field, on the return trip. "Papa Harris was Air Chief Marshal Harris, chief of Bomber Command.

V for Victor's captain came back from the operations room with the news that there would be ops. That settled the discussion. You seemed to be aware, without noticing anything in particular, of a kind of tension that gripped the men, like they were pulling in their belts a notch or two to get set for the job ahead.

And with the news, everybody got busy, the aircrews, the ground crews, the mechanics, the WAAFs, the cooks. The ships already had a basic bomb and fuel load on board, and the additional loads were sent out in ammunition trailers and fuel trucks. The perimeter track lost its usual deserted appearance and looked like a well-travelled highway, with trucks and trailers, buses and bicycles hurrying out to the dispersal points. It was just like the preparation at any bomber base before taking off for enemy territory – but going over the big city was something different. These men had been there before. They knew what to expect.

In the equipment room, June, the pint-sized WAAF in battledress, was an incongruous note. Over a counter as high as her chin, she flung parachutes, harnesses and Mae Wests. The crews grabbed them and lugged them out to the ships. You kept thinking they ought to be able to get somebody a little bigger for the job she was handling.

In the briefing room, the met officer gave the weather report and the forecast over enemy territory. There would be a considerable cloud over the target. The men grinned. An operations officer gave a talk on the trip. The route was outlined on a large map of Germany on the front wall. It looked ominously long on the large-scale map. He pointed out where the ground defences were supposed to be strong, and where fighter opposition might be expected. He gave the time when the various phases should be over the target. He explained where the "spoof" attacks were to be made, and the time. He told the men what kinds of flares and other markers the Pathfinders would drop. There was the usual business of routine instructions, statistics and tactics to be used. The Group Captain gave a pep-talk on the progress of the battle of Berlin. And all the while, that tape marking the route stared you in the face and seemed to grow longer and longer.

Outside, it was hazy and growing more so. But this was nothing new. The men were convinced that the weather was always at its most variable and its dampest and haziest over their field. What could you expect? Ops would probably be scrubbed after all. Hell of a note.

In the fading light the planes were silhouetted against the sky. They looked, on the ground, slightly hunched and menacing like hawks. Seeing them there, in the half-light, you would never guess how easy, and graceful they are in flight. Nor would you realize when you saw them soaring off the runway, what an immense load they take up with them. It is only when you see the open bomb bay, on the ground, that you get some idea of a Lancaster's destructive power. The open bomb bay seems like a small hangar. The 4,000lb blockbuster in place looks like a kitten curled up in a large bed. It is a sobering sight.

In the evening a few of the men tried to catch a few winks; most of them just sat around talking. The operational meal followed. It was only a snack, but it was the last solid food anyone would get until the fresh egg and bacon breakfast, which has become a ritual for the proper ending of a successful mission.

As there was still some time to wait before take-off, V for Victor's crew sat around the ground crew's hut near the dispersal point, warming themselves by the stove or chewing the rag with the ground crew.

The Wingco came around to make a last-minute check-up. The medical officer looked everyone over. The engineer officer checked the engines.

The minutes crept by until at last the time came to get into the planes. The deep stillness of the night was awakened by the motors revving up, one after another, until each one was lost in the general roar. The crews scrambled into the planes and took their places. The great ships were guided out of their dispersal area by the ground crews, who gave a final wave as the Lancs moved off slowly down the perimeter track. They appeared more menacing than ever creeping along in the dark with their motors roaring.

One by one they turned into the runway and noisily vanished into the night.

From now on until they would return, the members of V for Victor's crew were a little world in themselves, alone and yet not alone. For all around them were other similar little worlds, hundreds of them, each with a population of seven, hurtling through space, lightlessly – huge, animated ammunition dumps. For its safety, each little world depended utterly and completely on its members – and a large dash of luck.

There was not much conversation over the intercom. When you're flying without running lights on a definite course, and surrounded by several hundred other bombers, you have no time for any pleasantries. The navigator was busy checking the air speed and any possible drift. Almost everyone else kept a lookout for other aircraft, both friend and foe. A friendly aircraft is almost as dangerous as an enemy plane, for, if two blockbusters meet in mid-air, the pieces that are left are very small indeed.

Occasionally the ship jolted from the slipstream of some unseen aircraft ahead, and frequently others overhauled V for Victor, passing by to port and starboard, above and below. V for Victor gained altitude very easily to maximum ceiling. She was a veteran of over 50 ops and had the DFC painted on her port bow to celebrate the fiftieth, but she had the vitality of a youngster. Blondy, the wireless operator, broke the silence. "Taff, the W/T had gone U/S."(the wireless is unserviceable).

The wireless is not used, except in an emergency such as ditching, but it is nice to know it's there. We went on. Occasionally, Taff, the pilot, would call into the intercom, Bob, are you OK?" There would be a silence for a moment while the rear gunner fumbled to turn on his intercom, until you wondered if he had frozen back there. Then, he'd sing out, "OK, Taff." He and the mid-upper gunner were the only two outside the heated cabin. Inside the cabin it was warm and snug. You didn't even need gloves. Jock, the navigator, wore no flying gear, just the Air Force battledress.

Up ahead the Pathfinder boys dropped the first route marker, flak shot up into the air, and the men knew that V for Victor was approaching the Dutch coast. An enormous burst of flame lit up to night off to port. "Scarecrow to starboard, the mid-upper gunner reported on the intercom. Jerry intended the "scarecrow" to look like a burning plane, but it did not take long to see that it was not.

Jock's Scotch accent came over the intercom. "Taff", we're eleven minutes late." "OK, we'll increase speed." The engineer pushed up the throttles. Everything was black again below. Occasionally, there was a small burst of flak here and there. "Plane to starboard below." "OK, it's a Lanc." As V-for Victor passed it you could see the bluish flames from the exhaust lighting the aircraft below in a weird ghostly manner. It was unpleasant to realize that our own exhausts made V for Victor just as obvious as the other plane. Away off to port bow a glow became visible. It looked like the moon rising, but it was the first big German searchlight belt, encompassing many cities. The beams were imprisoned under the cloud. "That will be Happy Valley" (the Ruhr), Jack said. Another route marker appeared ahead. "Tell me when we are over it," the navigator replied. Shortly, the bomb-aimer said, "we're bang over it now." "Taff, we're nine minutes late.

The navigator took a couple of astro sights to get a fix. From this he could determine the wind and the drift of the plane. Another searchlight belt showed up to starboard. It was enormous, running for miles and miles. It was all imprisoned under the cloud, but it was an evil-looking sight just the same. The top of the clouds shone with millions of moving spots, like so many restless glow worms, but the impression was much more sinister – like some kind of luminous octopus. The tentacle-like beams groped about seeking some hole in the cloud, some way of clutching at you as you passed by protected by the darkness. The continuous motion of the searchlights caused a rippling effect on the clouds, giving them an agitated, angry, frustrated appearance. Once in a while, one found a rift and shot its light high into the sky. Flak came up sparkling and twinkling through this luminous blanket. V for Victor jolted violently from a close burst but was untouched. It passed another Lanc, which was clearly silhouetted against the floodlit clouds.

Another leg of the trip was completed. The navigator gave the new course over the intercom and added, "Seven minutes late." "OK, Jock. Mac, make it 165." V for Victor passed plane after plane and occasionally jolted in the slipstream of others. A third searchlight belt showed up, this one free of cloud. It was a huge wall of light and looked far more impenetrable than a mountain. It seemed inconceivable that any plane could pass through and reach the opposite side. You thanked your lucky stars that this was not the target. To fly out of the protecting darkness into that blaze of light would be a test of courage you would rather not have to face. Nevertheless, there were some facing it right now. The flak opened up and the searchlights waved madly about. It was a diversionary attack, the "spoof". You watched in a detached, remote sort of way. It seemed very far away and did not seem to concern you at all. Until suddenly, one beam, which had been vertical, slanted down and started to pursue V for Victor, and you realized that it did concern you, very intimately. The second ticked by as the beam overtook the plane. But it passed harmlessly overhead and groped impotently in the darkness beyond.

"Four minutes late," Jock called over the intercom. The target itself, the big city, came into view like a luminous patch dead ahead. It was largely hidden by cloud and showed few searchlights. It seemed so much less formidable than the mountain of light just behind, that it came as a sort of anticlimax. Surely, you felt, this cannot be the big city, the nerve-centre of Europe's evil genius. It was quiet. There was no flak as yet, no flares, and just the handful of searchlights. You tried to imagine what it was like on the ground there. The sirens would be about to sound, the ack-ack batteries would be standing ready, the searchlights already manned. You wondered if the people were in shelters.

But it was too much an effort. It was too remote. Your problems were flak, fighters, searchlights and whether you are on the course and on time. What happened below was an entirely different problem, which had nothing to do with you. What happened below might just as well be happening on Mars. V for Victor's little world was simply hovering off this planet and leading a life of its own.

Ever so slowly, V for Victor crept up on the target. The two worlds were coming inevitably together. But it still had the quality of unreality. It was like a dream, where you are hurrying somewhere and yet cannot move at all. Nevertheless, Victor was passing plane after plane and jolted in somebody's slipstream now and again. The other Lancs looked ominous bearing down on the target, breathing out blue flame as they approached.

The minute of the attack came and still the target was quiet. One minute ticked by. Still quiet. The engineer opened up the throttles to maximum speed and increased the oxygen supply. Still quiet. The whole attack was a minute or two late. Winds probably. Suddenly, the whole city opened up. The flak poured up through the clouds. It came in a myriad little lights. It poured up in streams of red as if shaken from a hose. It went off in bright, white puffs.

The Pathfinders had arrived. In another moment, they had dropped the target indicators, great shimmering Christmas trees of red and green lights. You couldn't miss. It would be impossible to miss such a brilliantly marked objective. Bright flashes started going off under the clouds. That would be the cookies of the planes ahead.

V for Victor started the bombing run. The bomb-aimer called the course now. "Left, left...Steady now....Right a bit....Steady....Steady....Cookie gone!" V for Victor shot upward slightly..."Steady....Incendiaries gone!" V for Victor surged forward again ever so slightly. "Stand-by, Taff." It was the voice of Bob, the tail gunner. "Fighter. Corkscrew starboard," the tail gunner called. Instantly, the pilot sent V for Victor over to starboard and rushed headlong downward. A stream of red tracers whipped out of the dark, past the rear turret and on past the wingtip, missing both by what seemed inches. A second later the fighter itself shot past after the tracers, a vague dark blur against the night sky. "Me109," Bob said calmly. V for Victor squirmed and corkscrewed over the sky of Berlin. You wondered how it could be possible to avoid all the other planes that were over the city. But the fighter was shaken off and V for Victor came back to a normal course again.

Down below through rifts in the cloud, you could see that Berlin was burning. The bright, white flame of the incendiaries showed up as a carpet of light, always growing. And flash after flash went off as the blockbusters fell. The dark, black shapes of many Lancasters could be seen all over the sky against the brilliant clouds below. They were like small insects crawling over a great glass window. It did not seem possible that these tiny black dots could be the cause of the destruction which was going on below. The insects crawled to the edge of the light and disappeared into the darkness beyond. They had passed safely through the target. V for Victor followed close behind.

Shortly, the course was set for the return, and Berlin was visible for many miles on the port quarter. The attack was over now and took only fifteen minutes. The ack-ack was silent. There was no flak flashing over the city. But the city was brighter than ever. The clouds were getting a reddish tinge, which showed that the fires had caught hold below.

And so the capital of Nazism dropped astern, obscuring the rising moon by its flames. The government which came into power by deliberately setting fire to its chamber of representatives, the government which first used wholesale bombing, and boasted of it, was now perishing in fires far more devastating than any it ever devised. It was perishing to a fire music never dreamed of by Wagner.

But it was impossible to connect V for Victor with the death struggles of Berlin. There was no time for contemplation. "Stand-by – Ju88 starboard – corkscrew," came Bob's voice. Again, with lightning speed, the pilot put V for Victor over and dived out of the way. The Ju88's tracer missed us and shot down another Lanc which had not been so fortunate.

After that, the route home was uneventful. Crossing the North Sea, V for Victor went into a gentle incline towards home base, as if by a sort of homing instinct.

The searchlights of England sent out a greeting of welcome. For miles along the coast they stood almost evenly spaced, vertical sentries guarding the island. Then they started waving downward in the direction of the nearest airfield. No doubt they were helping home a damaged bomber. How different they were from the menacing tentacles over the German cities.

V for Victor arrived over the home field. The wireless operator called the base over his repaired equipment. He said simply, "V for Victor." The clear voice of a girl came pleasantly over the intercom. "V-Victor, prepare to pancake." The short, business-like message in service slang was a wonderful welcome home. V for Victor circled the field, losing altitude. "V-Victor in funnels." "V-Victor, pancake," the girl's voice said.

V for Victor touched down gently, ran down the flare path and turned off on the perimeter track. "V-Victor clear of flare path." The ground crew met V for Victor and acted as guide back into the dispersal area. "How was it?" "A piece of cake," someone said. The crew got out, collected their gear, the parachutes, Mae Wests, the navigator's bag, the guns etc., and then, as one man, lit up cigarettes. The pilot walked around the plane looking for any damage. There was one small hole through the aileron, but it was too dark to see it then. The bus arrived and the crew clambered in with all the gear and were taken back to the locker room. June was there and gathered in all the stuff over the counter and staggered away, lost from sight under a mound of yellow suits and Mae Wests.

Then back to the briefing room, where a cup of hot tea with rum in it was waiting. Each captain signed his name on the board as he came in. Crew by crew, the men went into the intelligence room, carrying their spiked tea with them. There were packages of cigarettes on the table, and everyone chain-smoked, lighting up from the butt of the previous one. The intelligence officer asked brief questions and the replies were brief, such as, "The heavy flak was light and the light flak heavy." It was all over in a very few minutes, and you went back to the briefing room and hashed over the trip with the other crews. No trouble, any of them, but there were gaps in the list of captains chalked on the board.

"It's like that," the Wingco remarked. "In night flying, you usually get back intact, or you don't get back at all. If you get coned, or a fighter sees you before you see it, then very often you have had it, but if somebody else gets coned, then it's that much easier for you." You thought of that other Lancaster the Ju88 got with the same burst that missed V for Victor. And you lit another cigarette.

The first signs of dawn were coming over the field now, and off in the distance on the bleak, windswept little knoll, V for Victor stood guard over the empty dispersal points, from which other men and ships had gone out a short while before. "....If someone else gets coned, then it's so much easier for you."

The fifth wartime Christmas passed in traditional fashion, and the Command remained stood-down until the 29th, when briefings took place for the first of what would be an unprecedented three Berlin operations in the space of five nights spanning the turn of the year. A force of 712 aircraft included 136 Lancasters of 1 Group, of which ten represented 576 Squadron and departed Elsham Wolds between 16.45 and 17.15 with F/L Smith the senior pilot on duty and W/C Clayton flying as second pilot to P/O Edie. It was from this juncture that the intolerable strain on the crews of successive long-range flights in difficult weather conditions began to manifest in some squadrons through the rate of early returns, which on this night reached forty-five or 6.3%, although only a modest seven from the ranks of 1 Group. Each bomb bay contained the standard cookie and incendiary bomb load as the 576 Squadron contingent flew out over Mablethorpe and joined up with the bomber stream over the North Sea to then proceed via the Dutch Frisian islands directly towards Leipzig. Having reached a point just to the north of that city, they turned to the north towards Berlin, while Mosquitos carried out spoof raids on Leipzig and Magdeburg. The Elsham Wolds squadrons were exempt from early returns and reached the target area to find ten-tenths cloud with tops at anywhere between 7,000 and 18,000 feet and red and green Path Finder release-point flares hanging over the city. Based on the 103 Squadron record, the 576 Squadron crews delivered their bombs from 20,000 to 23,000 feet either side of 20.15 and for the first time in six operations, all returned safely.

At debriefings, crews reported a considerable red glow beneath the clouds, which remained visible for a hundred miles and gave the impression of a concentrated and successful assault. This was not entirely borne out by reports from local sources, which revealed that the main weight of the raid had fallen onto southern and south-eastern districts and also into outlying communities to the east, and that 388 buildings had been destroyed, although none of significance, and ten thousand people had been bombed out of their homes. Eleven Lancasters and nine Halifaxes failed to return, a loss-rate of 2.4% for the former and 3.5% for the latter.

During the course of the month the squadron participated in six operations and launched forty-seven sorties for the loss of seven Lancasters and crews, a disturbing 15% of those dispatched. It had been a testing end to a year which had brought major successes and advances in tactics, but it had also been a year of high losses, particularly among the Stirling and Halifax squadrons. While "window" (aluminium-backed paper strips designed to swamp enemy radar with false returns) had been an instant success, when introduced to operations during the Gomorrah series of attacks on Hamburg in July, it had also caused the Luftwaffe to rethink and reorganise and the night-fighter force emerging from the ruins of the old system was a leaner, more efficient and altogether more lethal beast than that of before. As far as the crews of Bomber Command were concerned, the New Year offered the same fare as the old one, which few would view with relish and the next three months would see morale at its lowest ebb as the winter campaign ground on. Gone were the days when a freshman crew would be eased into battle with nickelling (leaflet) and gardening (mining) trips, now one's maiden operation could be to Berlin, and that was, indeed, the fate that awaited those about to leave the training units and join a frontline squadron.

January 1944

The change of year was not destined to effect a change in the emphasis of operations, and this was, no doubt, a disappointment not only to the hard-pressed crews of Bomber Command but also to the beleaguered residents of Germany's capital city. Proud of their status as Berliners first and Germans second, they were a hardy breed and just like their counterparts in London during the Blitz of 1940, would bear their trials with fortitude and humour and would not buckle under the constant assault from above. "You may break our walls", proclaimed banners in the streets, "but not out hearts", and the most popular song of the day, "Nach jedem Dezember kommt immer ein Mai", "After every December there's always a May", was played endlessly over the airwaves, its sentiments hinting at a change in fortunes with the onset of spring. Harris allowed the Berliners little time to enjoy New Year, and as New Year's Day dawned, plans were already in hand to continue the onslaught. Before it ended, the first of 421 Lancasters, 117 representing 1 Group, would be taking off and heading eastwards to arrive over the city as the clock showed 03.00 hours on the 2nd.

Take-off had actually been delayed because of doubts over the weather, and this meant that insufficient hours of daylight remained to allow the planned outward route over Denmark and the

Baltic. Instead, the bomber stream would adopt the previously used almost direct route across Holland and northern Germany, but return as originally planned more circuitously, passing east of Leipzig, before racing across Germany between the Ruhr and Frankfurt and traversing Belgium to reach the Channel near the French port of Boulogne. 576 Squadron's eight Lancasters were each loaded with a cookie and nineteen SBCs of varying sizes containing a variety of incendiaries, before departing Elsham Wolds between 23.45 and 00.20 and heading for Mablethorpe with F/L Smith the senior pilot on duty. *At this stage in the squadron's development, the person responsible for record-keeping, probably the adjutant, was not given to recording more than basic details of operations, something, sadly, that would not change, and the bombing heights and times cited in this work, therefore, are either approximated or borrowed from other units, principally 103 Squadron.* The force was gradually depleted by twenty-nine early returns, ten of them from 1 Group's ranks, but none from Elsham Wolds. The 103 Squadron crews of F/L Churchill and F/O Russell-Fry would be performing a new role of "wind-finders", in which selected crews from each group were charged with the task of ascertaining wind strength and direction at regular intervals during the flight to transmit back to HQ, where the data would be collated, averaged and rebroadcast to the bombers as an aid to navigation. It would prove to be a largely useful tool but would reveal major limitations under unusual and extreme conditions.

The bomber stream covered the four-hundred-mile leg from the Dutch coast to Berlin in under two hours without once catching a glimpse of the ground through the dense cloud, and it was no different at the target, which was completely obscured by a layer of ten-tenths cloud with tops in places as high as 19,000 feet. The Path Finders had to employ skymarking (Wanganui), which was somewhat scattered, and the 576 Squadron crews aimed for these parachute flares, based on the 103 Squadron record, from 20,000 to 23,000 feet between 03.03 and 03.16. They observed the glow of fires and smoke rising through the cloud tops and a huge explosion was witnessed at 03.07, which lit up the clouds for three seconds, but it was impossible to assess what was happening on the ground. It was established, ultimately, that the operation had been a failure, which had scattered bombs across the southern fringes of the city causing only minor damage, while the main weight of the attack had fallen beyond the city boundaries into wooded and open country. The disappointment was compounded by the loss of twenty-eight Lancasters, six of them belonging to 1 Group, but none from Elsham Wolds.

During the course of the 2nd, a heavy force of 362 Lancasters and nine of the new Mk III Hercules-powered Halifaxes was made ready for a return to Berlin that night. There was snow on the ground as the crews tumbled out of bed late in the afternoon to attend briefing, many still tired following the almost-eight-hour round trip the night before and some in a mutinous frame of mind at being back on the order of battle again so soon. 1 Group contributed 116 Lancasters, the eight belonging to 576 Squadron receiving the standard cookie/incendiary bomb load before departing Elsham Wolds in two phases between 23.30 and 00.15 with F/L Smith the senior pilot on duty. They flew out over Mablethorpe and crossed the Dutch coast near Castricum on course for a point south-east of Bremen, followed by a dogleg to the north-west and finally a ninety degree change of course to the south-east in the Parchim area to leave a ninety-mile run to the target. The force was depleted by a massive sixty early returns, 15.7% of those dispatched, and twenty-eight were from 1 Group, fifteen of them, including 576 Squadron's P/O Henningham and crew, responding in error to a recall signal sent to Polish Wellingtons on their way to the Biscay coast for mining duties. A few were defeated by severe icing conditions, while the crews of Sgt Blackie and F/Sgt Marsden suffered engine issues and some others abandoned their sorties because of minor technical problems that might have seen them carry on had they been fully rested.

The route changes worked well to throw off the night-fighters, but they would congregate in the target area after the controller correctly identified Berlin as the target forty minutes before zero-hour. Ten-tenths cloud with tops at 16,000 feet forced the bombing to take place on the red skymarkers with green stars or on the glow of fires, the 576 Squadron crews carrying out their attacks from 17,000 to 23,000 feet between 02.45 and 03.10. Smoke was reported to be rising through 20,000 feet as the bombers turned away, but it was not possible to make an accurate assessment of the outcome and the impression was of an effective attack, when, in fact, it had been another failure. Bombs had been scattered across the city and destroyed just eighty-two houses for the loss of twenty-seven Lancasters, most of which had fallen victim to night-fighters in the target area. For the third operation running, 576 Squadron welcomed all of its crews home, while one from 103 Squadron was posted missing.

After three trips to the "Big City" in five nights, it would now be left to the Mosquitos of 8 Group's Mosquito squadrons to disrupt the residents' sleep with cookies until the final third of the month, allowing Harris to turn his attention on the 5th upon the Baltic port-city of Stettin, which had not been attacked in numbers since the previous April. Located some thirty miles south of the Baltic coast at Swinemünde, Stettin, now Szczecin in Poland, lies on the River Oder at the end of an inland sea, which at the time was known as the Stettiner Haff. A highly industrialised city, it was home to many war industry concerns including the Stoewer automobile works and the Oderwerke A.G Stettin U-Boot and A.G Vulkan shipyards. It was also the site of numerous forced workers' camps, although to what extent this was known by the Allies is uncertain. It was to be another predominantly Lancaster affair involving 348 of the type accompanied by ten Halifaxes, 1 Group putting up 113 aircraft and 576 Squadron eleven, each with a cookie in the bomb bay and a slightly reduced number of incendiaries to compensate for the additional fuel requirements for the round trip. They departed Elsham Wolds between 23.30 and 00.05 with S/L Attwater the senior pilot on duty, and in contrast to the previous operation, a modest four from 1 Group turned back early on this night. The bomber stream found itself in thick cloud at cruising altitude, some struggling to find a clear lane even when as high as 23,000 feet, but on the plus side, they all benefitted from a Mosquito diversion at Berlin, which kept the night-fighters off the scent.

Stettin was found to be partially visible through five-tenths thin cloud with tops at around 10,000 feet, and crews were able to identify some ground features before focusing on H2S-laid flares and green TIs, which the 576 Squadron crews bombed from 21,000 to 23,500 feet between 03.46 and 03.59. Returning crews provided the intelligence section with accounts of a highly accurate and concentrated attack, which seemed to leave the entire city on fire. The Berlin diversion was successful in keeping most of the enemy fighters away, but fourteen Lancasters and two Halifaxes failed to return, among the former three from Elsham Wolds, two belonging to 576 Squadron. DV333 was shot down over north-eastern Germany by a night-fighter while outbound, with fatal consequences for F/L Smith and three of his crew, the four survivors, including a second pilot under instruction, falling into enemy hands. ND416 crashed in the town of Pasewalk, some twenty miles west-north-west of Stettin, and there were no survivors from the crew of P/O Henningham RAAF. Post-raid reconnaissance and local sources confirmed heavy damage in central and western districts, where 504 houses and twenty industrial buildings had been destroyed, a further 1,148 houses and twenty-nine industrial buildings seriously damaged and eight ships sunk in the harbour.

The arrival of the moon period allowed further respite from operations, and batches of crews were given a forty-eight-hour pass over the ensuing week. Snowfalls and freezing conditions made life difficult for ground personnel, but they were able to keep Lancasters flying for training purposes, while the Halifax units further north would spend three weeks in virtual hibernation apart from isolated mining forays. When briefings finally took place on the 14th, there was doubtless some relief to see the red tape on the wall maps terminate some way short of Berlin. It led, in fact, to Braunschweig (Brunswick), the historic, culturally significant and highly industrialised city situated some thirty-five miles to the east of Hannover, which was home among other war production sites to Volkswagen, and aircraft and motor components factories. It had not been attacked by the Command in numbers before, and on this night, would face a force which at take-off numbered 496 Lancasters and two Halifaxes. 1 Group supported the operation with 151 Lancasters, of which nine represented 576 Squadron, and they each received a bomb load of a cookie, supplemented by eighteen assorted SBCs of incendiaries, before departing Elsham Wolds between 16.20 and 16.45 with S/L Attwater the senior pilot on duty.

They set course via Mablethorpe for the Frisian Island of Texel, losing the services of F/L Johnson and crew to engine failure shortly after crossing the enemy coast, and they bombed Texel as a last resort target on the way back to Elsham Wolds. The others entered Germany north of Meppen, where they were met by part of the enemy night-fighter response, which would harass the bomber stream all the way to the target and back. They skirted the Hannover defence zone, before settling on the final leg to the target, where complete cloud cover topped out in places at around 15,000 feet and dictated the use of red skymarkers with green stars, at which the 576 Squadron crews aimed their cookies and incendiaries from 20,000 to 22,500 feet between 19.15 and 19.30. The enemy night-fighters scored consistently and accounted for the majority of the thirty-eight missing Lancasters, many coming to grief around Hannover, which was the fate of both missing 576 Squadron aircraft. LM381 was south-west of Hannover when exploding and throwing clear F/L Morren and his flight engineer as the sole survivors, while ME585 crashed at Bruchhausen south of Cologne on the way home and took with it the crew of Sgt Mann. The attack almost entirely missed the city, falling mostly onto outlying communities to the south, and was reported locally as a light raid. This would be a continuing theme in future attacks up to the autumn, as Braunschweig enjoyed something of a charmed life, leading to a belief among the populace that the surrounding villages were being targeted intentionally, in an attempt to drive the residents into the city, before a major operation destroyed it with them in it!

The Path Finders, in particular, had been taking a beating since the turn of the year, with 156 Squadron, the 1 Group representative in the force, alone losing fourteen Lancasters and crews in just three operations, four and five on Berlin, and five again on Braunschweig. This was creating something of a crisis in Path Finder manpower, particularly with regard to experienced crews, and a number of sideways postings took place between the squadrons to ensure a leavening of experience in each one. One of the solutions was to take the cream from the crews emerging from the training units, rather than wait for them to gain experience at a main force squadron.

Fog persisted from the 15th onwards, and a thaw set in on the 17th to ease conditions, but no flying took place at Elsham Wolds until air-tests on the 20th in preparation for the night's operation to Berlin. It was to be a maximum effort, and the Halifax squadrons, which had appeared to be in hibernation since late December, were roused from their slumber so that 264 of them could join 495 Lancasters to constitute the Path Finder and main force elements, while two small Mosquito elements carried out spoof raids on Kiel and Hannover. 1 Group weighed in with 144 Lancasters, ten of them made ready by 576 Squadron and loaded with a cookie and eighteen SBCs of 4lb and 30lb incendiaries, before departing Elsham Wolds between 15.50 and 16.20 with F/Os Morgan and Shearer the only commissioned pilots on duty. Accompanying the crew of Sgt Bodger was a Mr Coggins, and in the absence of further explanation, it must be assumed that he was another war correspondent. It was a rare pleasure for crews to be taking off in daylight, and while climbing out they observed dozens of other Lancasters rising up into the dusk to join them from the neighbouring stations. They turned their snouts towards Mablethorpe and set course for the west coast of Schleswig-Holstein at a point opposite Kiel, rendezvousing with the other groups over the North Sea and all the time shedding individual aircraft as a hefty seventy-five of them turned back.

The remainder made landfall over the Nordfriesland coast, before turning to the south-east on a more-or-less direct course for Berlin and soon found themselves hounded by night-fighters. The advent of "window", had forced the Luftwaffe Nachtjagd to develop new tactics and out of this was borne the "Sahme Sau" or "Tame Boar" system of running commentaries, which actively vectored night-fighters from their beacon assembly points to the bomber stream, rather than wait for the bombers to pass through a box as in the former "Himmelbett" system. The enemy controller had fed a proportion of his resources into the bomber stream east of Hamburg, and they would remain in contact until a point between Leipzig and Hannover on the way home, although, curiously, the 1 and 5 Group brigades experienced little of this and would lose just four Lancasters between them. The two Mosquito diversions had been completely ignored by the Luftwaffe controller, who knew well in advance that Berlin was to be the target.

The Path Finders arrived over the Müritzsee to the north of Berlin with a sixty-mile run-in to the aiming point, which they found this to be concealed beneath the same ten-tenths cloud that had accompanied them for the entire outward leg. The tops of the cloud lay beneath the bombers at up to 15,000 feet as the main force crews carried out their attacks on red skymarkers with green stars, those from 576 Squadron from 20,000 to 23,500 feet between 19.32 and 19.55. On return, the crews commented on the lack of flak activity over Berlin and reported the glow of large fires under the cloud and smoke rising through the tops. Thirty-five aircraft failed to return, twenty-two of them Halifaxes, which represented an 8.3% casualty rate compared with 2.6% for the Lancasters. It took a little time for an assessment of the operation to be made because of continuing cloud over north-eastern Germany, by which time four further raids had been carried out. It seems from local reports that the eastern districts had received the heaviest weight of bombs in an eight-mile stretch from Weissensee in the north to Neukölln in the south, although no details of destruction emerged.

On the following day, the city of Magdeburg was posted to host its first major attack of the war, having, in fact, been a regular destination for small forces as far back as the summer of 1940, when the Command targeted a ship lift at the eastern end of the Mittelland Canal at its junction with the River Elbe and the important Braunkohle A.G synthetic oil refinery (hydrogenation plant), both located in the same Rothensee district to the north of the city centre. Situated some fifty miles from

Braunschweig and slightly to the south of east, it was on an increasingly familiar route as far as the enemy night-fighter controllers were concerned, and within easy striking distance of the night-fighter assembly beacons. In an attempt to deceive the enemy, a small-scale diversion was planned at Berlin involving twenty-two Lancaster of 5 Group and twelve Mosquitos of 8 Group. 1 Group contributed 132 Lancasters, nine of them made ready by 576 Squadron and loaded with the standard cookie and incendiary mix, before departing Elsham Wolds between 19.25 and 20.15 with F/O Morgan the senior pilot on duty. They flew out over Mablethorpe to a point over the North Sea some one hundred miles off the west coast of Schleswig-Holstein, before turning to the south-east to pass between Hamburg and Hannover. Enemy radar was able to detect H2S transmissions during night-flying tests and equipment checks, and the night-fighter controller was, thereby, always aware of an imminent heavy raid. On this night, the night-fighters were able to infiltrate the bomber stream even before the German coast was crossed and the "Tame Boar" system provided a running commentary on the bomber stream's progress, enabling the fighters to latch onto it and remain in contact. The final turning-point was twenty-five miles north-east of the target, from where fires could be seen caused by twenty-seven main force aircraft, driven by stronger-than-forecast winds to arrive ahead of schedule and containing crews anxious to get the job done and get out of the target area as soon as possible. They bombed using their own H2S without waiting for the TIs to go down, and this, together with very effective enemy decoy markers, compromised the Path Finder efforts to achieve concentration after their initial red target indicators went down at 22.50.

The conditions over Magdeburg varied according to the time of arrival, the early birds encountering seven to nine-tenths thin cloud at around 6,000 feet, while those turning up towards the end of the raid found the northern half of the city completely clear with cloud over the southern half only. The main force crews experienced a mixture of eight-tenths cloud and relatively clear skies, and in the face of fairly modest opposition, those from Elsham Wolds bombed on green TIs from 21,500 to 23,000 feet between 22.57 and 23.27, all gaining the impression that the attack was concentrated around the markers. Returning crews from other groups reported explosions and fires or their glow, and smoke beginning to rise as they turned away. A number reported a flash some twelve minutes after bombing that lit up the clouds for seven seconds, and two large explosions were witnessed at 23.15. Fires that initially seemed to be scattered, became more concentrated as the crews headed for home and the impression was of a successful operation. While all of this was in progress, the diversionary force arrived at Berlin, some seventy miles away to the north-east, and found a layer of eight to ten-tenths cloud at 10,000 feet, through which the bombing took place. The 5 Group ORB expressed the opinion that the diversion had succeeded in the early stages in reducing the impact of the Nachtjagd, although this was not borne out by the figures. In the absence of post-raid reconnaissance and a local report, the outcome at Magdeburg was not confirmed and it is generally believed now that most of the bombing fell outside of the city boundaries. While Elsham Wolds welcomed all of its sons home, elsewhere, a record fifty-seven aircraft failed to return, thirty-five of them Halifaxes, and this provided another alarming statistic of a 15.6% loss-rate compared with 5.2% for the Lancasters.

The end of the month would bring the final concerted effort to destroy Berlin and involve three trips in the space of an unprecedented four nights, this hectic round of operations beginning on the 27th, after five nights of rest since the bruising experience of Magdeburg. An all-Lancaster heavy force of 515 aircraft was assembled, 1 Group responsible for 149 of them, ten belonging to 576

Squadron, which departed Elsham Wolds between 17.10 and 17.45 with S/L Attwater the senior pilot on duty and each bomb bay containing a cookie and seventeen assorted SBCs of incendiaries. After climbing out and passing over Mablethorpe to rendezvous with the rest of the group, they set course on a complex route that would take the bomber stream towards the north German coast, before swinging to the south-east to enter enemy territory over the Frisians and northern Holland. Having then feinted towards central Germany, suggesting Leipzig as the target, the force turned north-east to a point west of Berlin, from where the final run-in commenced. The long return route passed to the west of Leipzig before turning due east to miss Frankfurt on its northern side and traverse Belgium to gain the Channel south of Boulogne. As they pressed on towards the target, a mining diversion off Heligoland and the dispensing of dummy fighter flares and route-markers partially succeeded in reducing the number of enemy night-fighters making contact.

It was, therefore, a relatively intact bomber force that approached the target over ten-tenths cloud with tops at 15,000 feet, conditions which required the Path Finders to use sky-marking, and it was the red Wanganui flares with green stars that led the Elsham Wolds crews to the aiming point, where those from 576 Squadron bombed from 20,000 to 23,000 feet between 20.30 and 20.55. At debriefings, crews reported the glow of fires and the appearance of a successful raid, but no detailed assessment was forthcoming. Of course, not all made it back to tell their stories at debriefing, and thirty-three Lancaster dispersal pans stood empty in dawn's early light. Among these was the one belonging to 576 Squadron's ME593, which crashed somewhere in the target area with fatal consequences for Sgt Ebsworth and his crew. Reports from Berlin described bombs falling over a wide area, more so in the south than the north, and damage to fifty industrial premises, a number of them engaged in important war work, while twenty thousand people were bombed out of their homes. A feature of the campaign was the number of outlying communities suffering collateral damage, and on this night sixty-one such hamlets recorded bombs falling.

The early time-on-target had allowed crews to enjoy a full night in bed and they were, hopefully, fully rested, when news came through on the 28th that many of them would be returning to the "Big City" that night. A heavy force of 673 aircraft was assembled, of which 432 were Lancasters and 241 Halifaxes, 125 of the former provided by 1 Group. 576 Squadron made ready nine Lancasters, which departed Elsham Wolds between 23.25 and 00.15 with S/L Attwater the senior pilot on duty and a cookie and thirteen SBCs in each bomb bay. They were routed out over Mablethorpe on course for southern Jutland, before turning south-east on a direct course for the target, with an almost reciprocal return and various diversionary measures to distract the night-fighter controller. Sixty-six crews turned back early, suggesting some adverse reaction to the back-to-back operations, and among these was 576 Squadron's F/O Shearer RNZAF and crew, because of an engine issue during the North Sea crossing. The remainder reached the target area to encounter ten-tenths cloud and a mixture of sky and ground-marking to aim at. The 576 Squadron crews delivered their bombs on red and green release-point flares from above 20,000 to 23,000 feet between 03.15 and 03.30, and huge explosions were reported at 03.15, 03.18 and 03.25, the second-mentioned one described by a 10 Squadron Halifax crew as lighting up the sky over a radius of fifty miles. Forty-six aircraft failed to return, twenty-six of them Halifaxes as the defenders fought back to exact another heavy toll of bombers. The single absentee from Elsham Wolds was 576 Squadron's ND386, which crashed in the Berlin defence zone, killing F/Sgt Hart and all but his navigator, who was taken into captivity. The impression gained from returning crews at debriefing was of a concentrated and effective attack, and this was partly borne-out by local reports of heavy damage in western and southern districts, where 180,000 people were bombed out of their homes. However, as had been the pattern throughout the campaign against Berlin, seventy-seven outlying communities had also been afflicted.

After a night's rest a force of 534 aircraft was made ready on the 30th for the final operation of this concerted effort against Berlin. 1 Group contributed 129 Lancasters, thirty of which were to act as Path Finder supporters, a role requiring them to accompany the 8 Group spearhead across the aiming point to "beef" up the numbers and make it harder for flak batteries to single out individual aircraft. They would then carry out a second pass to deliver their bomb loads. 576 Squadron's eleven Lancasters had a cookie and fourteen assorted SBCs of 4lb and 30lb incendiaries winched into position and departed Elsham Wolds between 16.25 and 17.04 with S/L Attwater the senior pilot on duty. After climbing out and crossing the coast at Mablethorpe, they joined with the rest of the force over the North Sea to follow a route similar to that adopted two nights earlier, losing the services of Sgt Murray and crew to engine trouble on the way. The bomber stream remained relatively free of harassment and on reaching the target was greeted by ten-tenths cloud at around 8,000 feet and the sight of Path Finder skymarking in progress. The 576 Squadron crews bombed on these from 20,000 and above, either side of 20.30, and all commented on the smoke rising through 12,000 feet and the glow of fires beneath the cloud, which, according to some, was still visible on the horizon from a hundred miles into the return flight.

Thirty-two Lancasters and a single Halifax were missing, ten of the former from the ranks of 1 Group, 576 Squadron's persistent record of losses continuing with the failure to return of P/O Childs and crew in veteran Lancaster W4245, which exploded over Königsberg, a town to the north-west of Giessen in central Germany. The flight engineer and navigator were flung out into space as the sole survivors, the latter, Sgt Bardsley, sustaining a severe blast injury, from which he made a full recovery in captivity, only to be killed by an Allied fighter-bomber attacking a column of marching PoWs on the 19th of April 1945. In return for the significant losses, according to local sources, central and south-western districts suffered heavy damage and serious areas of fire. Other parts of the city were also hit, while many bomb loads were again scattered liberally onto outlying communities, and at least a thousand people lost their lives. 112 heavy bombers and their crews had been lost to the Command as a result of these three operations, and with the introduction of the enemy's highly efficient Tame Boar night-fighter system, the advantage had swung firmly back in the defenders' favour.

Two further heavy raids would be directed at Berlin before the end of the winter offensive, one in February and the other in March, but they would be almost in isolation. There is no question that Germany's capital city had been sorely afflicted by the three latest operations, but it remained a functioning administrative and war materials producing centre and showed no signs of imminent collapse. Harris had failed in his stated aim to bring an end to the war by destroying Berlin, but in truth, it was never a realistic expectation. Berlin was no Hamburg, developed over hundreds of years with tightly packed houses in narrow streets, where fire could spread more rapidly than it could be extinguished. Berlin was modern, built of concrete and steel, with wide thoroughfares and open spaces that acted as natural firebreaks, each attack creating further firebreaks and invoking the law of diminishing returns. Ultimately Berlin was too big, too far and too well-defended, and it was being attacked at a time when the weather was at its worst and the enemy night fighter force performing at its most lethal.

During the course of the month the squadron took part in eight operations, launching eighty-nine sorties for the loss of seven Lancasters and crews.

February 1944

Bad weather during the first two weeks of February allowed the crews to draw breath and the squadrons to replenish. Harris had intended to maintain the pressure on Berlin and would have launched a further attack had he not been thwarted by the conditions, and as a result, the time was filled with training, mining operations and lectures. When the Path Finder and main force squadrons next took to the air, it would be for a record-breaking effort to Berlin on the 15th, which would also be the penultimate operation of the campaign, and indeed of the war by Bomber Command's heavy brigade against Germany's capital city. The force of 891 aircraft represented the largest non-1,000 force to date, and, therefore, the greatest-ever to be sent against the "Big City", and it would be the first time that more than five hundred Lancasters and three hundred Halifaxes had operated together. The bomb bays of this huge armada would convey the greatest-ever tonnage of bombs to any target to date, and in order to ensure that as much of it as possible reached its destination, extensive diversionary measures included a mining operation in Kiel Bay ahead of the arrival of the bombers, a raid on Frankfurt-an-Oder to the east of Berlin by a small force of 8 Group Lancasters and, finally, Oboe Mosquitos attacking five night-fighter airfields in Holland. 1 Group contributed 161 Lancasters, a dozen of them representing 576 Squadron, each carrying a cookie and eighteen assorted SBCs of incendiaries as they departed Elsham Wolds between 17.00 and 17.25 with S/Ls Attwater and Haig the senior pilots on duty and W/C Clayton flying as second pilot with the former. A Flight commander, S/L Douglas Haig, had only recently arrived on posting to begin a second tour of operations, his first having been on Hampdens with 5 Group's 144 Squadron in 1940/41. They flew out over Mablethorpe to join up with the rest of the 1 Group squadrons on a course for the western coast of Denmark, and after traversing southern Jutland, entered Germany via the Baltic coast between Rostock and Stralsund on a direct heading for the target. After delivering their bombs, they were briefed to return south of Hannover and Bremen and cross Holland to the gain the North Sea via the known gap in the defences at Egmond.

The force had been depleted by seventy-five early returns by the time that the remainder homed in on the target, twelve of these "boomerangs" belonging to 1 Group, while those reaching the target encountered ten-tenths cloud at around 10,000 feet, which concealed it from view. The H2S-equipped crews, including some of those from Elsham Wolds, were able to confirm their positions, while the others relied on the Path Finders' red release-point flares with green stars and red and green TIs on the ground. The 576 Squadron crews bombed on these from 20,000 feet and above between 21.15 and 22.00 and on return reported the markers to be highly effective and well-concentrated. The burgeoning glow beneath the clouds convinced them that they had taken part in a successful operation, and this was borne out by local reports, which confirmed that the 2,642 tons of bombs had caused extensive damage in central and south-western districts but also had spilled out into surrounding communities. A thousand houses and more than five hundred temporary wooden barracks were destroyed and important war-industry factories in the Siemensstadt district were damaged in return for the loss to the Command of forty-three aircraft, made up of twenty-six Lancasters, (4.6%) and seventeen Halifaxes, (5.4%). Perhaps slightly disturbing was the fact that eight of the missing Halifaxes were Mk IIIs, only one fewer than the nine now obsolete Mk II/Vs.

Berlin had been posted as the target on the 16th and 18th, but both operations were cancelled, and when orders were received on the 19th to prepare for another major assault that night, the target was revealed as Leipzig, where four Messerschmitt aircraft factories were among the principal attractions. The heavy squadrons were able offer 816 aircraft, 561 Lancasters and 255 Halifaxes, 1 Group detailing 171 Lancasters, of which the fifteen representing 576 Squadron were each loaded with a cookie and eighteen assorted SBCs. They departed Elsham Wolds between 23.10 and 23.50 with S/Ls Attwater and Haig the senior pilots on duty and headed out via Mablethorpe to rendezvous with the rest of the force over the North Sea. They were aiming for the Dutch coast near the fishing port of Harlingen, and a 49 Squadron flight commander returning early described a scene of chaos over the North Sea, with aircraft flying in every direction, the wiser crews with their navigation lights on but most without and he claimed to have witnessed three aircraft exploding, possibly as a result of collisions. A proportion of the night-fighter force was waiting for the bomber stream as it closed on a pinpoint at Groningen, having passed close to the "wasps' nest" night-fighter aerodrome at Leeuwarden, while other night-fighters had been drawn away by a mining diversion off Kiel. This left plenty available to shadow the bomber stream as it continued on south of Bremen and north of Hannover, and it was at this stage, as they adopted a south-easterly course, that sections of the bomber stream became embroiled in a running battle with night-fighters that continued all the way into eastern Germany. It could have been during this leg that S/L Haig and crew were attacked five times and claimed the destruction of one of their assailants and damage to another, without themselves sustaining any damage.

Inaccurately forecast winds caused some aircraft to arrive at the target ahead of schedule, forcing them to orbit while they waited for the Path Finders to arrive, and the local flak batteries accounted for around twenty of these, while four others were lost through collisions. The 576 Squadron crews arrived to find ten-tenths cloud with tops at around 10,000 feet and bombed on green Wanganui flares and red and green TIs from 20,000 feet and above between 04.00 and 04.25. It seems that there was a brief period during the attack when skymarking stopped and led to some scattering of bombs, but the marker-flares were soon replenished with the arrival of more backers-up and a considerable glow beneath the cloud remained visible for some fifty minutes into the return journey, giving the impression of a successful assault. When a large forced returned to home airspace, the often-overlapping circuits could become severely congested and the potential for collision was enormous. Such was the fate of two 103 Squadron Lancasters in the Elsham circuit, one crash-landing on the airfield without injury to the occupants, and the other crashing more heavily killing five of the occupants. 576 Squadron's absent aircraft was DV386, which disappeared without trace with the crew of F/Sgt Kirk, one of seventeen lost from the ranks of 1 Group. When all of those aircraft returning home had been accounted for, there was a massive shortfall of seventy-eight, a record loss by a clear twenty-one aircraft. Forty-four Lancasters and thirty-four Halifaxes had failed to return, with a loss-rate of 7.8% and 13.3% respectively, prompting Harris to immediately withdraw the less-efficient Merlin-powered Mk II and V Halifaxes from further operations over Germany, which at a stroke, removed a proportion of 4 and 6 Groups' fire-power from the front line until they could be re-equipped with the Mk III. In the meantime, the Mk II and V operators would focus their energies for the remainder of the month on gardening duties.

Despite the recent heavy losses and the consequent depletion of available numbers, a force of 598 aircraft was made ready on the 20th for an operation that night against Stuttgart, which would be the first of three against the city over a three-week period. 1 Group was able to offer 170 Lancasters, of which eleven belonged to 576 Squadron, each receiving a bomb load of a cookie and eighteen assorted SBCs, before departing Elsham Wolds between 23.15 and 23.59 with no pilots on duty above the rank of flying officer. They flew south to exit England over Beachy Head on course to make landfall on the other side to the north-east of Dieppe, and at some point, lost the services of F/Sgt Gipson when a member of the crew became unwell. The cloud remained at ten-tenths with tops at 8,000 feet all the way from the French coast to southern Germany, a North Sea sweep and a diversionary raid on Munich two hours ahead of the main activity persuading the Luftwaffe to deploy its forces early and allowing the bomber stream to push on unmolested to the target. By the time it hove into view, the cloud had thinned to five to eight-tenths at around 6,000 feet and the excellent visibility enabled the crews to draw a bead on the Path Finder red and green sky-markers and similar-coloured TIs on the ground. The 576 Squadron crews bombed from 20,000 feet and above between 04.00 and 04.15, observing many large fires, and on return reported that the glow from the burning city was still visible from 250 miles into the return flight. Despite some scattering of bombs, local sources reported that central districts and those in a quadrant from north-west to north-east had sustained extensive damage, and a Bosch factory was one of the important war industry concerns to be hard-hit. In contrast to twenty-four hours earlier, a modest nine aircraft failed to return.

In an attempt to reduce the prohibitive losses of recent weeks, a new tactic was introduced for the next two operations. A force of 734 aircraft was assembled on the 24th for an operation to the centre of Germany's ball-bearing production, Schweinfurt, situated some sixty miles to the east of Frankfurt in south-central Germany. Four factories, the Kugelfischer-Georg-Schäfer, Fichtel & Sachs, Vereinigte Kugellagerfabriken A.G and Deutsche Star GmbH, produced between them 50% of Germany's ball-bearing output and had been targeted by the American Eighth Air Force, most notoriously in August and October 1943 at a total cost of 120 heavy bombers. The plan called for 392 aircraft to depart their stations between 18.00 and 19.00 and to be followed into the air two hours later by 342 others in the hope of catching the night-fighters on the ground refuelling and re-arming as the second wave passed through. While this operation was in progress, extensive diversionary measures involving more than three hundred other aircraft were put into effect, including one by 179 from the training units conducting a North Sea sweep and another by 110 Halifaxes and Stirlings mining in northern waters. 1 Group contributed seventy Lancasters to the first wave and eighty-six to the second, of which fifteen were made ready by 576 Squadron for inclusion in the first phase, while 103 squadron took the late shift. Each Lancaster lifted a cookie and eighteen assorted SBCs into the air from the Elsham Wolds runway between 18.00 and 18.25 with S/L Haig the senior pilot on duty and followed the familiar route over Reading to Beachy Head to begin the Channel crossing. The first phase bombers reached the target to find three-tenths cloud at 3,000 to 4,000 feet, with haze spoiling the vertical visibility for some, while others described excellent visibility and the aiming point clearly identified by red and green TIs and already established fires towards the south-western edge of the town. The 576 Squadron crews carried out their attacks from 20,000 feet and above between 23.00 and 23.30 and two columns of black smoke were observed to be rising through 5,000 feet as they turned away. As they retreated towards the west they left behind them developing fires, and at debriefings the consensus was of an effective, if, somewhat scattered first phase attack.

The burgeoning fires were visible to the approaching second wave crews at 00.40 when eighty some miles distant, although, remarkably, some even claimed first seeing the glow of fires from the earlier raid at a distance of two hundred miles. The visibility in the target area remained good for the second-phase crews, despite the rising smoke, and bombing took place from under almost cloudless skies onto red and green TIs from 20,000 to 24,000 feet between 01.00 and 01.30. All indications suggested an effective raid, but it was discovered after an analysis that both phases of the operation had suffered from undershooting after some Path Finder backers-up had failed to press on to the aiming point. In that regard, it was a disappointing night, but an interesting feature was the loss of 50% fewer aircraft from the second wave in comparison with the first, in an overall casualty figure of thirty-three, and this suggested some merit in the tactic of splitting the force.

The main operation on the following night was directed at the beautiful and culturally significant southern city of Augsburg, situated around thirty miles north-west of Munich. It was home, among other war-supporting industrial concerns, to a major Maschinenfabrik Augsburg Nuremberg (M.A.N) diesel engine factory, which had been the target for the epic low-level daylight raid by 44 and 97 Squadrons in April 1942. On this night, 594 aircraft were divided into two waves, 1 Group providing 102 Lancasters for the early shift, of which fifteen were made ready by 576 Squadron and loaded with a cookie and eighteen SBCs of 4lb and 30lb incendiaries. They departed Elsham Wolds between 18.00 and 18.30 with S/L Attwater the senior pilot on duty, and for the third operation running, began the Channel crossing at Beachy Head and made landfall on the other side north-east of Dieppe. They traversed north-eastern France over ten-tenths cloud and entered Germany near Strasbourg to find the cloud dissipating, to the extent that on arrival at the target, it was possible for crews to gain a visual reference. The Path Finders' red and green TIs were in the bomb sights as the 576 Squadron crews carried out their attacks from 20,000 to 23,000 feet either side of 22.45, and fires were beginning to take hold as they turned away.

The second wave crews were drawn on by the glow in the sky from a hundred miles away and arrived to find visibility still good despite copious amounts of smoke rising through 10,000 feet. The loss of twenty-one aircraft seemed to confirm the benefits of splitting the forces, and this tactic would remain an important part of Bomber Command planning for the remainder of the war. It had been a devastatingly destructive attack on Augsburg, in which all facets of the plan had come together in near perfect harmony to spell disaster for this lightly defended historical treasure trove. Its heart was torn out by blast and fire that destroyed almost three thousand houses along with buildings of outstanding historical significance, and centuries of irreplaceable culture was lost forever. There was also some industrial damage, and around ninety-thousand people were bombed out of their homes.

During the course of the month the squadron took part in five operations and launched sixty-eight sorties for the loss of a single Lancaster and crew, in stark contrast to the carnage of the previous month.

March 1944

March would bring an end to the winter campaign, but a long and bitter month would have to be endured first before any respite came from long-range forays into Germany. The crews had enjoyed a few nights off when the second raid of the series on Stuttgart was posted on the 1st, for which a force of 557 aircraft was made ready, including eighty Lancasters representing 1 Group, a somewhat depleted number after the station commanders at Binbrook and Elsham Wolds expressed concerns about the likely weather conditions for returning aircraft and cancelled their involvement. The Path Finders employed a combination of sky and ground-marking, which became scattered, and the bombing was directed between two main concentrations. It was not possible to assess the accuracy of the attack, although a column of smoke had reached 25,000 feet by the end of the raid and large fires were evident from the glow on the horizon visible from up to 150 miles away. The presence of thick cloud all the way there and back made conditions difficult for enemy night-fighters and a remarkably modest four aircraft failed to return. It was eventually established that the raid had been an outstanding success, which had caused extensive damage in central, western and northern districts, where a number of important war-industry factories, including those belonging to Bosch and Daimler-Benz, had sustained damage.

At the end of the first week, the Halifax brigade, particularly the older variants withdrawn from operations over Germany, fired the opening salvoes of the pre-invasion campaign, the purpose of which was to dismantle by bombing thirty-seven railway centres in France, Belgium and western Germany. It began on the night of the 6/7th at Trappes marshalling yards, situated some ten miles west-south-west of Paris and continued at Le Mans in north-western France on the following night. 5 Group was in the process of developing a new low-level marking technique and would be active over the ensuing nights practicing its craft at French aircraft factories with such success, that the group would soon gain a virtual independence from the main force and be given its own target marking force. For the other groups, however, there was no employment following Stuttgart, until a return to that city in mid-month, and now that the Mk III Halifax was becoming available in larger numbers, the Command was quickly returning to full strength. The Elsham Wolds crews had been alerted to operations on the 4th, 5th, 6th and 10th, but each was cancelled before briefings took place.

A force of 863 aircraft was assembled on the 15th, a number that included a record 190 Lancasters provided by 1 Group, thirteen of them belonging to 576 Squadron, each of which received a bomb load of a cookie and thirteen SBCs of incendiaries, before departing Elsham Wolds between 18.30 and 19.35 with F/Ls Davison, Morgan, Shearer and Underwood the senior pilots on duty and W/C Clayton flying as second pilot to W/O Whalley. They rendezvoused with the rest of the force as it passed over Reading on its way to the exit point at Selsey Bill, and it was an elongated bomber stream that crossed the Normandy coast at 20,000 feet over broken cloud with clear conditions above. By this time, P/O Thomas and crew had become one of seven 1 Group "boomerangs" after experiencing an engine issue, leaving the rest of the bomber stream to maintain a course parallel with the frontiers of Belgium, Luxembourg and Germany as if heading for Switzerland. The German frontier was crossed between Strasbourg and Freiburg, after which the route turned towards the north-east for the run-in to the target and it was during this final leg that the night-fighters managed to infiltrate a section of the stream and score heavily. Adverse winds were responsible for the Path Finders' arrival up to six minutes late to open the attack, when they employed both sky and ground-markers in the face of seven to ten-tenths cloud at between 8,000 and 15,000 feet. The Wanganui flares drifted in the wind, marking an area to the north-east of the River Neckar, while the TIs landed far apart in the north and south of the city. The 576 Squadron crews bombed on whatever markers presented themselves, mostly red TIs, from 20,000 feet and above either side of 23.30, observing smoke rising to bombing altitude and a spread of fires, including two large ones ten miles apart. It would be established later that some of the early bombing had been accurate, but that most of it had undershot and fallen into open country, a disappointment compounded by the loss, mostly to night-fighters, of thirty-seven aircraft, eight from the ranks of 1 Group, but none from Elsham Wolds.

A force of 846 aircraft was made ready on the 18th, for the first of two heavy raids on the city of Frankfurt in south-central Germany, which 1 Group supported with a new record of 194 Lancasters, eighteen of which belonged to 576 Squadron. Each received a bomb load of a cookie and eighteen assorted SBCs, before departing Elsham Wolds between 18.40 and 19.15 with S/L Attwater the senior pilot on duty and heading for Orford Ness on course for the Franco/Belgian frontier. They benefitted from favourable weather conditions as they pressed on across France and into Germany, where they encountered a layer of haze 20,000 feet thick over the target, and according to most, no more than three-tenths cloud. This allowed the Path Finders to employ the Newhaven ground marking technique (blind marking by H2S, followed by visual backing-up), and the 576 Squadron crews confirmed the accuracy of the marking by referring to their own H2S, as a result of which, they were not misled by decoy fires north of the city. The 576 Squadron crews carried out their attacks on red and green TIs from 20,000 feet and above either side of 22.00, and witnessed a large explosion at 22.05, before flying home confident that their efforts had been worthwhile. They had, indeed, contributed to an outstandingly successful raid, during which, 5 Group alone had dropped more than one thousand tons of bombs for the first time at a single target. Local reports calculated that six thousand buildings had been destroyed or seriously damaged in predominantly eastern, central and western districts, and this was in return for the loss of twenty-two aircraft, just two of which were from 1 Group.

Frankfurt was named again on the 22nd as the target for that night, and 194 crews of 1 Group learned at briefings that they were to be part of another huge force of 816 aircraft, the seventeen belonging to 576 Squadron each receiving a bomb load of a cookie and eighteen assorted SBCs of 4lb and 30lb incendiaries. They departed Elsham Wolds between 18.35 and 19.10 with F/Ls Davison, Morgan, Shearer, Slater and Underwood the senior pilots on duty, and after climbing out above the station, flew out over Woodbridge near the Suffolk coast to make landfall on the French coast at Dunkerque and, thereafter, head directly for the target. F/L Underwood and crew had been outbound for around two hours when abandoning their sortie, the rear gunner having struggled in vain to close his turret doors, which, when open, prevented the turret from rotating. The others arrived at the target to find five to six-tenths thin, low cloud at around 4,000 feet and Paramatta marking (blind marking by H2S) in progress and focused their attention on the release-point flares and red and green TIs marking out the aiming point. They bombed from 20,000 to 23,000 feet either side of 22.00, after which a massive rectangular area of unbroken fire was observed across the centre of the city, the glow from which could be seen, according to some, from two hundred miles into the return flight. At debriefings, crews reported numerous searchlights lighting up the cloud, and moderate to intense flak that reached up to the bombers' flight level.

Local reports confirmed the enormity of the devastation, which was particularly severe in western districts and left this half of the city without electricity, gas and water for an extended period. More than nine hundred people lost their lives and a further 120,000 were bombed out of their homes at a cost to the Command of twenty-six Lancasters and seven Halifaxes, a loss-rate of 4.2% and 3.8% respectively. It was a bad night for senior officers, 207 and 7 Squadrons losing their commanding officers, while Bardney's station commander, G/C Norman Pleasance, failed to return in a 9 Squadron Lancaster. What was about to happen over the next week and a half, however, would overshadow anything that had gone before and would certainly not fall within what might be considered acceptable.

It was more than five weeks since the main force had last visited the "Big City", and 811 aircraft were made ready on the 24th for what would be the final raid of the war upon it by RAF heavy bombers. 1 Group put up 184 Lancasters, of which the nineteen belonging to 576 Squadron each received a bomb load of a cookie and sixteen SBCs of 4lb and 30lb incendiaries, before departing Elsham Wolds between 18.35 and 19.05 with F/Ls Davison, Morgan, Shearer, Slater and Underwood the senior pilots on duty. They set course via Mablethorpe for the west coast of Jutland near Ringkøbing, heading, thereafter, to a point on the German Baltic coast near Rostock, and when north-east of Berlin, they adopted a south-westerly course for the bombing run. Once clear of the defence zone homebound, the returning bombers were to dogleg to the west and then north-west to pass around Hannover on its southern and western sides, before heading for Holland and an exit via the Castricum coast. The extended outward leg provided a time-on-target of around 22.30, but an unexpected difficulty would be encountered, which rendered void all of the meticulous planning.

The existence of what we now know as "Jetstream" winds was unknown at the time, and the one blowing from the north with unprecedented strength on this night pushed the bomber stream south of its intended track. Navigators, who were expecting to see the northern tip of Sylt on their H2S screens, were horrified to find the southern end, which meant that they were thirty miles south of track and about to fly over Germany rather than Denmark. The previously mentioned "wind-finder" system had been set up for precisely this eventuality, but the problem on this night was that the wind-finders refused to believe what their instruments were telling them. Winds in excess of one hundred m.p.h had never been encountered before, and fearing that they would be disbelieved, many modified the figures downward. The same thing happened at raid control, where the figures were modified again, so that the information rebroadcast to the bomber stream bore no resemblance to the reality of the situation.

The bomber stream had by now become depleted by the early return of fifty-three aircraft for a variety of reasons, ten of them from the ranks of 1 Group, among which was 576 Squadron's F/L Underwood and crew because of an engine issue. Many of those pressing on commented on the inaccurate wind information received during the outward journey, and having arrived in the target area, found that the Path Finders were up to ten minutes late in opening the raid, a situation confirmed by the voice of the Master Bomber exhorting them to hurry up. Crews reported a variety of cloud conditions from three to ten-tenths at between 6,000 and 15,000 feet, but most were able to pick out the red and green TIs on the ground, and if not, found red Wanganui flares with green stars to guide them to the aiming point. The 576 Squadron crews confirmed their positions by H2S before bombing from 20,000 feet and above from around 22.20, observing what appeared to be a scattered attack in the early stages, until fires began to become more concentrated in three distinct areas. Large explosions were witnessed at 22.42 and 22.54, while all around, the defences filled the sky with heavy flak bursting at up to 24,000 feet and light flak batteries attempted to shoot out the skymarkers. In contrast, night-fighter activity was described by the 5 Group ORB as unusually quiet. There was a shock awaiting the Command as the returning aircraft landed to leave a shortfall of seventy-two, and it would be established later that two-thirds of them had fallen victim to the Ruhr flak defences after being driven into that region's defence zone by the wind on the way home.

576 Squadron's LM438 was being kept aloft by the power from two engines as it began final approach, after being shot-up by flak and a single-engine fighter, and as it landed in the hands of F/L Shearer a third engine gave out, resulting in a minor crash, which the crew and Lancaster survived without further major damage. Less fortunate were the crews of F/O Brooke and F/Sgt Collis, who failed to return in LM469 and LM471 respectively. It is believed that the former was well to the south of the intended track while outbound, when it exploded and crashed near Naunhof in the Leipzig defence zone, killing all but the wireless operator, who was taken into captivity. The latter was homebound and had been blown into the Ruhr defences, when it crashed three miles to the north of Duisburg city centre with the pilot and flight engineer still on board, leaving the five survivors to fall into enemy hands. Post-raid analysis revealed that the wind had also played havoc with the marking and bombing and had pushed the attack towards the south-western districts of the capital, where most of the damage occurred, while 126 outlying communities also received bombs. During this long and bitter campaign against Germany's capital city, 576 Squadron had participated in twelve main force operations and dispatched 121 sorties for the loss of nine aircraft, a 7.4% casualty rate, fifty-seven men having lost their lives and thirteen taken prisoner. (The Berlin Raids. Martin Middlebrook).

1 Group captured two Berlin campaign records, both by 460 Squadron RAAF, the crews of W/O Douglas and F/L Wales having completed fourteen of the sixteen Berlin raids since the November resumption, the former the most by a first-tour crew and the latter by a second-tour crew. While the bombs had been falling on Berlin, the "Great Escape" was taking place at Stalag Luft III at Sagan in Poland, and seventy-six men managed to exit the tunnel before the seventy-seventh was spotted. All but three were recaptured and fifty of them murdered by the gestapo on Hitler's orders.

On the 26th, S/L Haig DFC & Bar was posted from the squadron on promotion to acting wing commander rank to assume command of 625 Squadron at Kelstern and was succeeded as A Flight commander by S/L Donald Garner, who arrived from 1656 Conversion Unit for what would be a brief period. Although Berlin had now been consigned to the past, the winter campaign still had a week to run, and two more major operations for the crews to negotiate, the first of which was posted on the 26th and would bring a return to the old enemy of Essen, for which a force of 705 aircraft was made ready. Harris had been waging a personal war against Essen since March 1942, within weeks of his enthronement as Commander-in-Chief, and it was a war he ultimately won, but only after enduring twelve months of frustration and failure until the advent of Oboe to operations in March 1943. His obsession with this Ruhr city was born out of the fact that it was home to the Krupp organisation, which had been the largest manufacturer of weapons in Europe since before the Great War, had a hand in all aspects of German war production from tanks to artillery and ship and U-Boot construction, and was given a controlling share in all major heavy engineering companies in Germany and the occupied countries. It also built manufacturing sites in other parts of Germany, many situated close to concentration camps, and employed vast numbers of forced workers in all of its factories. Once known as "Die Waffenschmiede des Reichs", the weapons-forge of the realm, its manufacturing sites in Essen included the Friedrich Krupp steelworks, the Friedrich Krupp locomotive and general engineering works, the Altenberg zinc works, the Presswerk plastics factory, the Goldschmidt non-ferrous metals smelting plant, six coal mines and ten coke-oven plants, all situated either within or close to the four Borbeck districts, in a segment radiating out from near the city centre as far as the Rhine-Herne Canal on the north-western boundary on the banks of the Emscher River. The steel and engineering works, alone, employed in the region of eighty thousand people, and the company's sites covered an area of more than two thousand acres, of which three hundred acres were occupied by factories and workshops. All of that production capacity required massive rail and canal access in the form of marshalling yards and its own harbour, and energy from at least four nearby power stations.

1 Group contributed 165 of the 476 Lancasters for this night's operation, sixteen of them provided by 576 Squadron, each of which received a bomb load of a cookie and eighteen SBCs of incendiaries, before departing Elsham Wolds between 19.25 and 20.10 with F/Ls Davison, Morgan, Slater and Underwood the senior pilots on duty. They climbed out over the station and set course via Mablethorpe for the Dutch coast to the north of Haarlem and Amsterdam, before swinging to the south-east on a direct run to the target. The crews of F/Sgt McIvor and F/O Wood turned back at the same time, the former because of an engine issue and the latter after the rear gunner passed out as a result of oxygen starvation. The others reached the target to find it covered by eight to ten-tenths cloud with tops in places as high as 14,000 feet, but Oboe performed well and enabled the Path Finders to mark the city with red and green TIs and Wanganui flares.

The 576 Squadron crews bombed from 20,000 feet and above between 22.00 and 22.20, before returning home, F/Sgt Wearmouth and crew after an eventful and tension-filled sortie. During the North Sea crossing outbound, the flight engineer, while attempting to feather the ailing starboard-inner engine, inadvertently feathered two, causing the Lancaster to lose height while he restarted the third engine. They managed to regain most of the lost altitude and continued on to the target, where they were badly shot up by a Ju88, but escaped, before fending off a second Ju88. On reaching the Channel homebound they lost a second engine but were picked up by a Mosquito and shepherded to West Malling, where they landed safely. Returning crews had been unable to assess the results of their efforts, but the impression was of a successful raid, based on a considerable glow beneath the clouds as they withdrew. Post-raid reconnaissance soon confirmed another outstandingly destructive operation against this once elusive target, thus continuing the remarkable run of successes here since the introduction of Oboe to main force operations a year earlier. Over seventeen hundred houses were destroyed in the attack, with dozens of war industry factories sustaining serious damage, and on a night when the night-fighter controllers were caught off guard by the switch to the Ruhr, the success was gained for the modest loss of nine aircraft.

The period known as the Battle of Berlin, but which was better referred to as the winter campaign, was to be brought to an end on the night of the 30/31st with a standard maximum-effort raid on Nuremberg. The plan of operation departed from normal practice in only one important respect, and this was to prove critical. It had become standard practice for 8 Group to plan operations and to employ diversions and feints to confuse the enemy night-fighter controllers. Sometimes they were successful and sometimes not, but with the night-fighter force having clearly gained the upper hand with its "Tame Boar" running commentary system, all possible means had to be adopted to protect the bomber stream. During a conference held early on the 30th, the Lancaster Group A-O-Cs expressed a preference for a 5 Group-inspired route, which would require the bomber stream to fly a long straight leg across Belgium and Germany to a point about fifty miles north of Nuremberg, from where the final run-in would commence. The Halifax A-O-Cs were less convinced of the benefits, and AVM Bennett, the Path Finder chief, was positively overcome by the potential dangers and predicted a disaster, only to be overruled. A force of 795 aircraft was made ready, of which 180 Lancasters were to be provided by 1 Group, sixteen of them representing 576 Squadron, and at briefings, crews were told of the route, wind conditions and the belief that a layer of cloud would conceal them from enemy night-fighters. Before take-off, a Meteorological Flight Mosquito crew radioed in to cast doubts upon the weather conditions, which they could see differed markedly from those that had been forecast. This also went unheeded, and from around 21.45 for the next hour or so, the crews took off for the rendezvous area, and headed into a conspiracy of circumstances, which would inflict upon Bomber Command its heaviest defeat of the war.

The 576 Squadron Lancasters each received a bomb load of a cookie and sixteen SBCs of incendiaries, before departing Elsham Wolds between 21.25 and 22.18 with F/Ls Davison, Slater and Underwood the senior pilots on duty. They headed via Southwold for the Franco/Belgian coast, and it was not long into the flight before they and the other crews began to notice some unusual features in the conditions, which included uncommonly bright moonlight, and a crystal clarity of visibility that allowed them the rare sight of other aircraft in the stream. On most nights, crews would feel themselves to be completely alone in the sky all the way to the target, until bang on schedule, TIs would be seen to fall, and other aircraft make their presence known by the turbulence of their slipstreams as they funnelled towards the aiming point. Once at cruising altitude on this night, however, they were alarmed to note that the forecast cloud was conspicuous by its absence, and instead, lay beneath them as a white tablecloth, against which they were silhouetted like flies. Condensation trails began to form in the cold, clear air to further advertise their presence to the enemy, and the Jetstream winds, which had so adversely affected the Berlin raid a week earlier, were also present, only this time blowing from the south. As then, the wind-finder system would be unable to cope, and this would have a serious impact on the outcome of the operation. The final insult on this sad night was, that the route into Germany passed close to two night-fighter beacons, which the enemy aircraft were orbiting while they awaited their instructions, unaware initially that they were about to have the cream of Bomber Command handed to them on a plate.

F/O Wood and crew had already turned back with an unserviceable rear turret by the time that the carnage began over Charleroi in Belgium, and from there to the target, the route was sign-posted by the burning wreckage on the ground of eighty Bomber Command aircraft. Unaware of what was going on around them, many crews speculated on the cause of what appeared to be numerous burning haystacks. LM470 was outbound at 20,500 feet when intercepted by the night-fighter of Lt Wilhelm Seuss of IV./NJG5 and shot down to crash at Oberweid, some fifteen miles east-north-east of Fulda in central Germany as the operation's fifty-seventh victim, and only F/L Underwood and his wireless operator survived to be taken into captivity. The wind-finder system broke down again, and those crews who either failed to detect the strength of the wind, or simply refused to believe the evidence, were driven up to fifty miles north of their intended track, and consequently, turned towards Nuremberg from a false position. This led to more than a hundred aircraft bombing at Schweinfurt in error on misdirected Path Finder TIs, and, combined with the massive losses sustained before the target was reached, this reduced considerably the numbers arriving at the primary target.

The remaining 576 Squadron crews arrived over Nuremberg to encounter eight to nine-tenths cloud with tops as high as 16,000 feet and bombed from 20,000 to 23,000 feet between 01.10 and 01.30. They aimed at red and green TIs and sky-markers after confirming their positions by H2S and observed many fires, the glow from which, according to some reports, remained visible for 120 miles into the return journey. Ninety-five aircraft failed to return home, twenty-one of them from 1 Group, and many others were written off in landing crashes or with battle damage too severe to repair. The shock and disappointment were compounded by the fact that the strong wind had driven the marking beyond the city to the east, and Nuremberg had, consequently, escaped serious damage.

At some point during the month, S/L Mervyn Attwater was posted to 156 Squadron of the path Finder Force, with which he would continue to serve with distinction, on occasions acting as Master and Deputy Master Bomber. He was succeeded as 576 Squadron's B Flight commander temporarily by F/L Underwood, until his failure to return as described above, and then by S/L Garner, who moved over from A Flight, allowing the promotion of F/L Davison to acting squadron leader rank as the new A Flight commander. During the course of the month the squadron undertook six operations and dispatched ninety-nine sorties for the loss of three Lancasters and crews.

Lancaster ED713 crashed 24th December 1943 with the loss of the crew.

Lancaster ED713 UL-W2 crash site 24th December 1943

Crew of Lancaster ED713
P/O Richard Hughes KIA, Sgt James Paton KIA, Sgt J Woodruff PoW, Sgt Donald A H Morris PoW -
Sgt John Gray KIA, F/Sgt Francis Rivett KIA, Sgt F H Lanxon PoW

F/Sgt Malcolm Western (AWM)   F/Sgt Albert Harris   (Greg Keays)
Crew of Lancaster DV342 which crashed near Berlin on the 16/17th December 1943. The pilot F/O R S McAra, Sgt J L Barrett, F/O G L Blackmore (below), F/Sgts A A Harris and M Western have no known grave while F/Sgt C Chapman and Sgt E Russom are buried in the Berlin War Cemetery.   (Aircrew Remembered)

LAC (later F/O) Geoffrey Blackmore, left, and a fellow Leading Aircraftman identified only as 'Ken', was killed in DV432 aged 21. (AWM)

Lancaster UL-A (Harry Holmes)

Lancaster D2 of C Flight (Harry Holmes)

576 Squadron Lancaster UL-B F/L O'Neill & crew   *(Harry Holmes)*

A 576 Squadron Lancaster landing at an airfield using the FIDO method of fog dispersal. (Harry Holmes)

A crashed Lancaster which damaged FIDO pipelines and burners upon crashing (Not 576 Squadron)

Sulzer pumps installed at Graveley, Huntingdonshire, to supply the FIDO (Fog Investigation and Dispersal Operation) petrol pipes on either side of the main runway.

P/O Bob Edie and Crews (Harry Holmes)

F/O Bodger & crew with Lancaster LL794 PM-P   (Harry Holmes)

576 Squadron

576 Squadron ground crew   (Harry Holmes)

576 Squadron Lancaster UL-B2   (Harry Holmes)

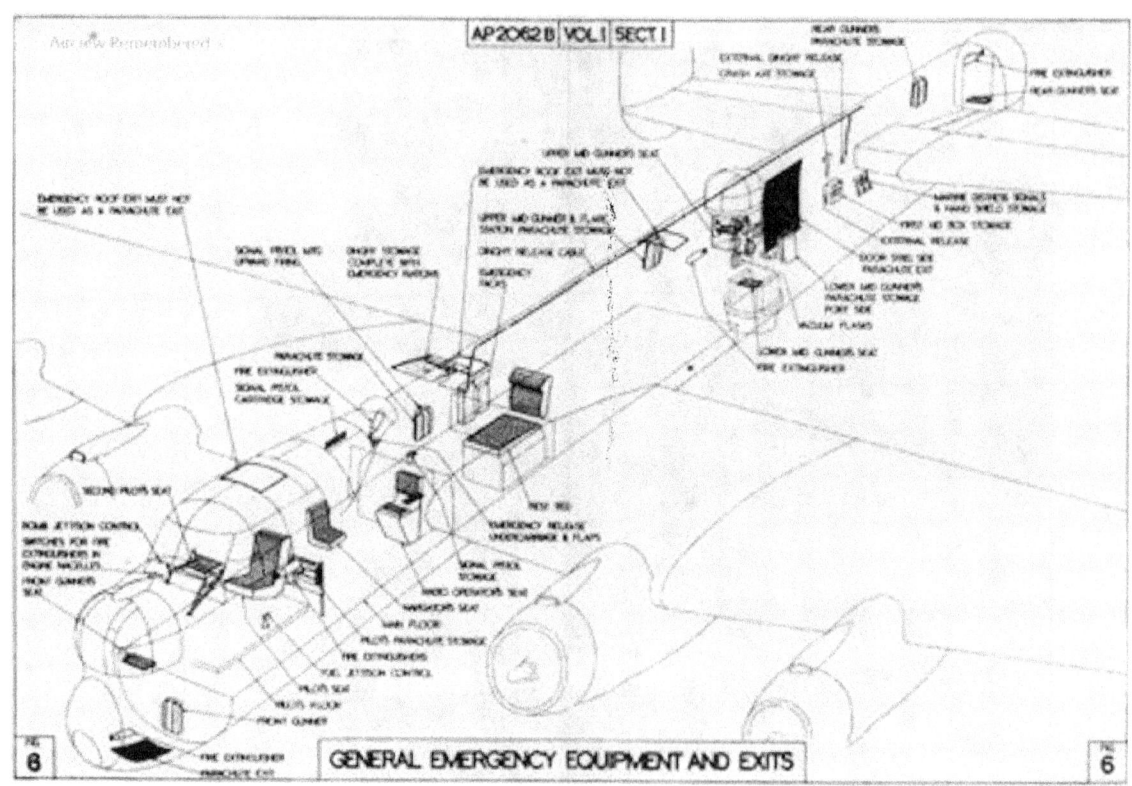
Lancaster interior schematic

Target Indicators over Berlin

The facade of a damaged building is demolished in Tauentzienstraße in Berlin-Charlottenburg.

Construction of splinter trenches. Soldiers are deployed in the Reich capital to dig splinter trenches in the public squares for the protection of the population against air terror in Dönhoffplatz. Berlin.

Lancaster ED888 UL-M2 P/O Bell crew's 100th operation 20th July 1944. (Harry Holmes)

Four members of 576 Squadron outside their hut RAF Fiskerton, Titch, Bert, Johnny, Harry. (AWM)

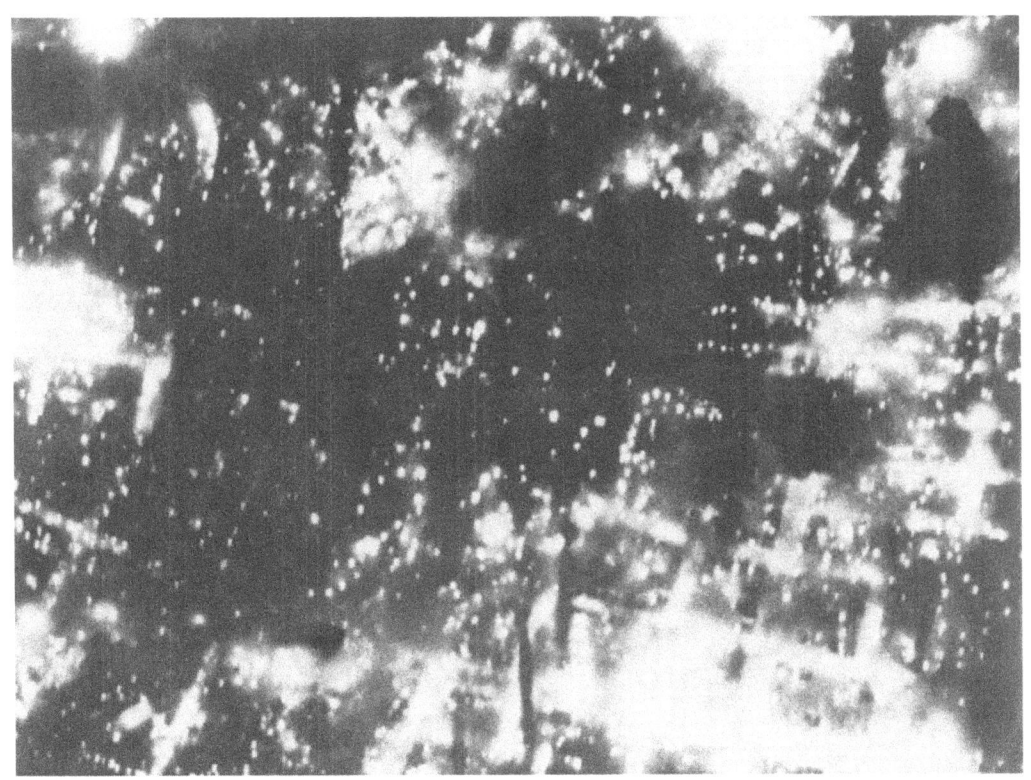

Braunschweig (Brunswick), Germany. 1944. Streets illuminated by fires as the result of night attacks on 14/15th October 1944 by RAF Bomber Command, when 800 tons of bombs, and incendiaries were dropped.

Aftermath of Magdeburg bombing

Lancaster ND375 UL-R and unidentified crew *(Harry Holmes)*

Lancaster ND521 UL-L2. Ground crew with possibly F/O G H Hardman in cockpit (Harry Holmes)

Interior of Augsburg Town Hall after the 25/26th February 1944 bombing.

576 Squadron Lancaster PA265 with possibly the Ryan crew who were lost March 1945 (Harry Holmes)

Lancaster JA868 UL-T2 with F/O A J L Ridge & crew (Harry Holmes)

Lancaster ME703 UL-N2 P/O Richard Reed (KIA 23rd May 1944) (Harry Holmes)

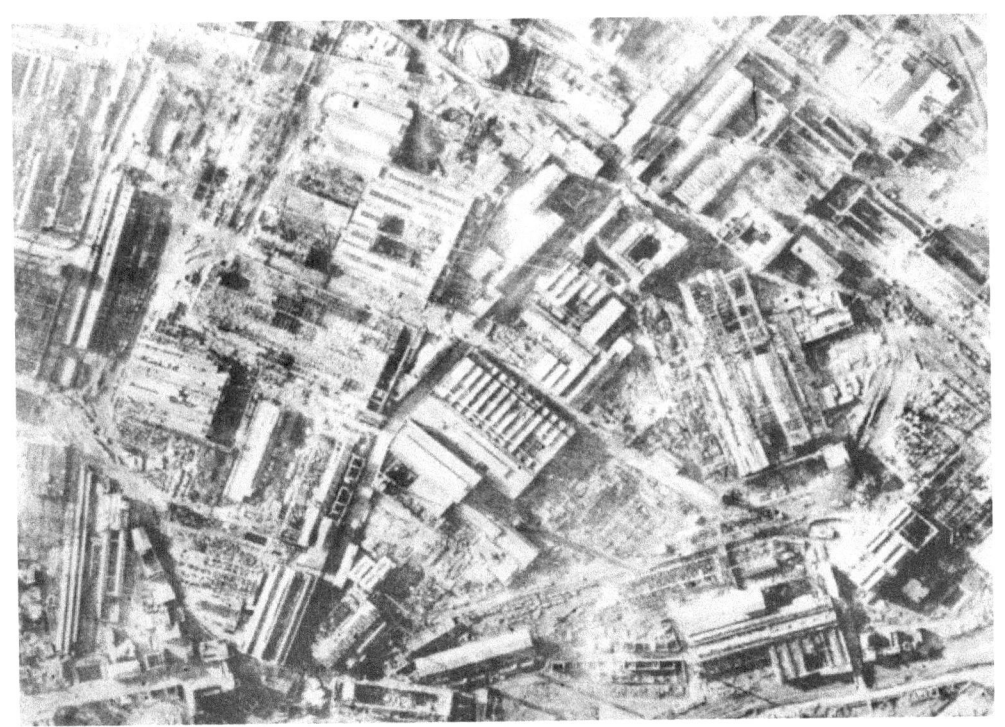

A large area of the great Krupp armaments works at Essen as it appeared after recent attacks by RAF Bomber Command in which aircraft of 576 Squadron took part.

Nuremberg

Lancaster UL-K2 'Killer' with unidentified crew (Harry Holmes)

The Smith crew and groundcrew of Lancaster ME671 UL-V2 on its dispersal at Fiskerton. (Harry Holmes)

Lancaster LM227 UL-I² 100 Operations (Harry Holmes)

Lancaster LM227 UL-I² take off (Harry Holmes)

April 1944

The winter campaign had brought the Command to its low point of the war and was the only time when the morale of the crews might have been in question, but what now lay before the hard-pressed men of Bomber Command was in marked contrast to that which had been endured over the seemingly interminable winter months. In place of the long slog to Germany on dark, often dirty nights, shorter range hops to France and Belgium in improving weather conditions would become the order of the day. However, these operations would be equally demanding in their way and require of the crews a greater commitment to accuracy to avoid casualties among friendly civilians. Despite this, a decree from on high insisted that such operations were worthy of counting as just one third of a sortie towards the completion of a tour, and until this flawed policy was grudgingly rescinded late in the war, a sense of injustice pervaded the crew rooms. In fact, the number of sorties to complete a tour would fluctuate up and down to a maximum of around thirty-eight between this point and the end of hostilities. Despite the horrendous losses of the winter campaign, the Command was in remarkably fine fettle to face its new challenge, with 3 Group gradually changing to Lancasters and the much-improved Hercules powered Halifaxes equipping 4 Group and most of 6 Group. Harris was now in the enviable position of being able to achieve what had eluded his predecessor, namely, to attack multiple targets simultaneously with enough strength to be effective. Such was the hitting-power now at his disposal, that he could assign targets to individual groups, to groups in tandem or to the Command as a whole, as dictated by operational requirements, and while invasion considerations were about to become the priority, Harris's favoured policy of city-busting would never entirely be shelved.

There would be an influx of new aircrew at Elsham Wolds during the course of the month, many arriving from 11 Base, which comprised the Heavy Conversion Units at Lindholme, Blyton and Sandtoft. On the 4th, Operational Instruction No 19 was issued by 1 Group HQ, stating that it was the intention to "train and operate suitable crews to act as target markers and assembly point markers for precision attacks by small forces of exclusively 1 Group aircraft". The instruction went on to state that these operations would be carried out "chiefly during moonlight periods", and generally when the bulk of the Command's main force squadrons were inactive. This mirrored in a small way 5 Group's march to independence, although, what would become 1 Group's Special Duties Flight was minor in comparison, and as events were to prove, would be relatively short-lived.

The weather at the start of the month was not conducive to operational flying, and Elsham Wolds was effectively stood down until the 9th, when the pre-invasion campaign got into full swing. Two operations were posted, one against the Lille-Delivrance goods station in north-eastern France assigned to 239 aircraft from 3, 4, 6 and 8 Groups, and the other targeting the marshalling yards at Villeneuve-St-Georges, on the southern outskirts of Paris involving 225 aircraft drawn from all groups. In addition to these operations, a large mining effort in the Baltic involved forty-seven and fifty-six Lancasters respectively from 1 and 5 Groups. Among thirty-six 1 Group Lancasters detailed for Villeneuve-St-Georges were four representing 576 Squadron containing the crews of P/O Thomas, S/L Garner and F/Sgts Thorpe and Wearmouth, who departed Elsham Wolds in that order between at 20.53 and 21.00, each with a bomb load of a dozen 1,000 and four 500-pounders beneath their feet. They began the Channel crossing at Selsey Bill, and having rendezvoused with the rest of the force, made landfall on the Normandy coast at around 14,000 feet under clear skies.

The target could be identified visually, but crews aimed for the Path Finder-laid red and green TIs, which when plotted later were found to have fallen a mile-and-a-half north-east of the aiming point. The 576 Squadron quartet delivered their hardware from 12,500 and above feet shortly before midnight in the face of little opposition, and many bomb bursts were observed along with orange explosions, and to those high above, the raid appeared to be highly successful. In fact, many bomb loads had hit adjacent residential districts, where four hundred houses had been destroyed or seriously damaged, and ninety-three people killed. This was far fewer than had died in the simultaneous operation at Lille, many miles to the north-east, where over two thousand items of rolling stock had been destroyed, and buildings and installations seriously damaged, but at a collateral cost of 456 French civilian lives. Civilian casualties would prove to be an unavoidable by-product of the campaign.

On the following day, Monday the 10th, a further five railway yards were posted as the targets for that night, four of them in France and one in Belgium, each assigned to an individual group. 1 Group was handed those at Aulnoye in the Haut-de-France region of north-eastern France, and for the first time would be employing its own target marking element and a Master Bomber and Deputy to back up the Path Finders. 130 Lancasters were made ready, plus two more for the Master Bomber pairing, and 576 Squadron supported the operation with fourteen aircraft, each of which was loaded with twelve 1,000 and four 500-pounders. They departed Elsham Wolds between 23.05 and 23.45 with F/L Davison the senior pilot on duty, still recorded in the ORB in his former rank, and lost the services before becoming airborne of F/Sgt Thorpe and crew after they deviated from the runway, fortunately without consequences. The others set course over ten-tenths cloud for Selsey Bill and the Channel crossing to the Seine estuary, overlooked by the port of Le Havre. There were no early returns, and as the French coast hove into view, the cloud gradually dispersed to leave clear skies and good horizontal visibility. At the target they encountered patches of thin, drifting cloud with tops at 6,000 feet and haze that presented challenging conditions in which to identify ground detail. The Path Finders opened the attack on the northern aiming point on time with green TIs, which the Master bomber assessed before directing the main force crews. He was carrying red TIs to remark the aiming point, if necessary, but the only reds to appear were employed at the southern aiming point. The 576 Squadron crews bombed mostly on green TIs from 12,000 feet and above either side of 02.30, and all but one returned safely to report too much conversation between the Master Bomber and Deputy, which apparently lasted for forty minutes. There was little opposition from the ground, but night-fighters were active over the target and at the French coast and seven Lancasters failed to return. Among them was 576 Squadron's LL830, which crashed east of Cambrai and west of Solesmes with no survivors from the crew of F/L Barnsdale. It proved impossible to assess the outcome, but reconnaissance and local sources confirmed a successful raid, in which 287 bombs had landed in the yards, damaging the engine sheds and thirty locomotives. Sadly, 340 houses were either destroyed or damaged and fourteen civilians were killed, and the Germans rounded up local civilians to pressgang into repairing the damage to get the yards working again before long.

Aachen was a major railway centre with marshalling yards at both the western and eastern ends, but the attack planned for the night of the 11/12th was clearly designed as a city-busting exercise for which a force of 341 heavy aircraft was drawn from 1, 3, 5 and 8 Groups. 576 Squadron made ready eleven of the ninety-five Lancasters representing 1 Group, and they were loaded with a dozen 1,000 pounders and two deep SBCs, each containing 150 rather than the standard 90 x 4lb incendiaries. They departed Elsham Wolds between 20.05 and 20.40 with F/L Davison the senior pilot on duty and S/L Garner flying as second pilot to F/L Morgan, and exited the English coast over the Norfolk resort of Sheringham. The bomber stream climbed to between 18,000 and 20,000 feet by the time it reached the Belgian coast at 3° East and maintained that altitude all the way to the target, where six to ten-tenths thin cloud was encountered that topped out at 12,000 feet. Red and green TIs identified the aiming point, and the 576 Squadron crews attacked it from 12,000 feet and above either side of 22.45, observing many bomb bursts and fires, which suggested that the attack was accurate. The bombers maintained height on the way home until fifty miles from the coast, at which position they began a gentle descent to exit enemy territory at 15,000 feet or above. Reports coming out of Aachen revealed this to be the city's worst experience of the war to date, with extensive damage in central and southern districts, disruption of its transport infrastructure and a death toll of 1,525 people in return for the loss of nine Lancasters, none of which was from 1 Group. However, post-raid reconnaissance revealed that the railway yards had not been destroyed and would require further attention.

On the 14th, the Command became officially subject to the orders coming from the Supreme Headquarters of the Allied Expeditionary Force (SHAEF), under General Dwight D Eisenhower, and would remain thus shackled until the Allied armies were sweeping towards the German frontier at the end of the summer. On the 15th, 300 (Masovian) Squadron, the last in 1 Group to relinquish the Wellington, was declared operational on Lancasters at Faldingworth, and would bring the passion and fierce determination of Polish airmen back to the frontline after spending much of the previous eight months undertaking gardening operations. 1 Group's Special Duties Flight, or SDF as it became known, was formed officially at Binbrook on the 18th under the command of S/L Breakspear, an experienced flight commander from 100 Squadron, a man who had recently been awarded a DFC following eleven trips to Berlin and to whom taking the war to Germany was a point of principle and pride. The other crews to be posted in were those of F/L Gillam, also from 100 Squadron, F/L Hull from 101 Squadron, F/L Russell-Fry from 103 Squadron, P/O Marks from 625 Squadron and P/O Stewart from 626 Squadron. F/Sgt Daley from 460 Squadron RAAF and P/O Knowles from 625 Squadron would be added to the unit three weeks hence.

It was on this day also that 83 and 97 Squadrons were posted on what amounted to a permanent transfer from the Path Finders to 5 Group along with the Mosquito unit, 627 Squadron. They would retain their Path Finder status and privileges but would spend the remainder of the war as part of 5 Group, 83 and 97 Squadrons to fulfil the heavy target marking role, while the Mosquitos would eventually take over the low-level marking role currently performed by 617 Squadron under W/C Leonard Cheshire. This was a major coup for AVM Cochrane and 5 Group and a bitter blow to AVM Bennett, the Path Finder Air Officer Commanding, whose relations had never been cordial, but this plunged them to new depths. Both were brilliant men, Bennett, an Australian, in particular, a man of the greatest intellect, who, despite his apparent total lack of humour, commanded the deepest respect and loyalty from his men. He and Cochrane possessed vastly different opinions on the subject of target marking, Bennett believing that a low-level method exposed the crews to unnecessary danger, while Cochrane insisted that the risks in a fast-flying Mosquito were negligible and would produce greater accuracy.

The Transportation Plan continued on the 18th with the briefing of 827 Lancaster and Halifax crews for attacks on marshalling yards at four locations in France, 1 Group assigned to Rouen in Normandy, for which 140 Lancasters were detailed, including seven from 300 Squadron on its Lancaster debut. 576 Squadron prepared fifteen Lancasters for this two-phase operation, loading each with twelve 1,000 and four 500-pounders, before sending them on their way from Elsham Wolds as part of the first phase between 21.15 and 21.50 with S/L Garner the senior pilot on duty. They headed south via Newbury to Selsey Bill under almost clear skies and lost the services of F/Sgt Thorpe and crew to a heating problem affecting the rear gunner. The fine conditions persisted as the remainder crossed the Channel and then the French coast near Dieppe with just twenty miles to cover to reach the target. In the light provided by Path Finder flares, the crews were able visually to identify the River Seine, the marshalling yards and railway track, and green warning flares guided them to the mark. The first phase attack on the southern aiming point proceeded seamlessly with the Path Finders and Master bomber fulfilling their roles faultlessly, and the 576 Squadron element delivering their attacks from 12,000 feet and above, observing numerous explosions, including a particularly large one at 00.18, which lasted a few seconds. The second phase assault on the northern aiming point took place two hours later and, only a little less effectively to leave the site in ruins and burning fiercely. F/L Wood and crew were attacked by an intruder in the circuit on return, their Lancaster sustaining some superficial damage but no crew casualties.

While the assault on railways in the occupied countries continued on the night of the 20/21st, a force of 357 Lancasters and twenty-two Mosquitos was drawn from 1, 3, 6 and 8 Groups to attack railway installations in Cologne. There were several major marshalling yards within the city, those at Kalk and Gremberg on the eastern side of the Rhine and Nippes and Gereon to the west, each within a relatively short distance of the city centre, which effectively turned the raid into a city-busting affair. 1 Group contributed a record 196 Lancasters, seventeen of them provided by 576 Squadron, each of which received a bomb load of a cookie and eighteen assorted SBCs of 4lb and 30lb incendiaries. They departed Elsham Wolds between 23.10 and 00.10 with F/Ls Morgan and Slater the senior pilots on duty, and with enemy intruders active over eastern England, were advised to find alternative routes to the departure point at Southwold. They made landfall on the Belgian coast at Knokke, and all reached the target area to find ten-tenths cloud with tops at 12,000 to 16,000 feet, through which it was impossible to see TIs on the ground, leaving them with no choice but to aim at late and scattered red and yellow Path Finder release point flares. The 576 Squadron crews carried out their attacks from 21,000 feet and above from around 02.05, and the flashes from many explosions were observed along with a red glow from the burgeoning fires. There was little opposition from the ground, but night-fighters were active over Belgium on the way home and ten combats were reported by 1 Group crews. Post raid reconnaissance and local sources confirmed an outstandingly destructive operation, during which a record 4,500 tons of bombs had been dropped mostly in northern and western districts. The catalogue of destruction included 1,861 houses or apartments, and 20,000 others were damaged, along with 192 industrial premises and 725 dwelling houses with commercial units attached. Many public buildings, including schools and churches, were caught in the bombing and more than 1,200 fires had to be dealt with.

A major night of operations on the 22nd called for three forces to be made available, the largest of 596 aircraft from all but 5 Group to target Düsseldorf for the first time for a year, while 5 Group tested its low-level marking system at Braunschweig and 181 aircraft from 3, 4, 6 and 8 Groups attended to railway yards at Laon. 1 Group contributed 178 Lancasters to the Ruhr raid, of which the fifteen belonging to 576 Squadron were given a similar bomb load to that for Cologne, before beginning the departure process from Elsham Wolds at 22.10. ND362 swung on take-off in the hands of F/Sgt Young and crew and hit the nose of P/O Thomas's ED767, causing both to be scrubbed from the order of battle, and LL794 also veered off the runway after bursting a tyre and experiencing a port engine fire. The flames were extinguished and W/O Puttock and crew walked away unscathed, but the incidents required a change of runway and the participation of the crews of F/Sgts Hordal and Thorpe and P/O Tomlin was cancelled. F/Sgt Wearmouth and crew were the last to become airborne at 23.20, and they caught up with the bomber stream as it flew out over Southwold under cloudless skies on the southern route to the Ruhr via the French coast. There, they were greeted by high cirrus cloud above 21,000 feet, which was present also in the target area and merged with the heavy condensation trails to betray the bomber stream's presence. The first Mosquito-borne Oboe red TIs went down between 01.14 and 01.15 and were immediately joined by concentrated greens delivered by the Path Finder heavy brigade, which were clearly visible through the industrial haze. The backers-up maintained the aiming point throughout the raid, and some of the experience crews would describe the marking as the best they had witnessed. The 576 Squadron crews carried out their attacks from 19,000 feet and above either side of 01.30, contributing to the total of 2,150 tons of bombs and gaining the impression that the entire city was on fire. By 01.23 a large volume of smoke was rising to meet the bombers and a large explosion at 01.45 was observed by some crews who were well into the homeward flight and would report at debriefing that the glow from the burning city was still visible from the Dutch coast. Night-fighters infiltrated the bomber stream over the target and on the way home, and twenty-nine aircraft failed to return, among them seven from 1 Group. Local sources confirmed the severity of the raid, which hit predominantly northern districts and destroyed or badly damaged more than two thousand houses and fifty-six large industrial concerns, while killing in the region of 1,200 people.

The main operation on the night of the 24/25th was against Karlsruhe in southern Germany, for which a force of 637 aircraft was assembled, while 5 Group targeted Munich in another test of its low-level marking system against a heavily defended urban target. 1 Group put up 179 Lancasters, of which the eighteen made ready by 576 Squadron received one of four bomb loads, depending on the role of the crew and its place in the bomber stream. Three loads included a cookie, supplemented with fifteen, seventeen or eighteen SBCs of incendiaries, while P/O Reed and crew were sitting on six 2,000-pounders for their role as a Path Finder supporter. This required them to accompany the 8 Group spearhead across the aiming point to "beef" up the numbers and make it harder for flak batteries to single out individual aircraft, after which they would carry out a second pass to deliver their bomb load. The 576 Squadron contingent departed Elsham Wolds between 21.35 and 22.20 with F/Ls Slater and Wood the senior pilots on duty, and according to the ORB, were given two routes, the first via Sheringham and the second via Beachy Head, presumably to converge as they approached the target. They flew out over small amounts of medium cloud as far as the Franco-German frontier, where they encountered a band of high cloud between 18,000 and 23,000 feet, which contained pockets of icing. Thin variable cloud persisted over the target to present the Path Finders with challenging conditions for target identification and marking, and they were a little late in opening the attack. Some crews bombed on their own H2S before the first TIs went down, and the altitude of the others determined whether or not they could see the red and green TIs on the ground. The 576 Squadron crews had been briefed to attack from 21,000 feet and above, but most came down to 18,000 feet, from where they gained a clear view of the marked area, while those above did not. Bombing took place from around 00.30 and fires were reported over a wide area with smoke rising through 12,000 feet as the attack ended.

On the 26th, briefings took place for an operation against Essen, for which a force of 493 aircraft was assembled from all but 5 Group, 1 Group contributing 175 of the Lancasters, eighteen belonging to 576 Squadron. Each received one of a variety of bomb loads, mostly including a cookie and incendiaries with the odd 1,000 and 500-pounder thrown in. They departed Elsham Wolds between 22.20 and 23.07 with S/L Garner the senior pilot on duty on course again for two exit points, one over Mablethorpe and the other over Sheringham, the former to make landfall over the Frisians and the latter over the Scheldt estuary to approach the target in a pincer movement from the north and south. A little broken cloud was encountered over the Frisians, but clear skies prevailed as the force progressed inland to find good visibility and only a little industrial haze at the target, while the defenders were aided by the formation of condensation trails. Many crews arrived in the target area ahead of the Path Finders and not all were prepared to wait for the attack to begin, which it did at 01.24 with red TIs that were soon backed up by a concentration of greens. The aiming point was well-maintained throughout the raid, during which the 576 Squadron crews carried out their attacks from 20,000 feet and above either side of 01.30, describing a good concentration of bomb bursts around the markers and a pall of smoke rising to a considerable height. The glow from the burning city remained visible for eighty miles and more, and returning crews were in no doubt that another devastating blow had been achieved. A modest seven aircraft failed to return, four from the ranks of 1 Group, including a 103 squadron Lancaster from Elsham Wolds.

The 27th saw a further three operations scheduled, two against railway yards at Aulnoye in France and Montzen in Belgium, and the night's largest effort against the small city of Friedrichshafen, situated on the northern shore of Lake Constance (Bodensee) on the border with Switzerland and close to the Austrian frontier. An all-Lancaster force of 322 aircraft was assembled, the main force element drawn from 1, 3 and 6 Groups with fifty-nine 8 Group Lancasters to provide the marking. At briefings, the 162 crews from 1 Group were told of the importance of Friedrichshafen to the German war effort as a centre of war production, particularly of tank engines and gearboxes. The eighteen 576 Squadron Lancasters received one of four bomb loads, three involving a cookie and SBCs of incendiaries and at least one a 1,000 and a 500-pounder, before departing Elsham Wolds between 21.10 and 21.55 with S/L Davison the senior pilot on duty. F/Sgt Thorpe and crew turned back early after losing an engine, while the others exited the English coast at Shoreham-on-Sea on course for the Normandy coast, and apart from ten-tenths cloud over the Channel, the outward route was completed under clear skies. The high-level cirrus over the target was no impediment to the crews' ability to establish their positions visually on Lake Constance, where zero hour for the main force was brought forward by ten minutes to 02.05, and the Path Finders opened the attack at 02.00 with green flares and green TIs. The 576 Squadron crews confirmed their positions by H2S before carrying out their attacks from 17,000 feet and above from around 02.00 in accordance with the instructions of the Master Bomber. They observed an accurate and concentrated pattern of bombing and many explosions and fires, and were confident that they had contributed to an outstandingly effective attack. It was not a one-sided affair, however, and having avoided to some extent contact with night-fighters on the way to the target, the bombers sustained heavy casualties at their hands in the target area. Eighteen Lancasters were lost, ten from 1 Group, including another belonging to 103 Squadron. A total of 1,234 tons of bombs had been dropped on Friedrichshafen, leaving an estimated 67% of its built-up area in ruins, several factories sustaining severe damage, while the tank gearbox plant was destroyed, thus dealing a severe blow to tank production.

The target on the 30th for 116 Lancasters was a Luftwaffe bomb and ammunition dump at Maintenon, situated some twenty miles to the west of Paris, for which a dozen 576 Squadron crews attended briefing to learn that this would be the first operation to be conducted exclusively by 1 Group with six Lancasters of the Special Duties Flight acting as the marker force. They departed Elsham Wolds between 21.25 and 21.50 with S/L Davison the senior pilot on duty and each Lancaster carrying eleven 1,000 and four 500-pounders. P/O Griffiths and crew were in LM527, which struck a fence with an undercarriage leg as it left the runway and damaged not only the landing gear but also the hydraulics system, which meant that they could not open the bomb doors to jettison the load for landing. They were left with no option but to abandon the Lancaster to its fate, presumably pointing its snout towards the North Sea before baling out safely. Meanwhile, the others flew out over Selsey Bill on course for the Normandy coast and so favourable were the conditions during the outward flight that crews were able to map-read their way to the target, where red spot fires marked out the aiming point, and when these had been obliterated by explosions, crews aimed for the centre of the smoke and flames. The 576 Squadron crews attacked from 6,000 feet and above either side of midnight in accordance with instructions from the Master Bomber, whose broadcasts were indistinct but sufficiently comprehensible, and a number of very large explosions confirmed the attack as an outstanding success, achieved without loss.

During the course of the month, the squadron took part in ten operations and dispatched 142 sorties for the loss of two Lancasters and one crew.

May 1944

With the invasion now just five weeks away, the new month would be devoted to attacks on railway targets and coastal defences, and in the case of the latter, the focus would be on the Pas-de-Calais region of France, to try to reinforce the enemy's mistaken belief that the landings would take place there. The month began with six small-scale operations over France on the night of the 1/2nd, three directed at railway targets and three at specific factories. The target for seventy-five Lancasters of 1 Group, six of them from the SDF, was the Berliet motor works in the Venissieux district of Lyons in east-central France, which was manufacturing lorries for the benefit of the enemy. 576 Squadron loaded its seven Lancasters with eleven 1,000-pounders and either a single or three 500-pounders, according to variant, and sent them on their way from Elsham Wolds between 21.15 and 21.35 with S/L Davison the senior pilot on duty and W/C Clayton flying as second pilot to P/O Blackie. They set course for Selsey Bill and then Cabourg on the French coast, and the excellent conditions persisted all the way to the target, which was bathed in bright moonlight with the vertical visibility marred only by a little ground haze as the first marker went down accurately at 00.47. However, the backer-up's first attempt fell wide of the mark, and he had to make a second pass, and this time the marker was deemed to be sufficiently accurate for the Master Bomber, S/L Breakspear, to call in the first wave of the main force at 01.02. The 576 Squadron ORB continues to provide incomplete information and the bombing heights and times are not recorded, but based on the records of other 13 Base units, bombing by the first wave took place on red spotfires from 8,000 to 10,000 feet, before the second wave was called in at 01.07, by which time smoke had enveloped the aiming point and concealed the spotfires from view. Cascading yellow TIs were then employed to guide the crews in, and the attack was concluded successfully without loss at around 01.15.

Briefings took place on 1 and 5 Group stations on the 3rd, for what would become a highly contentious operation that night against a Panzer training camp and transport depot at Mailly-le-Camp, situated some seventy-five miles east of Paris in north-eastern France. The units based there posed a potential threat to Allied forces as the invasion unfolded and needed to be eliminated. The events of the operation proved to be so controversial, that recriminations abound to this day concerning the quality of leadership provided by the 5 Group Master Bomber, W/C Laurence Deane of 83 Squadron, and marker leader, W/C Leonard Cheshire of 617 Squadron. Although the grudges by 1 Group aircrew against them can be understood in the light of what happened, they are unjust and based on emotion and incorrect information, and it is worthwhile to examine the conduct of the operation in some detail. W/C Cheshire was appointed as marker leader and was piloting one of four 617 Squadron Mosquitos, while W/C Deane was overall raid controller with S/L Sparks as his deputy. Deane and Cheshire attended separate briefings, and neither seemed aware of the complete plan, particularly the role of the 1 Group Special Duties Flight from Binbrook, which was assigned to mark its own specific aiming point for an element of the 1 Group force provided by 460 and 625 Squadrons.

A force was assembled consisting of 346 Lancasters and fourteen Mosquitos of 1 and 5 Groups and two 8 Group Mosquitos, 1 Group providing 140 Lancasters for Target A, the military camp, and thirty-three, including four from the SDF, to attack Target B, the tank repair depot. 576 Squadron contributed eighteen Lancasters, each of which was loaded with a cookie and sixteen 500-pounders, before departing Elsham Wolds between 21.30 and 22.22 with S/L Davison the senior pilot on duty. They began the Channel crossing at Beachy Head on course under clear skies and in bright moonlight to make landfall north-east of Dieppe, before tracking south-east to the final turning point north of the target. It seems that 576 Squadron's ME586 was shot down during the final leg to the target, crashing some six miles west-north-west of the town of Epernay, still forty miles short of Mailly, with fatal consequences for P/O Whalley DFC and four of his crew, while the flight engineer and navigator survived to fall into enemy hands.

The excellent conditions persisted as the force arrived in the target area and began to orbit awaiting instructions, while confusion was already beginning to influence events. W/C Cheshire and S/L Shannon were in position before midnight, and as the first flares from the 83 and 97 Squadron Lancasters illuminated the target below, Cheshire released his two red spot fires onto the first aiming point at 00.00½ from 1,500 feet. Shannon backed them up from 400 feet five-and-a-half minutes later, and as far as Cheshire was concerned, the operation was bang on schedule. A 97 Squadron Lancaster also laid markers accurately, to ensure a constant focal point, prompting Cheshire to pass instructions to Deane to call the bombers in, and it was at this stage of the operation that matters began to go awry. A communications problem arose, when a commercial radio station, believed to be an American forces network, jammed the VHF frequencies in use. Deane called in the 5 Group element, elated that everything was proceeding according to plan, but nothing happened. He checked with his wireless operator that the instructions had been transmitted and called up S/L Sparks, who was also mystified by the lack of bombing. A few crews from 5 Group's 9, 207 and 467 Squadrons had heard the call to bomb, and did so, but for most, the instructions were swamped by the interference. Some 5 Group crews realised that R/T was jammed and bombed between 00.11 and 00.17 causing smoke to begin drifting across the target area.

The four SDF aircraft, led by F/L Hull, were in position by this time, but the initial green spot flare was assessed by Hull to have overshot by a thousand yards, and a second was misplaced by five hundred yards. The deputy marker leader laid a third marker which was judged to be accurate, and at 00.11, the first dozen of twenty-nine Lancasters from 460 and 625 Squadrons followed up with accurate bombing from 6,500 to 9,000 feet, before the target became obscured by smoke. As a result of this, and the fact that the 5 Group attack had commenced close by, the remaining seventeen 1 Group aircraft assigned to the "special target" were diverted to assist in the attack on the main site. W/C Deane then attempted to control the operation by W/T, which also failed.

Post raid reports are contradictory, and it is impossible to establish an accurate course of events, particularly when Deane and Cheshire's understanding of the exact time of zero hour differed by five minutes. Remarkably, it also seems, that Deane was unaware that there were two aiming points, or three, if one includes 1 Group's Special Duties Flight. Cheshire, initially at least, appeared happy with the early stages of the attack, and described the bombing as concentrated and accurate. It seems certain, however, that many minutes had passed between the dropping of Cheshire's markers and the first main force bombs falling, during which period, Deane was coming to terms with the fact, that his instructions were not getting through. As the 1 Group crews became increasingly agitated at having to wait in bright moonlight with evidence of enemy night-fighters all around, some of them inevitably joined in the bombing.

Now a new problem was arising as smoke from these first salvoes began to obliterate the entire camp, and Cheshire had to decide whether or not to send in Fawke and Kearns to mark the second aiming point. His feeling, and that of Deane, as it later transpired, was that it was unnecessary, as the volume of bombs still to fall into the relatively compact area of the target would ensure destruction of the entire site, despite which, he ordered them in. By 00.16, the first phase of bombing should have been completed to leave a clear run for Fawke and Kearns across the target, but the majority of 5 Group crews were still on their bombing run, a fact unknown to Cheshire, who asked Deane for a pause in the bombing to allow the two Mosquitos to go in. As far as Cheshire was concerned, there was no response from Deane, who would, anyway, have been confused by mention of a second aiming point. Deane's deputy, S/L Sparks, eventually found a channel free of interference, and did, in fact, transmit an instruction to halt the bombing, both by W/T and R/T, and some crews reported hearing something. While utter chaos reigned above, Kearns and Fawke dived in among the falling cookies at 00.23 and 00.25 respectively, to mark the second aiming point on the western edge of the camp. At 2,000 feet, they were lucky to survive the turbulence created by the exploding 4,000 pounders, when 4,000 feet was considered to be a minimum safe height.

They were not entirely happy with their work, but F/O Edwards of 97 Squadron dropped a stick of markers precisely on the mark, and S/L Sparks was then able to call in the 1 Group main force along with any from 5 Group with bombs still on board, and it was at this time that the 576 Squadron crews attacked from 6,000 feet and above between 00.25 and 00.32. It was described in the 550 Squadron ORB as resembling the starting gate at the Derby as a headlong dash began to reach the aiming point, get rid of the bomb's and turn for home. Meanwhile, the night-fighters continued to create havoc among the Lancasters milling around in the target area close to a night-fighter assembly beacon just a few miles from the target, and picked off Lancasters with impunity, Hptm Helmut Bergmann alone downing no fewer than six bombers in thirty minutes. As burning aircraft were seen to fall all around, some 1 Group crews, particularly those from Australia, who, not restrained by RAF protocol, succumbed to their anxiety and frustration and in a rare breakdown of R/T discipline, let fly with comments of an uncomplimentary nature, many of which were intended for, and indeed, heard by Deane. 576 Squadron's P/O Reed and crew came under attack twice from a Ju88, which left ME703 severely damaged with the rear turret burnt out, its occupant beyond help and, according to the ORB, the mid-upper gunner missing. Despite the damage, which included a compromised undercarriage, the wounded Lancaster made it back to base and landed safely at 03.45. Sadly, for the survivors of this crew, it would be but a temporary reprieve. P/O Blackie and crew also reported an encounter with a Ju88, which the gunners claimed as destroyed.

Despite the problems, the operation was a major success, which destroyed 80% of the camp's buildings and 102 vehicles, of which thirty-seven were tanks, while over two hundred men were killed. Forty-two Lancasters failed to return, however, twenty-eight of them from 1 Group, and 460 Squadron RAAF was 1 Group's most afflicted unit with five Lancasters and crews unaccounted for. At debriefings crews reported the presence of a large number of night-fighters, particularly ME410s, with rocket projectiles well in evidence, and on the 5 Group station at Spilsby, the former 103 Squadron flight commander, S/L Blome-Jones, now of 5 Group's 207 Squadron, described the situation as a complete shambles and chaos, the controller as inefficient and the discipline of some crews as bad. Others voiced the opinion that this was a trip worthy of counting as more than one-third of a sortie.

On the following day, an inquest into the conduct of the raid revealed that the wireless transmitter in Deane's Lancaster had been sufficiently off frequency to allow the interference from the American network to mask the transmission of instructions and prevent the call to bomb from reaching the main force crews. The 1 Group A-O-C, AVM Rice, decided that he would not participate in further operations organised by 5 Group, which was probably not a blow to Cochrane, who was confident that his group did not need back-up.

Following a two-night break, 1 Group detailed fifty-two Lancasters, including four from the SDF, to attack an ammunition dump at Aubigne-Racan, situated some twenty miles south of Le Mans in north-western France. 576 Squadron briefed the crews of F/L Shearer, F/O Stansel, P/O Tomlin, W/O Young and Sgt Stedman and filled their Lancasters' bomb bays with eleven 1,000 and four 500-pounders each, before dispatching them from Elsham Wolds between 00.12 and 00.25. The 13 Base commander, Air Commodore Ivelaw-Chapman, had a particular interest in the raids on French targets and decided to experience one at first hand as second pilot to F/L Shearer, while the Binbrook station commander, G/C Hughie Edwards VC, was also flying on this night in a 460 Squadron Lancaster. They flew out over Shoreham-on-Sea over a layer of stratus cloud at 4,000 feet from the midpoint of the Channel to the French coast, and thereafter enjoyed clear skies and bright moonlight all the way to the target. The assembly point was inadequately marked, but smoke, explosions and red spotfires clearly indicated the target without the need for instructions from the Master Bomber, and based on the records of other units, the 576 Squadron quintet attacked from 7,500 feet and above either side of 02.45. Large explosions were witnessed, and smoke was rising through 9,000 feet as they turned for home confident in the success of their efforts. Absent from debriefing was the crew of F/L Shearer RNZAF, four of whom were members of the RAAF, and all but one of them lost their lives when ND783 was brought down. Bomb-aimer, Sgt Ford RAAF, was spirited away by partisans and retained his freedom, while the only other survivor, A/C Ivelaw-Chapman, was taken into captivity, as the most senior Bomber Command officer ever to fall into enemy hands.

The following night brought further attacks on ammunition dumps, coastal defences and airfields, for which 1 Group detailed two forces, one of fifty-one Lancasters, including one from the SDF, assigned to the aerodrome at Saint-Jacques-de-la-Lande to the south-west of Rennes and another of fifty Lancasters plus four from the SDF to attack a nearby ammunition dump at Bruz. 576 Squadron made ready nine Lancasters, loading each with a cookie and sixteen 500-pounders, and dispatched them from Elsham Wolds between 21.30 and 21.45 with pilots of pilot officer rank the most senior on duty. They pinpointed on Bridport and crossed Torbay to begin the Channel crossing at Start Point, making landfall on the French side near Saint-Brieuc. They arrived in the target area to find clear skies and bright moonlight, despite which, the marker crews experienced difficulty in locating the aiming point and the main force had to wait to be called in. The first bombs on the western aiming point fell a little to the south, and the Master Bomber did his best to correct the aim, but the results, a few fires but no explosions, were a little disappointing in comparison with the previous night's attack. The bombing of the eastern aiming point began four minutes later and was hampered by smoke drifting across to conceal the spotfires, some of which was from the attack on the airfield. Based on the records of other units, the 576 Squadron crews carried out their bombing runs from 11,000 and 12,000 feet at around 00.15 and returned safely, uncertain as to the effectiveness of their efforts. Post-raid reconnaissance suggested that most of the bombs had fallen wide of the mark and onto a village.

The focus of more than four hundred crews on the night of the 9/10th was upon seven coastal defences, most of them in the Pas de Calais in an effort to maintain in German minds the belief that the invasion would come there. However, while one of the 1 Group targets, three light batteries on the foreshore at Mardyck, was indeed, near Dunkerque, the other, a heavy gun emplacement, was at Merville-Franceville-Plage, close to what would be the British and Canadian Sword and Juno Beaches on D-Day. 13 and 14 Bases provided fifty-three Lancasters for the former, including ten representing 576 Squadron, while fifty-six from 12 Base attended to the latter, three of them from the SDF. The Elsham Wolds Lancasters each received a bomb load of eleven 1,000 and four 500-pounders, which the 576 Squadron participants lifted into the air between 22.10 and 22.40 with F/Os Stansel and Stockdale the senior pilots on duty. The route took them via Orford Ness to a point on the French coast between Calais and Dunkerque, and they arrived at the target under clear skies and bright moonlight that afforded excellent visibility. The "Musical Paramatta" (blind marking by H2S) marking technique was employed to great effect and the 576 Squadron crews delivered their bombs onto the markers from 11,000 feet and above between 00.10 and 00.16. Sticks of bombs were observed to fall across the markers, and one battery was seen in the flash of a nearby explosion of what was believed to be an ammunition dump.

All 1 Group bases contributed to a raid by sixty Lancasters on railway yards at Dieppe on the night of the 10/11th, one of five separate operations in the Transportation Plan involving in total more than five hundred aircraft. The six-strong 576 Squadron element departed Elsham Wolds between 22.25 and 22.45 with S/L Davison the senior pilot on duty and eleven 1,000 and four 500-pounders in each bomb bay. They arrived in the target area to encounter haze that prevented a visual identification of the aiming-point, but green TIs were clearly visible, and their accuracy checked by crews individually by H2S, before bombing was carried out from 10,000 feet and above between 00.04 and 00.17. Four of the operations were concluded successfully, but there was no post-raid reconnaissance at Dieppe and the outcome remained unclear. Six 103 Squadron crews were briefed for mining duties on this night in the Rosemary garden in the Heligoland Bight, each of their Lancasters carrying six 1,500 parachute mines for delivery by H2S from 12,000 feet. A photograph of an H2S screen taken on a Leica camera was back-plotted to confirm the accuracy of the drops, something that might have been of interest to 576 Squadron, which would shortly embark on its first foray into the dark and mysterious world of mining.

Six operations were mounted on the night of the 11/12th, four of them against railway yards in France and Belgium, and the largest, by 5 Group, directed at a military camp at Bourg Leopold in north-eastern Belgium. The objective for a 1 Group contingent of 105 Lancasters was the nearby marshalling yards at Hasselt, for which 576 Squadron made ready a dozen of its own and loaded each with eleven 1,000 and four 500-pounders, before sending them on their way from Elsham Wolds between 21.35 and 22.06 with F/L Slater the senior pilot on duty. F/O Basil Templeman-Rooke was embarking on a second tour, having served his first with 100 Squadron, and his rise through the ranks would be impressive and rapid, leading to command of 170 Squadron at Hemswell in February 1945. They set a course via Orford Ness to the Scheldt estuary and proceeded to the target over patches of cloud, which had dispersed by the time they arrived. The forecast winds proved to be inaccurate, causing some crews to arrive late, and all found the vertical visibility to be compromised by thick haze, which blotted out all ground detail. No TIs were seen while the Elsham Wolds crews were in the target area, but flares had been dropped in large numbers and thirty-nine aircraft from other stations bombed on these. Having been unable to establish the position of the aiming point, the Master Bomber called a halt to proceedings at 00.07 and sent the force home with bomb loads intact, by which time some crews had picked up a transmission from the Master Bomber at a different target, calling for the bombing of red T.Is. Confirmation of the recall was received from group immediately, thereafter, but was believed by some to be an enemy trick and a proportion of these decided to add their bombs to those from 5 Group at Bourg Leopold. Night-fighters were active and five Lancasters failed to return, two of them belonging to 103 Squadron.

1 Group detailed twenty Lancasters from 12 and 13 Bases on the 12th for mining duties in the Rosemary garden in the North Sea's Heligoland Bight, thus providing 576 Squadron with its first opportunity to experience a non-bombing role. The laying of parachute mines by air had been introduced to Bomber Command operations by 5 Group Hampdens during the ill-fated Norwegian campaign in mid-April 1940 and was given the code-name "gardening". The entire enemy-held coastline from the Pyrenees in the south-west to the Baltic port of Königsberg in the north-east, and even the northern Italian coast, was divided into gardens, each with a horticultural or marine biological name. The process of delivery was known as planting, and the mines, themselves, were referred to as vegetables, and it would not be long before the other bomber groups joined in to create a spiders' web of mines in chains across all of the sea-lanes employed by the enemy. By war's end, Bomber Command would have sunk and damaged more enemy vessels than the Royal Navy. The crews of F/O Presland DFC and P/O Reed departed Elsham Wolds at 22.20 in company with two 103 Squadron counterparts and set a course via Mablethorpe slightly north of east to the

target area, which was found to be under clear skies but concealed by haze up to 7,000 feet. Positions were established by H2S, and the six mines in each bomb bay were delivered into the briefed locations from 12,000 feet shortly after midnight.

At some point during the evening, P/O Parkinson and crew took off from Elsham Wolds on a Bullseye exercise (cross-country) in ND403 and disappeared without trace.

On the 15th, the same two 576 Squadron crews were detailed to join eighteen others from 1 Group for mining duties in the Forget-me-not garden in Kiel Bay, for which they departed Elsham Wolds at 22.00 and 22.05. P/O Reed and crew abandoned their sortie during the climb-out when their H2S and Gee failed, leaving the Presland crew to head out over Mablethorpe and track across the North Sea to make landfall on Jutland's western coast. They reached the Baltic, and it is not known whether it was outbound or on the way home that ME576 was shot down by a night-fighter to crash at Gamtofte, some four miles east-north-east of Assens on the western coast of Denmark's Fyn Island with no survivors among the eight occupants, including a second pilot under instruction.

Minor operations held sway until the 19th, when five railway yards and two gun emplacements were posted as the targets for that night, 1 Group assigned to the marshalling yards in the Les Aubrais district of Orleans on the northern bank of the Loire, for which it detailed 105 Lancasters from 13 and 14 Bases to join forces with thirteen Lancasters and four Mosquitos of 8 Group. 576 Squadron loaded each of its fifteen Lancasters with eleven 1,000 and four 500-pounders and dispatched them from Elsham Wolds between 21.45 and 22.18 with S/L Davison the senior pilot on duty. They flew south over Reading, before beginning the Channel crossing at Beachy Head and making landfall on the French side between Fecamp and Dieppe, benefitting throughout from excellent conditions. At the target, the Path Finder element delivered an accurate marking performance, which was exploited by the main force crews to produce an outstandingly successful outcome. The 576 Squadron crews delivered their attacks from 8,000 feet and above either side of 00.45 in accordance with the master Bomber's instructions and returned safely.

In a complete change of objective on the 21st, Duisburg was posted as the target for the first time since the previous May, and a force of 510 Lancasters and twenty-two Mosquitos was drawn from 1, 3, 5 and 8 Groups for the task, of which a record 207 of the former belonged to 1 Group. 576 Squadron made ready eighteen of its Lancasters, each of which received a bomb load of a cookie and eighteen SBCs of 30lb incendiaries and took off from Elsham Wolds between 21.55 and 22.50 with S/L Davison the senior pilot on duty. They had been instructed at briefing to adhere to the plan for the outward route, which involved a few aircraft from 3 Group gaining height as they adopted a north-westerly course as far as Sleaford, distracting the enemy radar operators and delaying the appearance of the force on screens for as long as possible. The groups were to rendezvous at 18,000 feet over the North Sea at 3° East to cross the enemy coast via the Dutch Frisians at 20,000 feet and climb to 22,000 or 23,000 feet, before increasing speed for the run across the target. All of the 576 Squadron participants reached the Ruhr, unaware that the Oboe Mosquito element had suffered a 50% rate of equipment failure, leaving eleven to dispense red Wanganui markers with-yellow-stars, which disappeared into the cloud tops almost before they could be seen. A number of crews commented on the data provided by the "wind-finder" system to be inaccurate, and this made it a challenge for some to establish their position. A steady stream of marker flares provided an aiming-point for the heavy brigade between 01.04 and 01.18, and the

576 Squadron crews carried out their attacks from just above the cloud tops at 20,000 feet and above sometime between 01.05 and 01.30. Returning crews were not enthusiastic about the outcome, and post-raid reconnaissance confirmed that a modest 350 buildings had been destroyed in the southern half of Duisburg, and 665 others had been seriously damaged. Twenty-nine Lancasters failed to return, demonstrating that the Ruhr had lost none of its sting since the campaign against it a year ago, and among the missing was 576 Squadron's DV365, which crashed homebound at Roosendaal-en-Nispen, a few miles short of the Scheldt estuary. Four of the occupants lost their lives, while F/O Stansel RCAF and two others survived to fall into enemy hands.

Just like Duisburg, Dortmund had not been visited by the heavy brigade for a year when it was posted on the 22nd to face an all-Lancaster heavy force of 361 aircraft drawn from 1, 3, 6 and 8 Groups, while 5 Group targeted Braunschweig. 1 Group made available 183 Lancasters of which seventeen represented 576 Squadron and took off from Elsham Wolds between 21.56 and 22.35 with F/L Wood the senior pilot on duty and each Lancaster loaded with a cookie and eighteen SBCs of 4lb and 30lb incendiaries. They climbed away into heavy cloud and severe icing conditions from 4,000 feet, which persuaded a considerable number of crews to abandon their sorties before reaching enemy territory. The 576 Squadron element flew out over Mablethorpe on course for the Frisian Island of Vlieland and was not represented among 1 Group's six "boomerangs". Those pressing on were rewarded with improving conditions and by the time that the target hove into view, the cloud had diminished to no more than two-tenths, and the attack opened punctually with red and green TIs and red flares with yellow stars. The 576 Squadron crews delivered their bomb loads from 20,000 feet and above between 00.45 and 01.00 and observed many fires, some with oily smoke, leading to a consensus among returning crews of an accurate and effective raid. Eighteen Lancaster failed to return, eleven from 1 Group, and three empty dispersals at Elsham Wolds told their own story.

The 576 Squadron absentee was ME687, which contained the highly decorated crew of P/O Reed DSO, who, it will be recalled, had returned from Mailly-le-Camp earlier in the month in a heavily damaged aircraft with a lifeless rear gunner and an empty mid-upper turret. For their gallantry and fortitude, the navigator and wireless operator had been awarded a DFC and the flight engineer and Canadian bomb-aimer a DFM, and the squadron gunnery leader, F/L Hill OBE, DFC, had been drafted in as the new rear gunner with Sgt Greenwood as his mid-upper counterpart. The Lancaster came down outbound at Hiddingsel, a small village five miles east of Dülmen, to the north of the Ruhr, and there were no survivors. Post-raid reconnaissance revealed that the main weight of the attack had fallen onto predominantly residential districts in the south-east of the city, where six industrial premises and more than eight hundred houses had been destroyed, and almost as many seriously damaged.

The main operation on the 24th involved 442 aircraft in a two-phase attack, ninety minutes apart, on marshalling yards at Aachen, Rothe-Erde in the east and Aachen-West. As the most westerly city in Germany, it was a major link in the railway network that would be a route for reinforcements to the Normandy battle front after D-Day. Other operations on this night were directed at coastal batteries, mostly in the Pas-de-Calais, and war-industry factories in Holland and Belgium. 1 Group contributed 116 Lancasters to the main event and fifty-four to an attack on a coastal battery at Le Clipon near Dunkerque, which was part of the deception plan. 576 Squadron's fifteen Lancasters each received a bomb load of eleven 1,000 and four 500-pounders, while their crews were attending briefing to learn that their aiming point was Aachen-West, for which they departed Elsham Wolds between 23.15 and 00.01 with B Flight's the newly promoted commander, S/L Slater, the senior pilot on duty. They exited the English coast at Orford Ness and made landfall near Dunkerque, before adopting a south-easterly course to pass to the south of Brussels and Liege, and then turning sharply to the north for the run to Aachen, benefitting from favourable weather conditions all the way. It was during this final leg that some aircraft were intercepted by night-fighters, and 576 Squadron's LM120 and NE171, containing the crews of P/O Langford and F/Sgt Thorpe respectively, were both shot down, crashing with such force with full bomb bays that only three and two crew members respectively were recovered for burial. The Path Finders, meanwhile, had reached the target and marked the aiming point employing the "Musical Paramatta" technique, blind marking by H2S, to establish a reference for the main force crews. Those representing 576 Squadron carried out their attacks from 21,500 feet and above, roughly between 02.20 and 02.30, while running the gauntlet of a heavy flak barrage and dodging night-fighters as they vacated the target area. According to photographic reconnaissance, the railway installations had escaped serious damage, and it would be necessary to go back, a major disappointment compounded by the loss of eighteen Halifaxes and seven Lancasters, four of the latter from the ranks of 1 Group.

In addition to the return to the Rothe Erde marshalling yards at Aachen on the night of the 27/28th was a second "return" visit, this one to the military camp at Bourg-Leopold in northern Belgium, which had been the target for an attack earlier in the month but had been abandoned because of poor visibility after half of the force had bombed. 1 Group supported both of the above with 110 and ten Lancasters respectively, while also providing fifty-seven for a return to the Merville coastal battery in the planned invasion area. 576 Squadron loaded its fifteen Lancasters with eleven 1,000 and four 500-pounders each and lost the first one to a burst tyre while taxiing to the runway. The others departed Elsham Wolds between 23.30 and 00.15 with F/Ls Templeman-Rooke and Wood the senior pilots on duty and flew out over Southwold on course for the Dunkerque area, joining up on the way with the rest of the 1, 3 and 8 Group force, which at take-off had numbered 162 aircraft. They enjoyed excellent conditions all the way to the target area, where a new tactic was to be employed during the final leg of the outward flight from the Dutch frontier to the target. The main force was to shallow dive at 1,400 feet per minute to reach a bombing height of 10,000 feet, while, at the same time, a spoof raid on Düsseldorf, some fifty miles to the north-east, would provide a distraction and hopefully draw off night-fighters. The Path Finders provided punctual and accurate marking, which provided the focal point for the 576 Squadron bomb-aimers as they released their hardware from 10,000 feet and above either side of 02.30, most clearly having ignored the designated bombing altitude. Enemy night-fighters were present in numbers and contributed to the downing of a dozen Lancasters, nine from the ranks of 1 Group and two on this occasion belonging to 103 Squadron.

Among three coastal batteries briefed to 181 crews on the 28th was one described as a field battery at Eu, located south-east of Le Treport at the eastern end of the Normandy coastline. 1 Group provided six SDF markers and the main force of fifty Lancasters, all from 12 Base, while Elsham Wolds remained inactive, having discharged its operational duties for the month. With the invasion now just a week away, operations on the 31st focused on railway targets, signals stations and coastal batteries. 1 Group detailed ninety-seven Lancasters for an attack on the marshalling yards at Tergnier in north-eastern France in company with an element of Lancasters and Mosquitos from

8 Group, for which 576 Squadron's former flight commander, S/L Attwater, acted as Deputy Master Bomber.

During the course of the month, the squadron took part in fourteen operations and dispatched 150 sorties for the loss of eight Lancasters and crews and two other crew members. It had been a sobering month for the Elsham Wolds community as a whole, which had to come to terms with the loss of twenty crews. On each station, a small team belonging to the Committee of Adjustment was on hand to remove all trace of missing men from their billets and gather their belongings to pass on to relatives. Within hours, the accommodation would be occupied by someone new, and this process became part of the fabric of life on a bomber station, the faces of the missing soon fading from the memory. Some of the lucky ones who evaded capture to return to a squadron within weeks or months, were generally astounded at how few faces they recognised.

June 1944

June was to be a hectic month which would make great demands on the crews, and the first week was dominated by unsettled weather, which caused concerns for the impending launch of Operation Overlord. The bombing of coastal batteries and signals stations was to be the priority during the first few days leading up to D-Day, and crews were briefed on the 1st for two sites, a battery at Brutelles and a radar-jamming station at Berneval-le-Grand, situated to the north and south respectively of the recently attacked site at Eu, well to the east of the landing grounds. In the event, both operations were cancelled, but the attack on the Berneval site was reinstated on the 2nd and handed to a 1 Group main force of 103 Lancasters, while sixty-three others targeted one of four heavy gun batteries near Calais as part of the deception plan. Fifteen 576 Squadron crews were briefed for Calais, while out on the dispersals each of their Lancasters was being loaded with eleven 1,000 and four 500-pounders, before being sent on their way from Elsham Wolds between 22.30 and 23.15 with F/L Wood the senior pilot on duty. They flew out over Orford Ness and made landfall near Dunkerque in poor weather conditions over ten-tenths cloud, having been told at briefing to bring their bombs home if the TIs could not be seen. In the event, an undisclosed but small number of 576 Squadron crews drew a bead on what they took to be the aiming point and bombed from 8,000 feet after 00.30, while most complied with the briefing instructions and returned their ordnance to the dump.

1 Group operations on the night of the 3/4th involved only sixty-one Lancasters from 13 Base squadrons, which were assigned to a railway-mounted heavy battery at Wimereux to the north of Boulogne in company with 113 other Lancasters and eight Mosquitos from 1, 3 and 8 Groups. The operation was in support of the deception plan, for which 576 Squadron loaded thirteen of its Lancasters with a cookie and sixteen 500-pounders and dispatched them from Elsham Wolds between 22.54 and 23.33 with F/L Rainey the senior pilot on duty. Conditions of low cloud and rain for both take-off and landing made this a testing operation, but there were no mishaps as they headed for the Kent coast near Dungeness to begin the Channel crossing. Clear skies greeted them over the target, where they bombed the mixed red and green TIs from 8,000 to 10,000 feet, before returning safely from another uneventful operation. There was one 576 Squadron casualty, P/O Mallard, the bomb-aimer in the crew of F/O Moss sustaining a serious flak wound, which was tended to by his crew colleagues and then in hospital.

The 5th was D-Day Eve, and during the course of that night, a record number of sorties would be flown against coastal defences and in support and diversionary operations. The weather had been a source of concern for the D-Day planners, and even as Operation Overlord was given the green light, massive uncertainty attended the final decision to go. Eighteen 576 and sixteen 103 Squadron crews attended the evening briefing at Elsham Wolds, where, as at every other station, no direct reference was made to the invasion but unusually, strict instructions were issued to observe briefed altitudes and a ban was placed on the jettisoning of bombs over the sea. They learned also that they would be among more than a thousand aircraft targeting ten heavy gun batteries along the Normandy coast, and that their specific objectives were at Crisbecq, on the Cherbourg peninsula to the north of the American Utah landing ground, and at St-Martin-du-Varreville, five miles to the south, which actually overlooked it. The 576 Squadron element was divided between the two targets, and as the crews took in the details at briefing, out on the dispersals each of their Lancasters was receiving a bomb load of eighteen 500-pounders. They were among the first to start the Bomber Command ball rolling and departed Elsham Wolds between 21.00 and 21.50 with F/Ls Rainey, Templeman-Rooke and Wood the senior pilots on duty and W/C Clayton flying as second pilot with the last-named.

They began the Channel crossing at Bridport over ten-tenths cloud with tops at around 6,000 feet and bright moonlight above, the cloudy conditions persisting as they pressed on to the targets, where the Path Finder Mosquitos employed the "Musical Paramatta" technique to mark the aiming points. Some TIs were seen to burst just above the cloud tops, otherwise crews focused on the glow of red TIs beneath, which seemed to cover quite a large area, and according to the 103 Squadron record, the bombing at Crisbecq was carried out from 8,000 feet and above at 23.35 and at St-Martin from 8,000 feet and above between 23.48 and 23.58. No results were observed, and all returned safely to report a quiet, uneventful operation, which was largely unopposed from the ground and in the air. Aircraft were taking off throughout the night, and those crews returning in dawn's early light were rewarded with a glimpse through gaps in the cloud of the greatest armada in history ploughing its way sedately across the Channel below. A total of five thousand tons of bombs was delivered during the course of these operations, and this was a record for a single night.

As the beachheads were being established during the 6th, preparations were put in hand to support the ground forces by attacking nine road and railway communications centres through which the enemy could bring reinforcements. 1 Group was handed two targets, marshalling yards at Acheres, situated in a loop of the Seine north-west of Paris, and two railway bridges at Vire near the American landing grounds south-east of St-Lô in Normandy, one by the railway station and the other over the river valley. Ninety-seven Lancasters were detailed for the former and 107 for the latter, and it was for Vire that nineteen 576 Squadron Lancasters departed Elsham Wolds between 21.30 and 22.30 with S/L Slater the senior pilot on duty and each crew sitting on eighteen 500-pounders. They flew south to Bridport over eight-tenths cloud with tops at 8,000 feet, which dispersed somewhat over the sea until reforming in the target area with a base at around 6,000 feet. The visibility below was good as the SDF element carried out the initial marking with red TIs, which were backed up with Path Finder greens at both aiming points, before the Master Bomber called in the main force crews at 00.37. Those from 576 Squadron bombed the red TIs from 3,000 feet and above from around 00.34, and the usual isolated undershooting aside, the attack appeared to be accurate, although drifting smoke hampered an assessment of the outcome. There was general agreement that the Master Bomber had played a valuable part in the proceedings and that little opposition came from the ground, but night-fighters were in evidence and some crews reported watching two aircraft go down in flames, while another saw one of the bridges to be completely wrecked. Two Lancasters failed to return to Elsham Wolds, one of them 576 Squadron's ME811, which was shot down by a night-fighter and crashed seven miles east-north-east of the target, taking the rear gunner with it. The likelihood is that he was killed during the engagement, while F/O Bain RCAF and the rest of his crew baled out, the pilot sustaining a broken right leg, but having the good fortune to fall into the hands of partisans, leaving only the Canadian navigator to be picked up by the enemy.

Elsham Wolds was not called into action on the 7th for operations by elements of 1, 5 and 8 Groups, one against a six-way road junction at Balleroy, situated between Bayeux and St-Lô, and the other a tank unit and ammunition dump hidden in the nearby Forêt-de-Cerisy. 1 Group provided eighty Lancasters for the latter as part of a force of 112 Lancasters and ten Mosquitos, and twenty in support of an attack on the Versailles Matelots railway centre.

There were no 1 Group operations on the 8th, and it was left to 13 and 14 Bases to provide a hundred Lancasters on the 9th to join three hundred other aircraft from 4, 6 and 8 Groups to bomb airfields south of the battle area at Flers, Le Mans, Laval and Rennes to prevent their use by the enemy to bring up supplies and reinforcements. The 1 Group target was at Flers, for which 576 Squadron loaded eighteen of its Lancasters with eighteen 500-pounders each and sent them on their way from Elsham Wolds between 00.05 and 01.10 with F/Ls Rainey, Sawyer and Wood the senior pilots on duty. The 1 Group contingent pinpointed first on Gravesend, before beginning the Channel crossing over Beachy Head with low cloud beneath and making landfall at Fécamp to the east of Le Havre. They reached the target to find "Musical Paramatta" marking in progress employing red and green TIs, which appeared to be accurate as the 576 Squadron contingent carried out their attacks from 3,000 feet and above between 03.15 and 03.25. Blinded by the cloud to events on the ground, it was not possible to assess the outcome, and little of value was passed on at debriefings.

The squadron was stood down on the 10th, when 101 Lancasters from 12 and 13 Bases were detailed for an operation against a railway junction at Acheres, one of four similar targets for the night along with Dreux, Orleans and Versailles, involving a total of 430 aircraft. All targets were believed to have been hit, but no details emerged. Elsham Wolds remained off the order of battle on the 11th, when four railway targets were earmarked for attention by elements of 1, 3, 4 and 8 Groups, among them the marshalling yards at Evreux, situated some twenty miles south of Rouen on the approaches to the battle area. A 1 Group force of 101 Lancasters carried out a successful operation against it based on clear and accurate Path Finder marking, and just one Lancaster failed to return.

Since beginning operations on Lancasters, a lack of Polish airmen had prevented 300 Squadron from operating two flights, as had been intended. A temporary solution was to form a second flight at Faldingworth under the command of S/L Misselbrook with ten RAF crews drawn from 101, 550, 576 and 626 Squadrons and four new crews from 1 Lancaster Finishing School. As they were settling into their new accommodation on the 12th, 193 other 1 Group crews were attending briefings for what at this time was a rare foray over Germany involving 286 Lancasters and seventeen Mosquito from 1, 3 and 8 Groups. The target was the Gelsenkirchener Bergwerke A.G synthetic oil refinery located in the Horst district of the Ruhr city of Gelsenkirchen, known to the RAF as the Nordstern plant and to the Germans as Gelsenberg A.G, and this operation would herald the start of a new oil campaign, which would continue to the last day of the bombing war. The briefing included a reference to a new method of dispensing "window", now at five bundles per minute, and while the crews took in the details, twenty 576 Squadron Lancasters were each receiving a bomb load of a cookie and sixteen 500-pounders, before being sent on their way from Elsham Wolds between 22.30 and 23.05 with the newly promoted S/L Templeman-Rooke the senior pilot on duty.

Conditions were excellent as they headed out over Mablethorpe on course for the Scheldt estuary and reached the target area to be greeted by clear skies with ground haze, and the first red Path Finder TIs falling at 00.55 some five miles south-south-east of the intended aiming point. This was surprising and frustrating, as a new version of Oboe had been made available for this operation and the errant markers attracted a considerable number of bomb loads, before further red and green TIs identified the true aiming point and brought the operation back on track. The 576 Squadron crews delivered their attacks from 19,000 feet and above between 01.00 and 01.13, and large explosions were observed at 01.05, 01.07 and 01.12 with smoke rising through 15,000 feet as the last of the bombers turned away. The glow from the burning refinery remained visible on the horizon from as far away as the Dutch coast, by which time night-fighters had taken a heavy toll, mostly as the homebound Lancasters crossed Holland. Seventeen of them failed to return home, 6% of those dispatched, and ten came from the ranks of 1 Group. In exchange for these considerable losses, all production at the plant was brought to a halt for several weeks at a cost to the German war effort of a thousand tons of aviation fuel per day. While this operation was in progress, 671 aircraft representing 4, 5, 6 and 8 Groups had been engaged in attacks on six communications targets, mostly railway-related, in France.

Minor operations on the following night enabled training to continue as new crews got to grips with H2S and "Village Inn", the code for the Automatic Gun-Laying Turret (AGLT), a radar device designed to prevent friendly fire incidents between bombers. It would not be introduced to operations until the autumn, but trials were under way in 1 Group. The 14th brought the Command's first daylight operation since the departure of 2 Group from Bomber Command twelve months earlier. The target was Le Havre, from where the enemy's E-Boats and other fast, light marine craft were posing a threat to Allied shipping supplying the Normandy beachheads. The two-phase operation was to be conducted by predominantly 1 and 3 Groups with 617 Squadron representing 5 Group and would take place in the evening under the umbrella of a fighter escort. The plan called for 617 Squadron's twenty-two Lancasters to target the concrete U-Boot pens with their recently introduced 12,000lb Barnes Wallis-designed Tallboy earthquake bombs just ahead of the main attack, for which 198 Lancasters of 1 Group would constitute the main force and bomb on Oboe markers provided by 8 Group. 3 Group would then follow up in the twilight to complete the destruction. The twenty 576 Squadron Lancasters each received a bomb load of eleven 1,000 and four 500-pounders, before departing Elsham Wolds into a lowering sun between 20.10 and 20.50, with S/L Slater the senior pilot on duty. They were greeted at the target by clear skies and accurate marking and delivered their payloads from 18,000 feet and above between 22.32 and 22.50, observing many explosions and greyish-white smoke rising through 12,000 feet as they headed back across the Channel. The 3 Group attack was equally destructive and few if any craft remained to pose a threat to the Allied shipping supplying the beachhead.

Other operations on this night were directed against railway installations at three locations in France, while elements of 4, 5 and 8 Groups attended to enemy troop and vehicle concentrations, referred to as "choke points" at Aunay-sur-Odon and Évrecy near Caen. A Path Finder presence was required at five locations, in addition to which, 8 Group sent thirty-five Mosquitos to attack the Hydrierwerke-Scholven A.G synthetic oil plant located in Gelsenkirchen's north-western suburb of Buer.

A force of 297 aircraft from 1, 4, 5, 6 and 8 Groups was assembled on the 15th to try to do to Boulogne what had been done to Le Havre twenty-four hours earlier, 1 Group providing 101 Lancasters in the absence of the Elsham Wolds squadron, whose contribution was cancelled at 19.00. Five to ten-tenths cloud lay over the target with tops at 11,000 feet and a base at around 3,000 feet, despite which, some crews were able to identify the breakwater and docks, but not the briefed aiming point. They were guided to the mark by red TIs, the first going down at 22.47 to be visible beneath the cloud, and the aiming point was backed up throughout the raid, during which a particularly large explosion occurred at 22.51 that was estimated to be on the south-western corner of the Bassin Loubet. The conditions hampered a detailed assessment of the outcome, but the raid was believed to be just as successful as at Le Havre, albeit at a cost of many civilian lives as collateral bombing hit the town.

Plans were put in hand on the 16th, to launch 829 sorties that night against a number of targets, including four flying-bomb launching sites in the Pas-de-Calais/Hauts-de-France regions of north-eastern France. Just three days earlier, the first V-1 flying bombs had landed on London, and this prompted a response in the form of a second new campaign to open during the month against this revolutionary new menace. The V-1 targets were of two types, launching sites in the form of small buildings shape like the letter J, which were attached to a launch ramp, and large concrete storage sites known in Bomber Command parlance as "constructional works", and many were, indeed, still under construction with additional work in progress to provide road and rail links. The largest single operation on this night was posted across 1, 4, 6 and 8 Group stations, which were ordered to prepare between them 321 aircraft to attack the synthetic oil plant at Sterkrade-Holten, a district of Oberhausen in the Ruhr, a plant known to the Germans as Ruhr-Chemie A.G. 1 Group's contribution to this operation amounted to one hundred Lancasters from 13 and 14 Bases, while fifty-four others from 12 Base were to target the Domleger "constructional works" situated ten miles north-east of Abbeville in north-eastern France.

576 Squadron loaded twenty-one Lancasters with a cookie and sixteen 500-pounders each and launched them from Elsham Wolds between 22.45 and 23.25 with F/Ls Stockdale and Wood the senior pilots on duty. They headed for the Scheldt via Sheringham, flying out over patchy cloud, and lost the services of Flt/O Charles Sawyer USAAF and crew to the failure of their navigational aids on the way. The cloud built over the Channel to leave a blanket of ten-tenths in the target area with tops at 7,000 to 10,000 feet, and when the cascading red TIs, were delivered blindly by H2S ("Musical Paramatta"), they disappeared quickly to leave a concentrated glow for the crews to aim at, leading to a suggestion that "Wanganui" parachute flares might have been a better option. The 576 Squadron crews delivered their attacks from 18,000 feet and above between 01.20 and 01.30

and returned with an expectation that the bombing had been scattered and ineffective. Their bombing photos revealed nothing but cloud, and it was left to post-raid reconnaissance and local sources to reveal there had been little impact on oil production. It had been an expensive endeavour for the Command, however, costing thirty-one aircraft, twenty-two of them Halifaxes, two-thirds having fallen victim to night-fighters. Three of 1 Group's seven missing Lancasters had taken off from Elsham Wolds, and two belonged to 576 Squadron. ME810 was shot down by a night-fighter to crash near Deelen aerodrome in Holland with no survivors from the recently promoted F/L Stockdale and crew, while PA997 was brought down by flak and crashed in the small town of Rhade on the northern rim of the Ruhr near Dorsten. P/O Puttock and four of his crew lost their lives and the flight engineer and wireless operator ended up in enemy hands. Meanwhile, some two hundred miles to the west, similarly unfavourable weather conditions also compromised the attack on the V-Weapon site, and the consensus was that if the TIs had been accurate, then the raid had been successful.

On the 17th, 317 aircraft of 1, 3, 4 and 8 Groups were assembled to attack railway targets at Aulnoye, Montdidier and St-Martin-l'Hortier, 1 Group detailing 101 Lancasters from 13 and 14 Bases for the first mentioned, located close to the Belgian frontier some forty miles south-east of Lille. 576 Squadron loaded each of its sixteen Lancasters with eighteen 500-pounders, including two with long delay fuses, and sent them on their way from Elsham Wolds between 23.25 and 23.55 with F/L Wood the senior pilot on duty. They flew out over Orford Ness to make landfall a little to the south of the Scheldt, and by the time that they were approaching the target, the excellent conditions had given way to cloud. The Master Bomber descended through it to 600 feet but could see nothing and sent the force home with their bombs, those with long delay fuses being jettisoned over the sea.

Operations were posted on each day from the 18th to the 21st, only for them to be cancelled at the last minute, on one occasion when seven belonging to 576 Squadron were actually airborne. It was a frustrating experience for the crews, who would have sat through a briefing and followed all of the procedures necessary before a major operation, including the build-up of tension, all for nothing and usually too late to be able to use the evening for leisure pursuits. On the 21st, 5 Group entered the oil campaign with operations against synthetic refineries at Wesseling, south of Cologne, and Scholven-Buer to the north-west of Gelsenkirchen, and lost forty-three Lancasters in the process, many to night-fighters on the way to the former. Two 101 Squadron ABC Lancasters from 1 Group also failed to return.

The transportation and V-Weapon campaigns continued side-by-side on the 22nd with attacks planned for marshalling yards in north-eastern France in the evening, but first, constructional works in the same region at Mimoyecques, Siracourt and Wizernes during the afternoon. 1 Group provided one hundred Lancasters for the Mimoyecques site, located some four miles from the French coast at Wissant, which was being constructed to house a V-3 super-gun, referred to by Hitler as the "London Cannon". Originally planned as one of two sites near Cap Gris Nez, each containing twenty-five barrels angled at fifty degrees and aimed at London, test failures and delays meant that a single three-barrel shaft stretching a hundred meters into the limestone hill, 103 miles from its target, was all that existed at the time. Each fifteen-meter-long smooth-bore barrel, which was designed on the multiple-charge principle to progressively boost the acceleration of the one-ton projectile as it travelled towards the muzzle, was to be capable of pounding London at the rate of hundreds per day without let-up. It was protected by a concrete slab thirty meters wide and five-and-a-half meters thick, which was correctly believed by the designers to be impregnable to conventional bombs.

Eighteen 576 Squadron Lancasters were each loaded with eighteen 500-pounders, before departing Elsham Wolds between 13.40 and 14.15 with S/L Slater the senior pilot on duty and flying out via Gravesend and Beachy Head to make landfall north-east of Dieppe. They were greeted at the target by largely clear skies, under which, in the absence of an abundance of TIs, they bombed visually from 10,000 feet and above between 15.45 and 15.48, achieving a reasonable degree of concentration but with little chance of success. Later that afternoon, 617 Squadron scored direct hits with 12,000lb Tallboy earthquake bombs, and provisional reconnaissance revealed four deep craters in the immediate target area, one causing a large corner of the concrete slab to collapse. The extent of the damage underground would not be apparent to the planners at Bomber Command until after the liberation of France, but the shafts and tunnels had also collapsed in on themselves, entombing those inside, who had believed themselves to be safe. The site was abandoned, and the weapon would never fire a single shell.

The railway targets that evening were at Reims and Laon and were assigned to 1 and 4 Groups respectively, both with a Path Finder element to provide the marking. 1 Group put up one hundred main force Lancasters and two SDF markers and completed the outward flight over patchy cloud that had built to nine-tenths in the target area with tops at around 6,000 feet. The red, green and yellow TIs disappeared into the cloud tops to leave a glow for the bomb-aimers to latch onto, but returning crews were unable to offer an assessment of their efforts and suspected a scattered raid.

W/C Clayton's tour as commanding officer came to an end on the 23rd on his posting to 14 Base and was succeeded by W/C Boyd Sellick DFC on his posting from 12 Base. A seasoned campaigner, Sellick's experience would add to the outstanding work of his predecessor in maintaining the highest operational standards and esprit-de-corps. Born in India, "Shrub" Sellick had joined the RAF in 1935 and spent the early war years serving in 3 Group, beginning with 214 Squadron on Wellingtons, and while it was still a reserve unit, he undertook its first operational sortie, with a colleague in a 9 Squadron Wellington on a "razzle" trip to the Black Forest in mid-June. *(Razzle was an unsuccessful incendiary device designed to set fire to forested areas.)* Having completed a tour with 214 Squadron as B Flight commander, he moved on to 15 Squadron in 1941 to fly Stirlings and was appointed commanding officer of 7 Squadron, the first Stirling unit, in April 1942, remaining in post until October.

Flying bomb sites and railway yards provided the objectives for more than six hundred aircraft on the night of the 23/24th, and while 5 Group went for marshalling yards at Limoges, 13 and 14 Bases were ordered to provide one hundred Lancasters and Binbrook six SDF markers for a raid on marshalling yards at Saintes, an important link in the railway communications with the port of Bordeaux and located a few miles inland from the Atlantic coast, south-east of La Rochelle. 576 Squadron loaded eighteen of its Lancasters with ten 1,000-pounders and two long-delay 500-pounders and dispatched them from Elsham Wolds between 21.40 and 22.15 with F/L Rainey the senior pilot on duty. They began the Channel crossing at Bridport and Start Point and skirted the Brest peninsula in favourable conditions that persisted for the entire flight, and once the Master Bomber had cancelled an errant spotfire, the bombing proceeded accurately and unopposed. The

576 Squadron crews delivered their attacks on green TIs from 6,000 feet and above either side of 02.00, before returning safely to report explosions.

Later, on the 24th, orders were received for 1 Group to provide a hundred Lancasters, predominantly from 12 and 14 Bases for an attack on a "constructional work" at les Hayons, situated fifteen miles south-east of Dieppe, one of three sites involving a total of 321 aircraft drawn from 1, 4, 6 and 8 Groups. The marking was accurate, but the excellent visibility almost rendered it unnecessary, as most crews were able to identify the aiming point visually, and a good concentration of bombing was achieved. As they were landing, 739 other crews were preparing to depart their stations to attack seven other flying bomb sites, among them a hundred 1 Group Lancasters predominantly from 13 Base and two SDF markers from Binbrook, whose target was "constructional works" at Flers in north-western France. Eighteen 576 Squadron Lancasters received a bomb load each of eighteen 500-pounders, including two with long-delay fuses, and departed Elsham Wolds between 01.10 and 01.55 with S/L Templeman-Rooke the senior pilot on duty. It was another night of fine weather conditions and moonlight, which was ideal for target identification and marking, but was also of help to the enemy night-fighter force. They set course via Beachy Head for the Normandy coast, passing over the battle area before reaching the target to find plenty of searchlights, but no flak, which suggested that the batteries were, indeed, working in conjunction with night-fighters. The marking was late, probably as the result of a big change in the forecast wind, but once underway it was accurate, and the 576 Squadron participants delivered their bomb loads onto the TIs from 13,000 feet and above from around 03.15, were prevented by haze from observing the outcome. The single missing Lancaster was 576 Squadron's JB460, which disappeared without trace with the crew of F/O Alcorn RAAF.

Elsham Wolds was stood down on the 25th, a day which began early for a hundred 1 Group Lancaster crews of 12 and 14 Bases, who had been briefed for an attack on "constructional works" at Ligescourt II, located fifteen miles inland from the coastal resort of Berck-sur-Mer. There were two targets to occupy 1 Group during the night of the 27/28th, marshalling yards at Vaires-sur-Marne, east-north-east of Paris for one hundred Lancasters and two SDF markers and "constructional works" at Chateau Bernapre for ninety-nine, including two from the SDF. Seventeen 576 Squadron Lancasters were loaded with eighteen 500-pounders each, before departing Elsham Wolds for the latter in a heavy shower between 01.10 and 01.50 with F/L Rainey the senior pilot on duty. They began the Channel crossing over cloud at Beachy Head and made landfall on the Normandy coast, by good fortune, finding large gaps in the cloud over the target to allow the yellow cascading and impact TIs to stand out clearly. The 576 Squadron crews bombed from 12,000 feet and above between 03.30 and 03.40, and on return reported the TIs to be somewhat scattered and the bombing to have lacked concentration, despite which, it seems, that all of the night's objectives were dealt with in a satisfactory manner.

The operation for the Elsham Wolds squadrons on the afternoon of the 29th was something of a rushed job after being called late and was a further attack on the "constructional works" at Domleger, located a dozen miles east-north-east of Abbeville. This was one of three flying bomb-related sites to be attacked by a total of 286 Lancasters from 1 and 5 Groups, 1 Group detailing ninety-eight Lancasters and ninety-nine for a similar target at Siracourt. 576 Squadron made ready eighteen of its Lancasters and loaded each with eleven 1,000 and four 500-pounders, before sending them on their way between 11.20 and 12.00 with F/L Wood the senior pilot on duty. They headed south to begin the sea crossing at Dungeness and complied with the instructions at briefing to remain below cloud level until reaching the enemy coast. The target area was found to be relatively free of cloud and the aiming point well-marked by the Path Finder Mosquito element, which enabled crews to bomb visually, those from 576 Squadron from 10,000 feet and above either side of 13.30 in accordance with the instructions of the Master Bomber, F/L Wiseman of 156 Squadron. They returned home confident in the effectiveness of their work, and at debriefing reported large explosions around the aiming point and fires emitting smoke.

The final operation of this hectic month began at first light on the 30th, when a hundred Lancasters from 13 and 14 Bases, including eighteen representing 576 Squadron, took off to attack a flying bomb launching site at Oisemont/Neuville-au-Bois, ten miles to the south of Abbeville. The 576 Squadron contingent departed Elsham Wolds between 05.30 and 06.05 with W/C Sellick the senior pilot on duty and each crew sitting on eleven 1,000 and four 500-pounders. They exited the English coast at Gravesend in initially good conditions, but on reaching the French coast the force encountered complete cloud cover, and the Master Bomber issued instructions to bomb on H2S. The 576 Squadron crews complied from 12,000 feet and above either side of 08.00 but were unable to assess the results and suspected that the effort had been scattered and not fully effective.

During the course of the month, the squadron took part in fifteen operations and launched a very creditable 267 sorties for the loss of four Lancasters and their crews. S/L Davison was posted from the squadron at the end of his tour and reverted to flight lieutenant rank for his duties as an instructor at 28 O.T.U.

July 1944

The new month began as June had ended, with flying-bomb sites providing employment for over three hundred aircraft on both the 1st and 2nd. Reconnaissance had revealed that the raids thus far on the "constructional works" at Oisemont/Neuville-au-Bois had failed to completely destroy the site, and another operation was scheduled for the afternoon of the 1st. In the event, complete cloud cover prevented any TIs from being observed by the 6 Group main force and bombing was carried out on estimated positions based on Gee and dead-reckoning (DR). Orders were received on the 2nd to return to the site in the early afternoon, for which 1 Group detailed fifty Lancasters from 12 Base, while a further 125 from 13 and 14 Bases targeted the previously attacked Domleger "constructional works". 576 Squadron loaded eighteen of its Lancasters with eleven 1,000 and six 500-pounders each, two of the latter containing long-delay fuses, and dispatched them from Elsham Wolds between 11.50 and 12.25 with F/Ls Moss, Rainey and Smith the senior pilots on duty. They began the sea crossing at Dungeness, picking up a Spitfire escort, and made landfall on the French coast near Eu, before swinging to the east for the run on the target, by which time the ten-tenths cloud accompanying them for the majority of the outward flight had dissipated to an extent to leave gaps over the aiming point. This meant that the Master Bomber's instruction to bomb on H2S could be changed during the course of the attack to aim for the red TIs, and the 576 Squadron crews delivered their ordnance accordingly from 13,000 feet and above either side of 14.15 in the face of only slight opposition from flak, gaining the impression of a concentrated raid.

Orders were received on 1 Group stations on the 4th to prepare for an operation that night against the marshalling yards at Orleans in the Loire Valley, some fifty miles south-west of Paris. A 1

Group force of 156 Lancasters was made ready, the SDF providing six for marking, while 576 Squadron contributed sixteen, each of which was loaded with eighteen 500-pounders before departing Elsham Wolds between 21.45 and 22.17 with S/L Templeman-Rooke the senior pilot on duty. They began the Channel crossing at Lyme Regis and made landfall on the approaches to Abbeville, before reaching the target to find a thin layer of cloud at 8,000 to 10,000 feet with clear visibility below aided by bright moonlight. The crews easily identified the assembly point, which had been marked with green TIs, and the marking of the aiming point commenced at 01.20, only for it to be observed in the light of illuminating flares that the TIs had fallen well to the east. This prompted the SDF to drop red spotfires at 01.27, which fell in two distinct groups, those to the south assessed by the Master Bomber as "bang on" the aiming point, and within three minutes of the first wave of bombing, the aiming point became obscured and had to be re-marked for the second wave. The 576 Squadron participants released their payloads from 6,000 feet and above between 01.30 and 01.37 and all returned home safely emphatic in their belief that the marshalling yards had been severely damaged, persuaded in part by one particularly large explosion at 01.37. P/O Cartwright and crew landed in southern England with the bomb-aimer, Sgt West, fatally wounded by flak over the target, and reported that the flight engineer had taken over his role to release the bombs. Absent from debriefing was the predominantly RCAF crew of P/O Baxter RCAF, who all lost their lives when LM532 crashed some seven miles south-south-east of the target.

The target for 154 Lancasters of 1 Group on the 5th was the marshalling yards in the city of Dijon in east-central France, an operation that created disappointment among the Binbrook crews, who were forced to miss the special dance open to all ranks and held in the airmen's dining hall in support of the "Salute the Soldier Week" campaign. The fourteen participating 576 Squadron Lancasters were each loaded with eight 1,000 and four 500-pounders, before departing Elsham Wolds between 20.55 and 21.20 with S/L Templeman-Rooke the senior pilot on duty. They flew out over the Bridport-Lyme Regis area with ten-tenths cloud below them topping out at 7,000 feet, and this persisted until halfway across the Channel, when it began to disperse to provide crews with visibility good enough to enable them to map-read their way from the French coast, west of Abbeville, all the way to their destination. They were greeted at the target by near perfect visibility, and the attack began with cascading yellow TIs delivered blind by H2S as a guide to the SDF marker crews. They fell around a mile to the north-west of the aiming point, and the Deputy Master Bomber, who arrived ahead of the Master Bomber, dropped one red and one yellow TI to within sixty yards of the mark, and the Master Bomber then arrived to back up with red spotfires. The main force crews were called in, bombing initially with great accuracy until smoke obscured the aiming point and the attack began to creep back towards the town. It proved difficult to re-mark the aiming point in the face of a spirited light flak defence at lower levels, but the Master Bomber maintained control of proceedings and the marshalling yards stood out clearly to the main force crews flying at a higher level out of range of the light flak. The 576 Squadron crews attacked from 6,000 feet and above either side of 02.00 and were diverted on return because of low cloud.

The 6th was devoted to daylight attacks on five V-Weapons sites involving 550 aircraft, of which a hundred Lancasters were provided by 1 Group predominantly from 12 Base for its target of "constructional works" in the Forêt-du-Croc, situated some five miles south-east of Dieppe. The Path Finders were punctual and accurate with their marking, and the initial bombing was seen to fall across the aiming point, before cloud drifted in, and crews had to aim at the glow of TIs.

During the course of the 7th, 467 aircraft from 1, 4, 6 and 8 Groups were made ready to carry out the first major operation in support of the Canadian 1st and British 2nd Armies, which were trying to break out of the Caen area. The targets initially had been German-occupied fortified villages, but this was changed to an area of open ground north of Caen. 1 Group contributed 192 Lancasters, eighteen of them provided by 576 Squadron, each of which had eleven 1,000 and four 500-pounders winched into their bomb bays before departing Elsham Wolds between 19.10 and 19.50 with S/Ls Slater and Templeman-Rooke the senior pilots on duty. The cloud that accompanied the bomber stream over England gradually dispersed during the sea crossing from Worthing to the Normandy coast, leaving small amounts of broken white stuff with a base at 7,000 feet. Excellent visibility prevailed, and ground features were clearly identified as the Path Finders opened the attack on time and with great concentration, the first red TIs going down at 21.46. These were backed-up until the aiming point was ready to receive the main force bombs, and it was not long, thereafter, that smoke and debris concealed the markers, the Master Bomber retaining control, however, and keeping the attack on track. A series of explosions between 21.52 and 22.03 suggested a successful outcome, contributed to by 576 Squadron's efforts from 2,500 feet and above either side of 22.00. A message from the 2nd Army awaited the returning crews, congratulating them on the accuracy of their work and thanking them for their efforts. However, the decision to change the aiming points ultimately proved to be counter-productive as the bombing blocked access roads in the northern suburbs of the city, rather than inflicting damage on German forces.

Operations were posted and cancelled over the ensuing days, and it was the 12th before 1 Group crews took to the air again in anger, when three railway targets were briefed out to 378 Lancaster crews of 1, 5 and 8 Groups, at Culmont for 5 Group, Revigny for 1 Group and Tours for 1 and 8 Groups. 1 Group committed a main force of a hundred Lancasters to each of its targets with an additional seven SDF aircraft assigned to the junction at Revigny, a town located south-east of Reims on the south-eastern edge of the Marne region. 576 Squadron loaded each of its nineteen Lancasters with seven 1,000 and four 500-pounders, before dispatching them from Elsham Wolds between 21.00 and 21.50 with W/C Sellick the senior pilot on duty. They climbed out into five tenths cloud and pointed their snouts towards the south to begin the Channel crossing at Bridport on what was a circuitous route via the Channel Islands, with landfall on the Brittany coast near St-Malo. From there they headed south-east, swinging south of Le Mans and Orleans and then turning to the north-east for the final leg to the target. Thin cloud in the target area at between 4,000 and 6,000 feet and haze below created challenges for the Master Bomber's efforts to establish his bearings, particularly as his H2S had failed. He was forced to carry out a DR run to drop a green TI on the assembly point, before calling upon the illuminator crews to dispense their flares in the hope that this would reveal the aiming point. Neither he nor his Deputy was able to locate it despite searching for fifteen minutes, and he had little choice but to abandon proceedings and send the force home. By this time, half of the force had bombed on DR or on flares and even on what they believed were red spotfires, but must have been burning aircraft, and among those delivering their bombs were an undisclosed number representing 576 Squadron from 2,500 feet and above.

ND859 was returning south of the intended track and is believed to have collided with a 44 (Rhodesia) Squadron Lancaster, which was homebound from the 5 Group raid on Culmont. It crashed shortly before 02.00 on high ground some sixteen miles south-west of Chaumont and nine miles north of the other Lancaster's crash site. P/O Hart and four of his crew lost their lives, while both gunners survived to fall into enemy hands, and were joined in captivity by two from the 44 Squadron aircraft, the rest evading a similar fate with the assistance of partisans. A collision also accounted for one of the four 103 Squadron Lancasters absent from their Elsham Wolds dispersal pans, one of them having been abandoned safely by its crew after it ran out of fuel. This completed a bad night for 1 Group, which registered the loss of ten Lancasters for no gain, and a sombre air pervaded Elsham Wolds as the community came to terms with the loss of twenty-eight familiar faces.

A second attempt on the railway junction at Revigny was scheduled for elements of 1 and 8 Groups on the 14th, and a force of 105 Lancasters assembled on 12 and 13 Base stations with five 101 Squadron ABC Lancasters from 14 Base to provide RCM cover. 576 Squadron briefed a dozen crews and loaded each of their Lancasters with seven 1,000 and four 500-pounders, before sending them on their way from Elsham Wolds between 20.58 and 21.20 with F/L Guilfoyle the senior pilot on duty. They climbed away through ten-tenths cloud and passed overhead unseen by the residents of Bridport as they made their way via the St-Malo coastal area, following the same route as for the previous raid. F/Sgt Greig and crew were contending with engine issues and turned back an hour before reaching the target, by which time the cloud had broken up during the trek across France to leave three to seven-tenths in the target area with a base at 6,000 to 8,000 feet. The Master Bomber and Deputy, respectively F/L Wiseman and S/L Davies from 8 Group's 156 Squadron, experienced great difficulty in establishing the location of the aiming point, despite a gap opening in the clouds right above it and the deployment of numerous flares. S/L Davies DSO apparently found it before being shot down by a night-fighter and, meanwhile, the main force crews orbited for a considerable time as they awaited instructions. Five aircraft bombed before the Master Bomber abandoned the operation, leaving the Elsham Wolds participants to set off for home with their bomb loads intact until the delayed-action bombs could be jettisoned into the sea. On the way, 576 Squadron's ND994 was intercepted by a night-fighter and shot down to crash at 02.24 at Loches-sur-Ource with no survivors from the predominantly RCAF crew of F/O Linklater RCAF. This was one of six 1 Group Lancasters to be lost, and half of them were from Elsham Wolds. At debriefings, some crews complained that they had clearly identified the target and could have carried out an attack, but this troublesome target would now be handed to 5 Group, which would succeed where 1 Group had failed, but at a great cost in aircraft and lives.

Sixteen 576 Squadron crews were called to briefing at midnight on the 17/18th to learn of their part in a tactical support operation to be carried out at dawn by a force of 942 aircraft, of which 201 of the Lancasters were to be provided by 1 Group. It was the start of the ground forces' Operation Goodwood, which was Montgomery's plan for a decisive breakout into wider France as a prelude to the march towards the German frontier. The aiming-points were five enemy-held villages of Colombelles, Mondeville, Sannerville, Cagny and Manneville, all situated to the east of Caen and standing in the path of the advancing British 2nd Army. The 1 Group target was Sannerville, for which the Elsham Wolds aircraft were loaded with eleven 1,000 and four 500-pounders, before taking off between 03.15 and 04.10 with S/L Templeman-Rooke the senior pilot on duty. They began the Channel crossing at Selsey Bill and by the time that they made landfall on the Normandy coast, the ten-tenths cloud had broken up to reveal the red and yellow TIs bang on the aiming point. Each aiming point was carefully controlled by a Master Bomber because of the close proximity of Allied troops and the 576 Squadron bomb-aimers had TIs in the bomb sights as they delivered their hardware from 3,000 feet and above between 05.45 and 06.00. The bombing was accurate and concentrated, and even after smoke and debris had concealed the aiming point, the TIs remained visible. All 1 Group aircraft returned safely after a highly successful operation and crews reported little opposition from the ground and none in the air. Of 6,800 tons of bombs delivered by RAF and USAAF aircraft on these targets, more than 5,000 tons had been dropped by the RAF.

Many of the crews involved in the morning activity were back in the briefing room during the late afternoon to learn of their respective targets for that night, when the Command would be committing almost a thousand aircraft again, principally against synthetic oil and railway objectives, but also on a variety of support and minor operations. The Wesseling synthetic oil refinery, or to give it its full title, the Union Rheinische Braunkohlen-Kraftstoff Aktien Gesellschaft, situated on the eastern bank of the Rhine south of Cologne, was to be the target for a force of 194 aircraft made up of a 6 Group main force of 153 Halifaxes and Lancasters with six ABC Lancasters from 101 Squadron for RCM cover, and twenty-nine Lancasters and six Mosquitos of 8 Group to provide the marking. At the same time, 153 Lancasters of 1 Group would be joined by four Lancasters and thirteen Mosquitos of 8 Group to target the Hydrierwerke-Scholven plant in the Buer district of Gelsenkirchen. The fourteen 576 Squadron Lancasters each received a bomb load of a cookie and sixteen 500-pounders, before departing Elsham Wolds between 22.55 and 23.40 with S/L Slater the senior pilot on duty. They climbed out through ten-tenths cloud, breaking into clear air at 6,000 feet, before passing over Mablethorpe on their way to landfall on the Dutch coast to the south of Zandvoort. The cloud began to disperse as they progressed towards the northern rim of the Ruhr and clear skies greeted them over the target with just a little industrial haze to compromise the vertical visibility.

The first red TIs went down a little early at 01.25 and thereafter, the aiming point was backed up to ensure a constant focal point, until, at 01.29, the markers were scattered by a huge yellow mushroom-shaped explosion, from which sheets of flame lit up the surrounding area for fifteen to twenty seconds. A column of black, oily smoke began to rise and had reached 18,000 feet by the end of the raid, the 576 Squadron crews having attacked from 20,000 feet and above between 01.30 and 01.33 in the face of moderate to intense flak and the usual array of searchlights. A post-raid analysis assessed that 550 bombs had fallen into the oil plant, but curiously, according to local sources, 40% of them failed to detonate. Despite this, the operation was successful and brought all production to a halt for a considerable period. A dozen 1 Group aircraft sustained flak damage, and twelve crews reported combats, while four failed to return, a modest figure for a target in the heart of the Ruhr.

A concentrated raid at Wesseling was confirmed by local reports, which told of one thousand high explosive bombs falling within the plant, destroying 20% of the installations and causing a substantial loss of production. The town was also hit, and 151 houses were destroyed, many of them in the estate occupied by the plant's workforce. It was on this night that 5 Group finally delivered a telling blow on the marshalling yards at Revigny, but at a cost of twenty-four Lancasters hacked out of the sky by night-fighters, mostly during the outward flight. *(For an account of the three raids on Revigny, read the outstanding book, Massacre over the Marne by Oliver Clutton-Brock).*

A daylight raid on "constructional works" at Wizernes, situated twenty-five miles east of Boulogne, was scheduled for the evening of the 20th and involved a hundred 1 Group Lancasters from 12 and 13 Bases. At the same time, six flying bomb launching sites were to be attacked by other groups for which a further 269 aircraft were detailed. The Wizernes site had already been subjected to many attacks and had, in fact, been effectively destroyed and abandoned a few days earlier after a visit from 617 Squadron, whose Tallboys had caused a landslip that knocked the huge concrete dome out of alignment. This was not revealed in photographs taken from above, however, and attacks would continue for the time being. 576 Squadron made ready nineteen Lancasters, each of which was loaded with eleven 1,000 and four 500-pounders and departed Elsham Wolds between 18.50 and 19.25 with S/L Templeman-Rooke the senior pilot on duty. They headed towards Southwold and then North Foreland in ten-tenths cloud with a base at 2,000 feet, which persisted as they made landfall on the Belgian coast near Knokke under the umbrella of a strong Spitfire escort. The cloud broke up in the target area to leave skies clear enough for the crews to identify the aiming point visually, those representing 576 Squadron bombing either visually or on accurately placed red impact TIs and cascading yellows from 13,000 feet and above either side of 21.00. All returned safely from what was a successful if, ultimately, unnecessary operation.

Meanwhile, ninety-three Lancasters from the group were preparing to attack the railway yards and a triangular junction at Courtrai (Kortrijk) in north-western Belgium that evening as part of a 1, 5 and 8 Group force of 302 Lancasters and fifteen Mosquitos. The first red TIs went down on time and were followed by many illuminating flares, which failed to highlight the aiming points, but their position in relation to the town suggested that they were in the right place. The first phase of bombing created so much smoke and dust that the aiming point was soon enveloped, prompting the Master Bomber to call a halt at 01.59.

On the afternoon of the 23rd, 189 crews attended briefings on all 1 Group operational stations to be told that, after a two-month break from city busting, Harris had sanctioned a major raid on the naval port of Kiel, which, as previously mentioned, was home to the Deutsche Werke, Germania Werft and Howaldtswerke shipyards, each producing U-Boots for the Kriegsmarine. A force of 629 aircraft was made ready, 576 Squadron contributing nineteen Lancasters, each loaded with a cookie, some supplemented with sixteen 500-pounders and others with six J-Type cluster incendiaries and eight 500lb general purpose (GP) bombs. They departed Elsham Wolds between 22.15 and 22.50 with S/L Slater the senior pilot on duty and after climbing out, headed for the coast at Mablethorpe to rendezvous with the rest of the bomber stream over the North Sea and form up behind an elaborate "Mandrel" jamming screen laid on by 100 Group. Having made landfall on the western coast of Jutland, the head of the bomber stream arrived unexpectedly and with complete surprise in Kiel airspace, rendering the enemy night-fighter controller confused and unable to bring his resources to bear. Kiel was covered by a nine to ten-tenths veil of thin cloud with tops at 5,000 feet, and a skymarking plan was put into action, which enabled the main force crews to bomb on the glow, first of the flares, and then of fires. Positions were confirmed by H2S, before the 576 Squadron crews aimed at the red and green "Wanganui" markers disappearing into the cloud tops from 19,000 to 21,500 feet either side of 01.30. Flak was mostly in barrage form and exploding at 15,000 to 22,000 feet but was not overly troublesome, and more concerning to F/L Rainey and crew was a single-engine enemy aircraft stalking them from between two hundred and six hundred yards. For whatever reason it did not open fire and was promptly shot down by the Lancaster's gunners. It was not possible to determine the outcome of the raid, but the glow of fires remained visible for a hundred miles into the return journey, which suggested an effective raid at a cost of just four aircraft. The success was confirmed by local reports, which conceded that this had been the town's most destructive raid of the war and had inflicted heavy damage on the port and U-Boot construction yards and cut off water supplies for three days and gas for three weeks. Many delayed-action bombs had been dropped, and these continued to cause problems for some time.

The first of three heavy raids on Stuttgart over a five-night period was posted on the 24th and a force of 614 aircraft assembled, 120 of the Lancasters provided by 1 Group's 13 and 14 Bases. 576 Squadron loaded each of its sixteen Lancasters with a 2,000-pounder and twelve J-Type cluster incendiaries and dispatched them from Elsham Wolds between 21.05 and 21.50 with S/L Templeman-Rooke the senior pilot on duty. P/O Ball and crew turned back early on because of an engine issue, leaving the others to begin the Channel crossing at Selsey Bill, from which point the cloud began to disperse and the Normandy coast was crossed under clear skies that persisted until the German frontier was reached near Strasbourg. There it built up again to ten-tenths, with tops in the target area at 10,000 feet, which demanded the deployment of skymarkers ("Wanganui") to mark out the aiming point and the Master Bomber to exercise effective control. The 576 Squadron crews bombed from 18,000 feet and above between 01.50 and 02.00 and were unable to assess the outcome, but the large glow of fires reflected in the clouds promoted the impression of a successful operation. Twenty-one aircraft failed to return, and among them was 576 Squadron's PB265, containing the crew of Flt/O Robert Sarvis USAAF, a Canadian-born American, who had joined the RCAF in April 1942. Six members of the crew were reported to be safe, either in Allied or partisan hands, but the fate of the pilot and the location of the crashed Lancaster was not discovered until 1989, when both were found at Liesville-sur-Douve on the Cherbourg peninsula.

There was an early start on the 25th for 1 Group forces of thirty and thirty-one Lancasters from 12 Base, which were assigned to act as the main forces at two flying bomb launching sites, at Ardouval II, a dozen miles south-south-east of Dieppe and Coquereaux, situated some fifteen miles to the east, each to be marked by 8 Group Mosquitos. Both operations were carried out in accordance with instructions from a Master Bomber and appeared to be accurate, the Ardouval site becoming obscured by smoke and dust by the end. Bombing photos revealed that both aiming points had been straddled, but that the main weight of the attacks had fallen short or wide.

That night, 560 aircraft, including 108 Lancasters of 1 Group, were sent back to Stuttgart, while 114 Halifaxes of 4 Group attended to the Krupp Treibstoffwerke synthetic oil plant at Wanne-Eickel, situated between Gelsenkirchen and Herne in the Ruhr, the latter supported by three Path Finder Lancasters and eight of the ABC variety provided by 101 Squadron. 576 Squadron loaded seven of its Lancasters with a 2,000-pounder and twelve J-Type cluster bombs for the main event and eight others with eighteen 500-pounders each for use against a flying bomb launching ramp at Bois-des-Jardins, located south of Amiens. The latter would join forces with two SDF Lancasters and fifteen of 460 Squadron RAAF, the only 1 Group unit not to contribute to the Stuttgart raid. The 576 Squadron main eventers departed Elsham Wolds between 21.20 and 21.30 with S/L Slater the senior pilot on duty and set course for Selsey Bill, where they met seven to ten-tenths cloud. F/Sgt Greig and crew dropped out early because of instrument failure, while the rest of the bomber stream followed the same route as for the previous Stuttgart raid and arrived in the target area under a cloud base at 17,000 feet. The marking was considered to be somewhat scattered but covered the target area, and the 576 Squadron participants carried out their attacks from 16,000 feet and above either side of 02.00. The glow of the burning city remained visible on the horizon for 150 miles into the homeward journey, which twelve aircraft failed to complete.

It was 00.30 before the first 576 Squadron Lancaster rolled down the runway at Elsham Wolds bound for Bois-des-Jardins and all eight were airborne by 00.55 with S/L Templeman-Rooke the senior pilot on duty. They began the Channel crossing somewhere near Brighton and made landfall to the north-east of Dieppe, before pushing the few miles inland to the target, the cloud thinning as they closed on it. The Master Bomber called the main force element down to the 9,000-foot cloud base to ensure a clear view of the red Path Finder TIs, which went down a little early and were assessed as being slightly misplaced, prompting the Master Bomber to drop four green TIs, which fell within two hundred yards of the aiming point at 02.53½. He called in the main force and instructed them to overshoot by two hundred yards, and the 576 Squadron crews complied from 8,000 feet and above shortly before 03.00 and returned home to report what appeared to be a successful outcome. This confidence was not supported by bombing photos, which revealed the attack to have fallen wide of the mark.

The night of the 28/29th would prove to be busy, eventful and expensive as the Command prepared for major operations against Stuttgart and Hamburg and a number of smaller undertakings involving a total of 1,126 aircraft. The final raid of the series on Stuttgart was to be prosecuted by an all-Lancaster heavy force of 494 aircraft drawn from 1, 3, 5 and 8 Groups, of which 159 Lancasters were provided by 1 Group. The annual last-week-of-July attack on Hamburg, 320 miles away to the north, was to be conducted by 307 aircraft, consisting of a predominantly 6 Group Halifax and Lancaster main force, with six ABC Lancasters of 1 Group's 101 Squadron to provide RCM cover and 8 Group Lancasters and Mosquitos to carry out the marking. The operation would take place a year and a day after the devastating firestorm raid during the Operation Gomorrah series.

576 Squadron briefed seventeen crews for Stuttgart, loading each of their Lancasters with a cookie and ten or eleven 500-pounders depending on their role, and dispatching them from Elsham Wolds between 21.05 and 21.40 with F/Ls Guilfoyle and Smith the senior pilots on duty. They flew out over the Sussex coast and followed the usual route for this target, crossing France in bright moonlight above the cloud layer and exposing themselves to the night-fighter hordes that had infiltrated the bomber stream from 5° East and had stayed in contact with it all the way to the target. It was the Luftwaffe's Nachtjagd that would gain the upper hand on this night and inflict a major blow upon Elsham Wolds, as its participants passed over the Grande-Est region of north-eastern France on the way in and out of the frontier region near Strasbourg. PB128 was probably the first of four 576 Squadron Lancasters to fall, crashing at 01.30 in the south-western suburbs of the town of Rheinstetten, south-west of Karlsruhe with no survivors from the crew of F/L Smith. Ten minutes later, and forty miles to the west on the French side of the frontier, LL905 came down with a wing on fire at Sarrewerden, killing F/O Mann DFC RCAF and three of his crew and delivering the three survivors into enemy hands.

A thin layer of up to ten-tenths cloud lay over Stuttgart, with tops in places at around 12,000 feet, and the Path Finders initially employed skymarker flares (Wanganui), which were quickly swallowed up. Most crews bombed on H2S, before scattered red and green TIs appeared on the ground in a line from north-west to south-east, and the Master Bomber attempted to persuade the main force crews to bomb the glow from a cluster of greens nearest to the aiming-point. A number of crews descended into clear air beneath the cloud base and reported green TIs at the southern end of the railway station at 01.56, by which time most of the 576 Squadron crews had carried out their attacks from 17,000 and above, and observed large explosions at 01.47, 01.51 and 02.05. On the way home, LL799 crashed some ten miles north-north-east from the centre of Strasbourg with fatal consequences for F/O Brown RAAF and four of his crew, while the two survivors joined their squadron colleagues in captivity. At around the same time, PB253 crashed five miles west of Epinal, and pilot, F/O Archibald RNZAF, alone of his crew survived, probably evading capture, although this is not confirmed. It was impossible to assess the outcome of the raid, but most returning crews reported it to be scattered, for which they blamed the weather conditions.

Thirty-nine Lancasters failed to return, seventeen from the ranks of 1 Group and nine from Elsham Wolds, although one of 103 Squadron's casualties was written off in a crash-landing at Little Harwood airfield in Buckinghamshire, and all crew members emerged unscathed from the wreckage. Another 103 squadron Lancaster was badly shot up and landed at White Waltham near Maidenhead in Berkshire with just the pilot, flight engineer and navigator on board, who reported that the other four members of the crew had baled out. At debriefing, crews described the intensity of the night-fighter activity, and ten combats were reported, with one enemy aircraft claimed as destroyed, two as probably destroyed and three as damaged. Some crews also reported being fired upon by other bombers, despite flying at the correct height and briefed course. The Hamburg force was also mauled by night-fighters while homebound and lost twenty-two of its number to bring the night's casualty figure to sixty-one aircraft.

The penultimate operation of a busy month for 576 Squadron was as part of a 1 Group force of 104 Lancasters assigned to two aiming points at Cahagnes in the Caumont-Villers-Bocage region of Normandy in support of the American 2nd army. A total of 692 aircraft was to be involved at six German positions, for which 576 Squadron contributed a dozen Lancasters, each loaded with twenty 500-pounders as they departed Elsham Wolds between 06.25 and 07.05 with F/Ls Masters, Moss and Rainey the senior pilots on duty. They began the Channel crossing at Selsey Bill over low cloud, which persisted all the way to the target, where it became necessary for the Master Bomber to call the main force crews down to below the cloud base. The 1 Group force was divided 34/70 between aiming points "E" and "F" and the 576 Squadron crews bombed the Oboe markers from 1,500 feet and above in accordance with instructions from the Master Bomber. The marking seemed well placed and the bombing concentrated, and the attacks were delivered unopposed, some of those returning to Elsham Wolds displaying the scars from the blast of their own bombs at such low level. The low cloud was responsible for the fact that only 377 aircraft delivered an attack and just two of the six aiming points were effectively dealt with.

The final operation of the month for Elsham Wolds was posted on the 31st and involved fifty Lancasters from 13 Base in an attack on the port area of Le Havre and any U-Boots sheltering therein, in company with two Lancasters and five Mosquitos of 8 Group. 576 Squadron loaded each of its ten Lancasters with eleven 1,000 and four 500-pounders and sent them on their way between 17.55 and 18.15 with F/Ls Guilfoyle, Masters and Moss the senior pilots on duty. They headed south to begin the Channel crossing at Brighton and arrived at the target under clear skies with excellent visibility that facilitated a visual identification of the aiming point. Moderate flak in the target area was focused on aircraft right over the target, and a 103 Lancaster was observed to receive a direct hit, which caused a wing to break away. Two parachutes were seen to deploy and these crewmen, the navigator and bomb-aimer, landed in the arms of their captors, while the others perished in the wreckage. The 576 Squadron crews bombed from 13,000 feet and above at around 02.00, and it is believed that one U-Boot was hit.

That night, ninety 1 Group Lancasters crews from 12 and 14 Bases were briefed to attack a flying bomb storage site in the Forêt-de-Nieppe, close to the Belgian frontier in north-eastern France, one of four storage and launching sites to be targeted by two hundred aircraft of 1, 6 and 8 Groups. Bombing took place on the glow of TIs through ten-tenths cloud, and post-raid reconnaissance revealed that only the 1 Group operation had been successful.

During the course of another busy month, the squadron took part in sixteen operations and dispatched 235 sorties for the loss of eight Lancasters and crews and one other airman.

Lancaster ND994 UL-F2 F/O R E Linklater & crew all KIA 15th July 1944
(Aircrew Remembered)

F/O R E Linklater Sgt SJ Kozlowski F/O D M Mackintosh

Sgt W M Beattie F/Sgt W J McCollum Sgt G R Sims
Also killed was Sgt J W G Pringle (FE). (Aircrew Remembered)

The funeral of the Linklater Crew. The crew were buried at Loches-sur-Ource by the local French villagers including dignitaries who wanted to express their sorrow and gratitude to the crew.

The Funeral of the Linklater Crew

F/O R Bastick & crew with Lancaster UL-J2   *(Harry Holmes)*

Lancaster NG273 UL-Y2. F/O W Holmes & crew   (Harry Holmes)

F/L Bertram Roberts and crew with Lancaster RA587 UL-U   (Harry Holmes)

Lancaster RA587 UL-U take off wave   (Harry Holmes)

Lancaster RA562 UL-B engine runs   *(Harry Holmes*

Lancaster RA562 UL-B.   *(Harry Holmes)*

RAF attacks on Villeneuve St Georges, a railway marshalling area south of Paris, destroyed a large quantity of enemy motor transport, tracked vehicles and mobile guns on their way to the fighting areas as well as wrecking loading platforms, October 1944.

The devastated marshalling yard at Aulnoye, France, following three raids by aircraft of Bomber Command during March-April 1944.

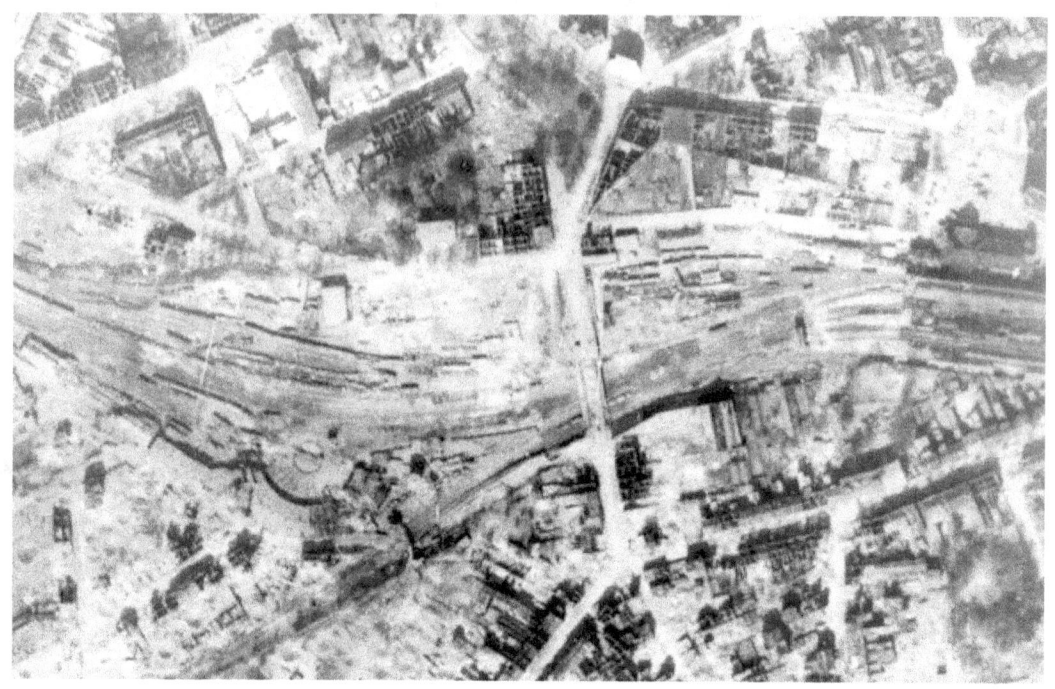

Aachen, Germany.
The main railway station and railyards at Aachen April 1944 after the attacks of RAF Bomber Command

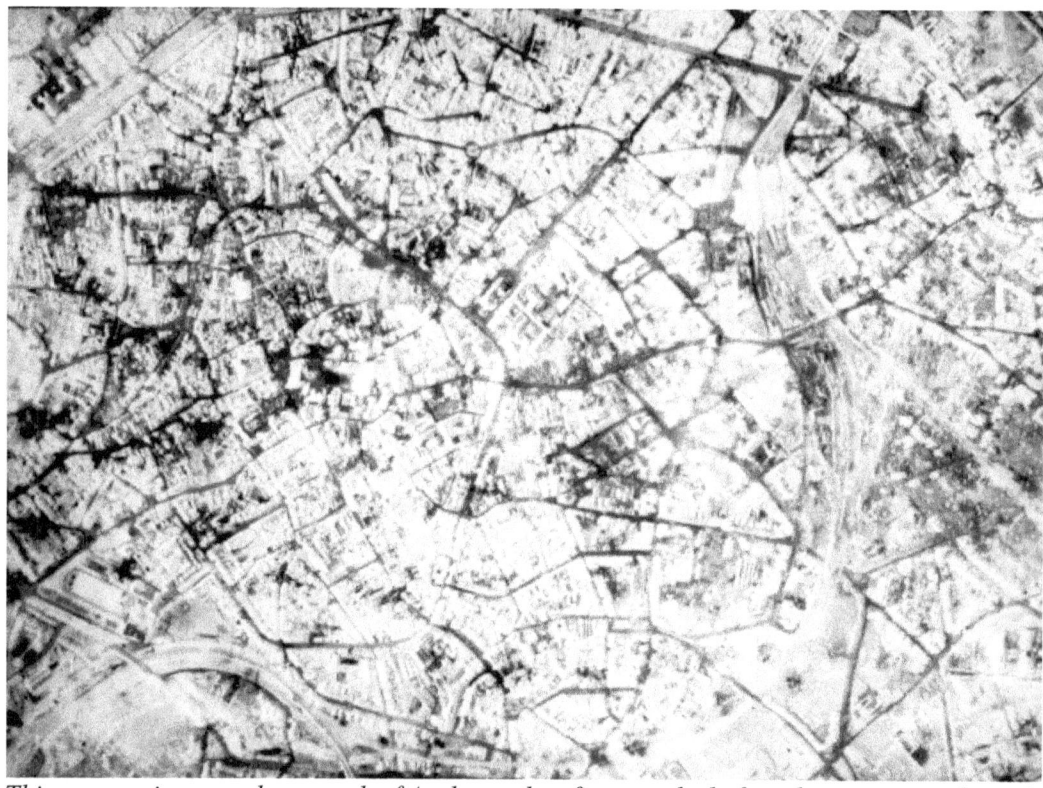

This reconnaissance photograph of Aachen, taken five months before the great assault on the city from the ground, shows the damage caused by the attacks of RAF Bomber Command.

Aftermath of Douai raid.

F/O R J Sarvis USAAF and his crew.
F/O Sarvis died when his Lancaster PB265 crashed in France on the 24th July 1944. The remaining crew, Sgts Balfour, Gordon, Weir, Coates, Reed and Clark had abandoned the aircraft, and all were eventually reported to be in safe hands. The wreckage was not found until 1989 (next page) and F/O Sarvis was buried in the US Military Cemetery Normandy.
(Aircrew Remembered)

Not realising there were human remains amongst the wreckage of the Lancaster, it was bulldozed off the road and it was not until a road widening scheme in 1989 that F/O Sarvis was discovered.

Lancaster UL-B2 of 576 Squadron in an RAF Fiskerton hangar.   (Harry Holmes)

Kangaroo nose art on a 576 Squadron Lancaster (AWM)

Rouen after the bombardments April 1944.

Cologne

Lancaster PD235 UL-N2
Lost 24th September 1944 with six of its crew - Sgt Vivian Price, F/O Jack Manser, F/O Dave Baker, (Pilot), F/L Ted Bennett, F/O Francis (Pete) Walker, and Sgt Donald Purse. Flight engineer F/O K G Playfoot evaded. *(Harry Holmes)*

Lancaster PB253 UL-A2 crash site of F/L J Archibald & crew KIA 29th July 1944.

Lancaster PB253 shot down 29th July 1944 with the loss of all crew except F/O J Archibald RNZAF who appears to have evaded. Crew: Sgt J R Cuthbert, Sgt J E Kearney, F/O P J Biollo RCAF, Sgt L Fielding, WO T P Barry, Sgt A Milne.
(Many thanks to Aircrew Remembered for these and the many other invaluable photographic contributions to this profile.)

F/O Peter Biollo RCAF KIA 29th July 1944. Aged 20 from Archibald Crew. (Aircrew Remembered)

W/OII Joseph Martel RCAF KIA 29th January 1944. From Archibald Crew (Aircrew Remembered)

The Childs Crew

Back L – R: F/Sgt Ronald Johnstone, Sgt Herbert Bowles, W/O Eric Bardsley, P/O Edward Childs and Sgt Victor White. Kneeling: Sgt Clifford Brewster and Sgt Clifford Giffard. Their Lancaster W4245 exploded in mid-air on the 30th January 1944 on a Berlin raid.

Dusseldorf, Germany. November 1944. Damage to Rheinmetall-Borsig Arms works in Dusseldorf after a raid in which 576 Squadron took part.

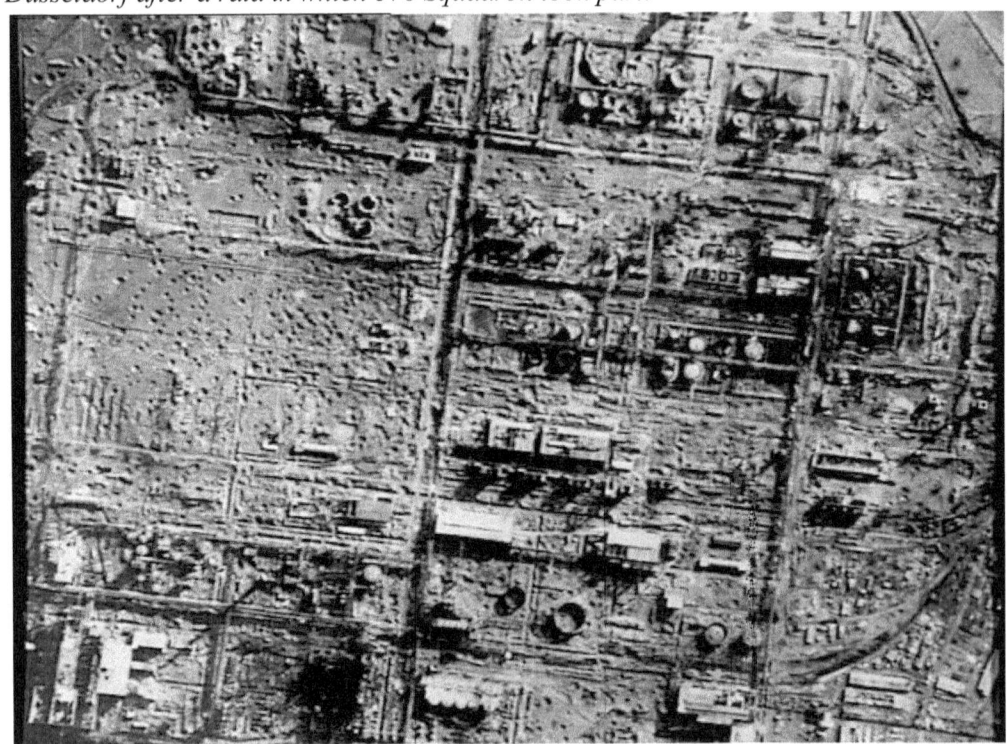
Zeitz, Germany. The Zeitz synthetic oil plant photographed by RAF reconnaissance a month after an Allied air attack on January 1944. The plant is a mass of debris amongst a dense concentration of craters. Most of the pipelines are broken, and all the vital parts of the plant have been hit. Large numbers of storage tanks and cooling towers are destroyed or damaged.

A Lancaster Bomber over the target during an attack on a flying bomb depot at Trossy St. Maximin, near Paris, France.

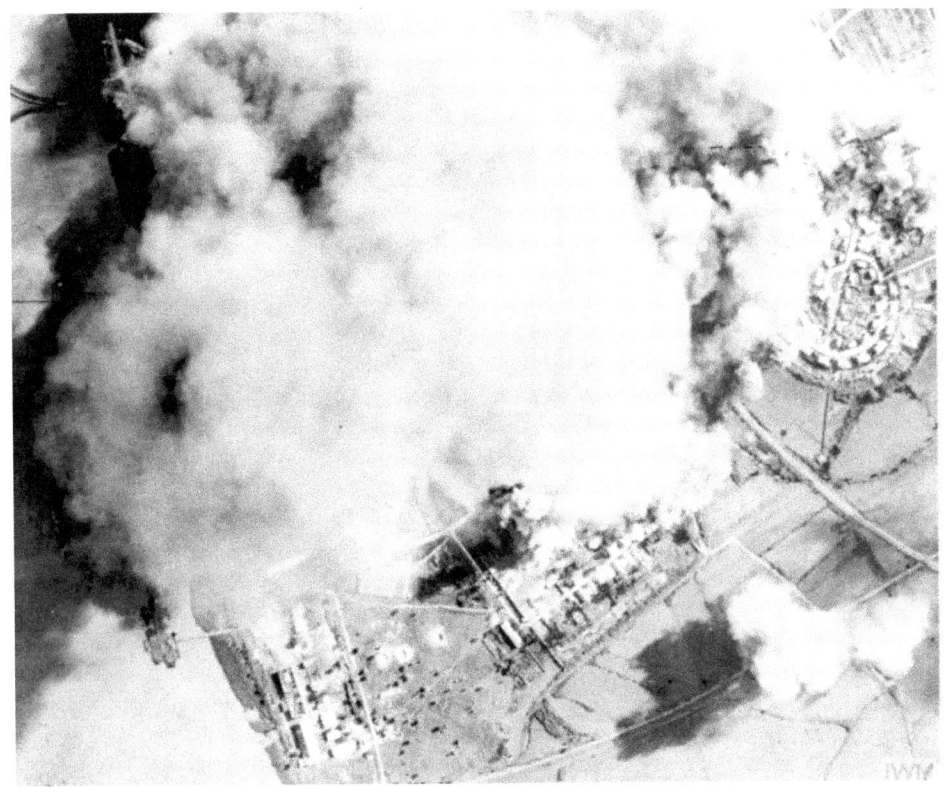

Attack on oil storage depot at Pauillac, 4th August 1944.

Bombing target: Karlsruhe

Friedrichshafen after air raid April 1944.

Before and after the raid on the Mailly-le-Camp Military Barracks 3/4th May 1944

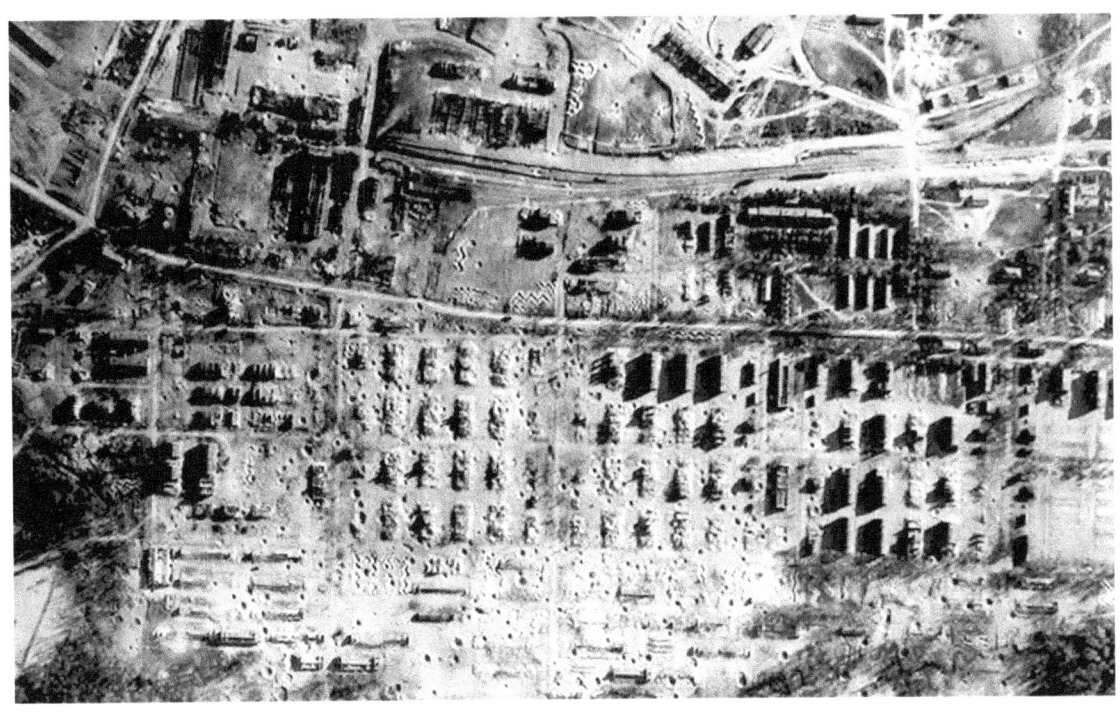

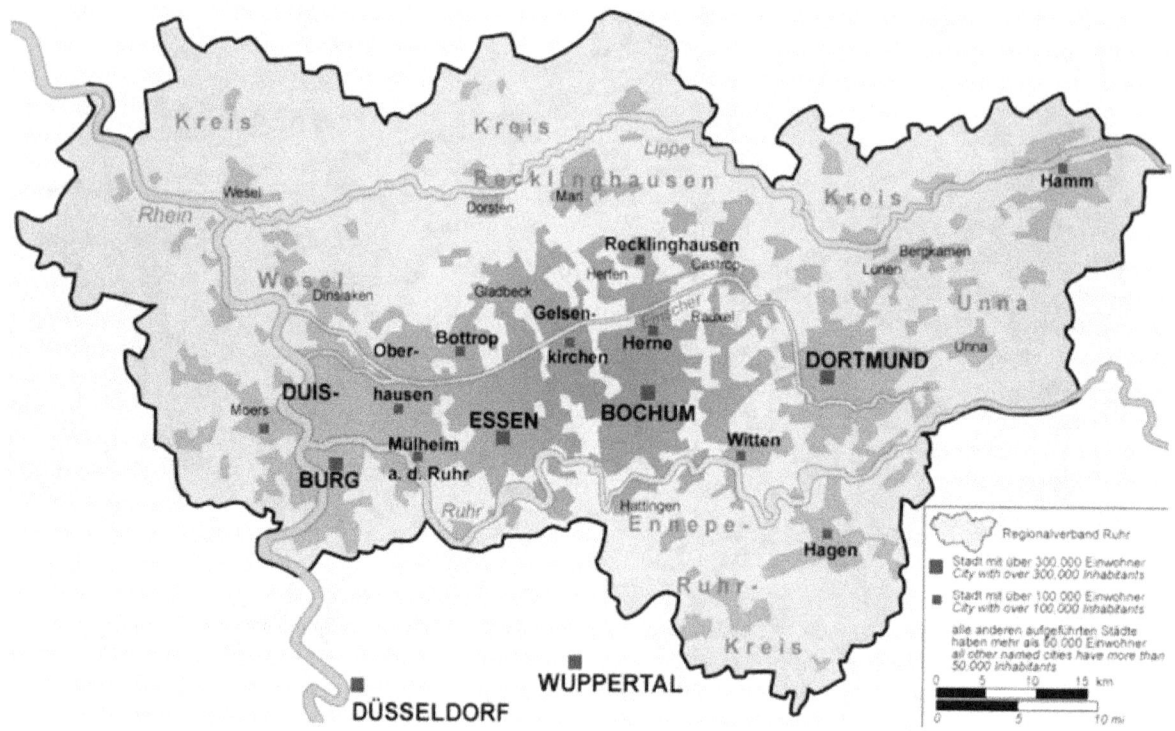

Main cities and towns of the industrial Ruhr.

Gelsenkirchen

Le Havre

Calais, France. 25th September 1944. Halifax aircraft bombing Calais. By the orders of Hitler, German garrisons in Le Havre, Boulogne and Calais were declared "Fortresses" and their defenders were expected to resist to the last. As a result of the intensive attacks by bombers, the German garrison surrendered after five days.

Le Havre

Sgt Anthony Raymond KIA 13th May 1944
(Aircrew Remembered/Philip Isbell)

ACM Sir Ronald Ivelaw-Chapman,
GCB, KBE, DFC, AFC

Mimoyecques showing the V3 sites

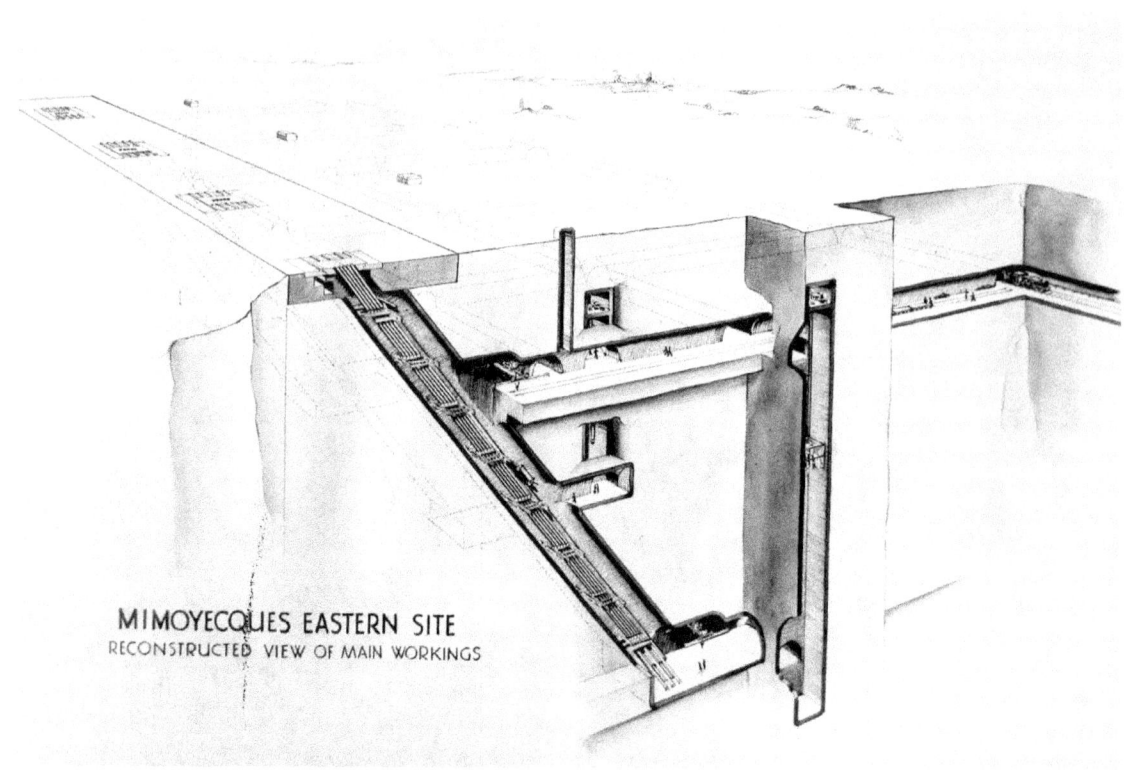

An RAF Handley Page Halifax flies over Mimoyecques on 6th July 1944 as exploding bombs send smoke and clouds of dust into the air.

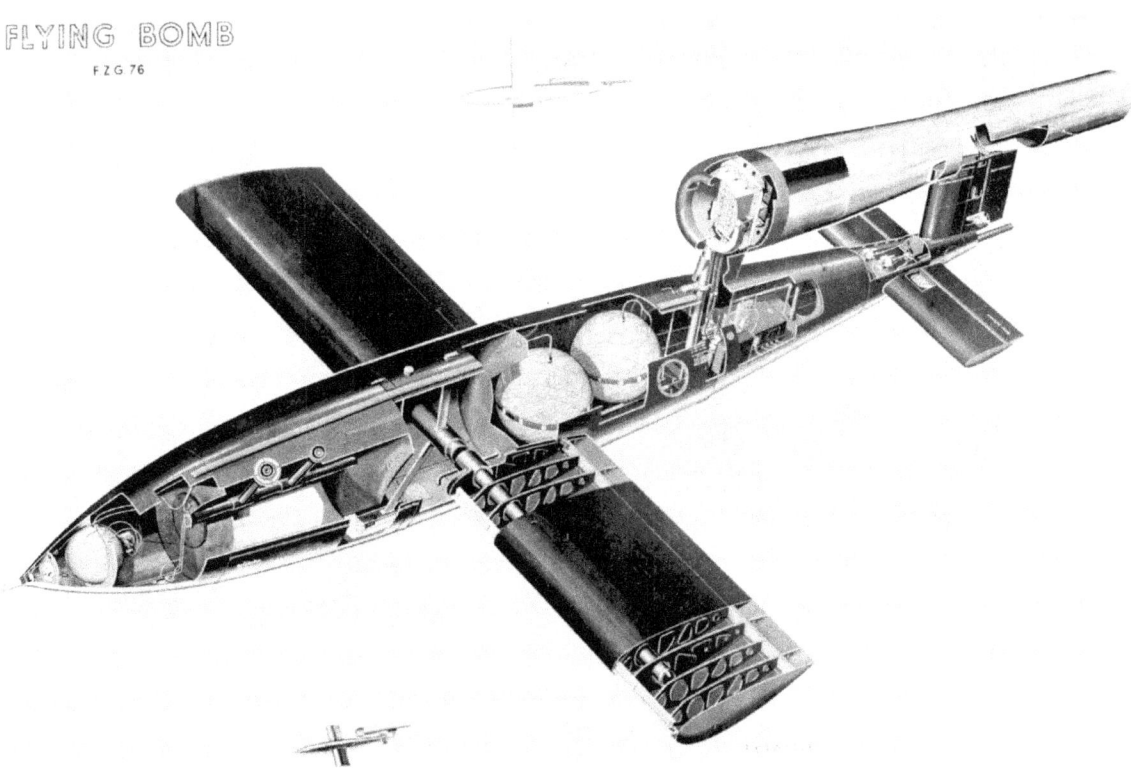

V-1 Missile

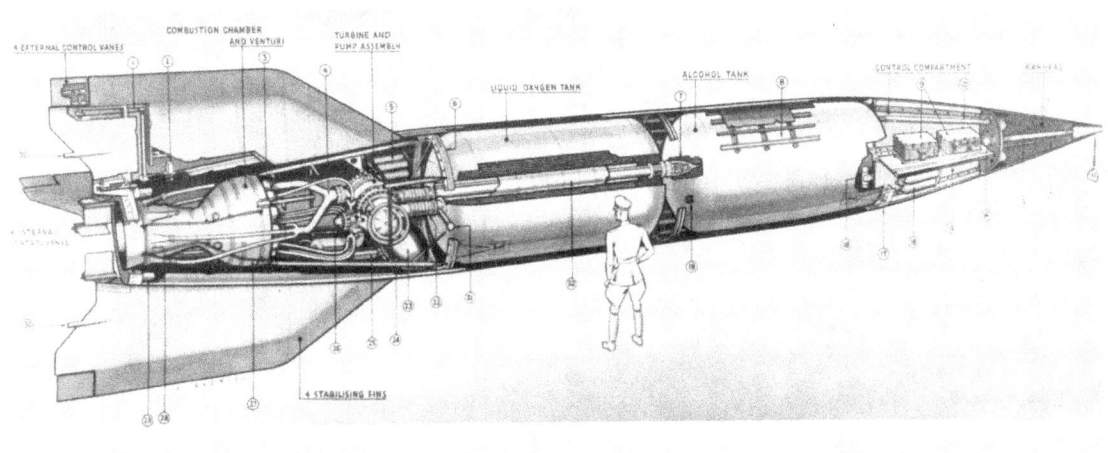

1. CHAIN DRIVE TO EXTERNAL CONTROL VALVE
2. ELECTRIC MOTOR
3. BURNER CUPS
4. ALCOHOL SUPPLY FROM PUMP
5. AIR BOTTLES
6. REAR JOINT RING AND STRONG POINT FOR TRANSPORT
7. SERVO-OPERATED ALCOHOL OUTLET VALVE
8. ROCKET SHELL
9. RADIO EQUIPMENT
10. PIPE LEADING FROM ALCOHOL TANK TO WARHEAD
11. NOSE PROBABLY FITTED WITH NOSE SWITCH, OR OTHER DEVICE FOR OPERATING WARHEAD FUZE
12. CONDUIT CARRYING WIRES TO NOSE OF WARHEAD
13. CENTRAL EXPLODER TUBE
14. ELECTRIC FUZE FOR WARHEAD
15. PLYWOOD FRAME
16. NITROGEN BOTTLES
17. FRONT JOINT RING AND STRONG POINT FOR TRANSPORT
18. PITCH AND AZIMUTH GYROS
19. ALCOHOL FILLING POINT
20. DOUBLE WALLED ALCOHOL DELIVERY PIPE TO PUMP
21. OXYGEN FILLING POINT
22. CONCERTINA CONNECTIONS
23. HYDROGEN PEROXIDE TANK
24. TUBULAR FRAME HOLDING TURBINE AND PUMP ASSEMBLY
25. PERMANGANATE TANK (GAS GENERATOR UNIT BEHIND THIS TANK)
26. OXYGEN DISTRIBUTOR FROM PUMP
27. ALCOHOL PIPES FOR SUBSIDIARY COOLING
28. ALCOHOL INLET TO DOUBLE WALL
29. ELECTRO-HYDRAULIC SERVO MOTORS
30. AERIAL LEADS

U.S. Army V-2 cutaway drawing showing engine, fuel cells, guidance units and warhead.

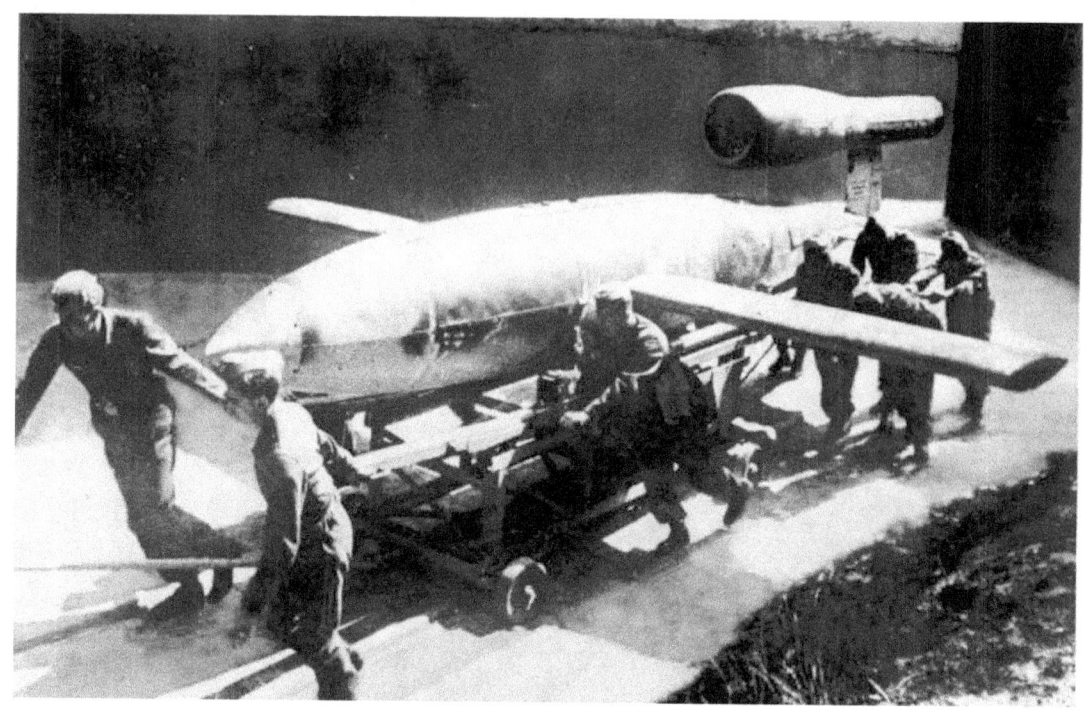

A V-1 is rolled to the launch site. The start is carried out by a compressed air system. With the help of a remote guidance procedure, the V-1 hits the ordered target. The consistently high speed, which was not achieved by any Allied fighter, is obtained from a rocket engine. Typically launched from sites like Domleger.

Aerial view after the bombardment in Vire, Normandy, 1944

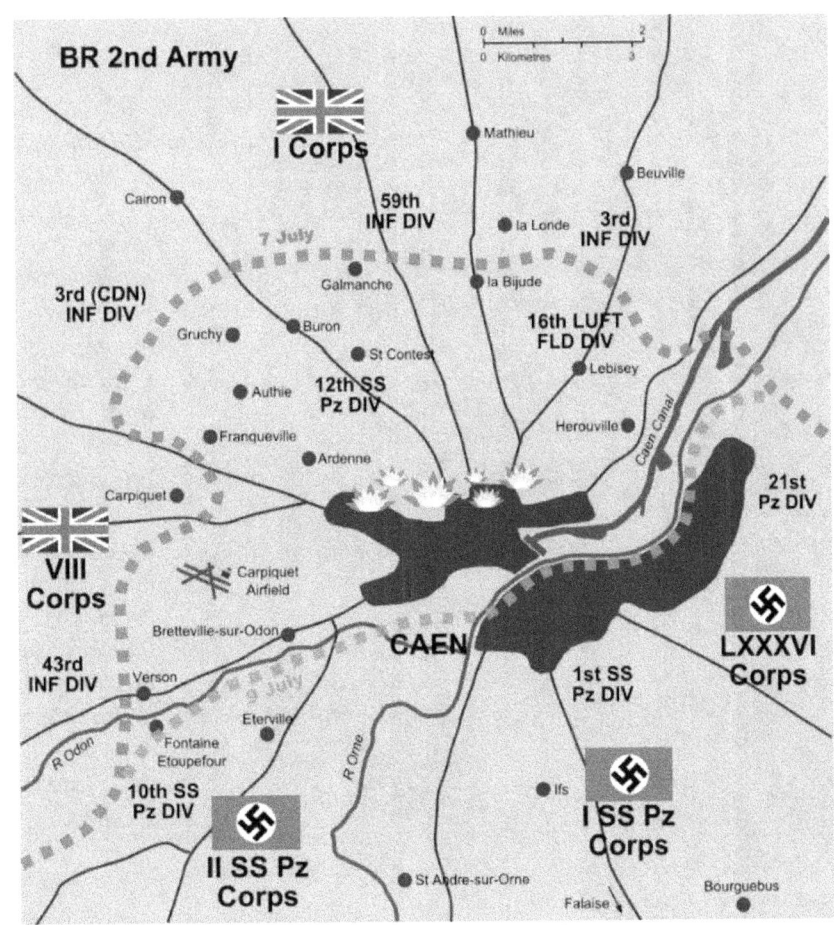

Map of Caen and the aiming points of the heavy bombers on the northern outskirts of the city. Below: A British soldier carries a little girl through the devastation of Caen, 10th July 1944.

A Handley Page Halifax of No. 4 Group flies over the suburbs of Caen, France, during a major daylight raid to assist the Normandy land battle during Operation Charnwood. 467 aircraft took part in the attack, which was originally intended to have bombed German strongpoints north of Caen, but the bombing area was eventually shifted nearer the city because of the proximity of Allied troops to the original targets. The resulting bombing devastated the northern suburbs.

A British soldier helps an elderly woman through the ruins of Caen after its bombardment by Bomber Command.

A Lancaster crew of 576 Squadron which raided Berlin eleven times. The crew in their flying kit are identified as, left to right: Sgt J R (Jock) Mearns (FE); F/O Gomer S (Taft) Morgan DFC, pilot, (both in back of a truck); P/O Neil Lambell DFC, RAAF (BA) (back to photographer); Sgt J R (Blondie) O'Hanlon W/Op; Sgt Stan S Greenwood (MUG), Sgt C E (Bob) Shilling (RG); F/L Edward (Jock) Graham DFC, (Nav). (AWM)

F/L Herbert Benson & crew and Lancaster UL-H2. December 1944   (Harry Holmes)

Flak tower during construction *Post-war Flak tower Heiligengeistfeld in Hamburg*

A 12.8 cm FlaK 40, the main guns of the Flak-towers, and its crew

August 1944

August would bring an end to the flying bomb offensive and also see a return to major night operations against industrial Germany. Flying bomb sites were to dominate the first half of the month, however, and would be targeted in daylight on each of the first six days. It began with the commitment of 777 aircraft to operations against thirteen flying bomb-related sites during the afternoon and evening of the 1st, although there were serious doubts about the weather conditions, which were poor over England. A 1 Group operation by fifty Lancasters of 13 Base against a "constructional works" at Belle Croix les Bruyeres involved a dozen 576 squadron aircraft, each loaded with a dozen 1,000 and four 500-pounders and departing Elsham Wolds between 18.45 and 19.00 with F/Ls Guilfoyle and Moss the senior pilots on duty. They exited the English coast at Orford Ness and encountered ten-tenths low cloud with tops at 2,000 feet, which completely obscured the ground, and as they crossed the French coast near Calais, the master Bomber aborted the operation and sent them home.

Elsham Wolds was not called into action when four small-scale operations against flying bomb sites were handed to individual 1 Group squadrons on the 2nd, the plan for which required each element to formate on two Path Finder Mosquitos, and bomb when the first Mosquito released its load. There was also a repeat of the recent attack on Le Havre for which fifty-one Lancasters were detailed.

On the following day, 1,114 aircraft were committed to attacks on flying bomb sites at Bois-de-Cassan, Forêt-de-Nieppe and Trossy-St-Maximin, and 1 Group was assigned to the last-mentioned, described in the 1 Group ORB as large "constructional works". This was one of many similar sites in the Hauts-de-France region and had been targeted by 5 Group on the previous day. 576 Squadron contributed fifteen Lancasters to the 1 Group force of 180 and loaded each of them with eleven 1,000 and four 500-pounders, before dispatching them from Elsham Wolds between 11.25 and 11.50 with F/Ls Guilfoyle, Masters and Moss the senior pilots on duty. They disappeared almost immediately into a very low cloud base hovering at around 300 feet, but this was in the process of breaking up as they began the Channel crossing at the Sussex coast over Bognor Regis to make landfall on the French side near Dieppe, where heavy flak brought down a 460 Squadron RAAF aircraft and damaged others. Those continuing on were forced to run the gauntlet of flak, largely from aerodromes, and on reaching the target, crews were confronted by three to seven-tenths cloud in a wedge between 3000 and 7,000 feet. Most were able to identify the target visually through the many gaps and bombed on their own reference, while others aimed for the red TIs or to port of the yellows in accordance with the clear instructions from the Master Bomber. The 576 Squadron participants delivered their attacks visually, based on the 103 Squadron record, from 11,000 to 14,000 feet from around 14.15, and the aiming point and markers were soon obscured by smoke. Twenty-seven 1 Group aircraft sustained flak damage, and one was seen to have half a wing sliced off by bombs from above.

The Bois de Cassan and Trossy sites were to be attacked again by elements of 6 and 8 Groups on the 4th, while 288 Lancasters of 1, 3 and 8 Groups were made ready for the long flight to the Bordeaux region of France's Biscay coast. The mighty Gironde estuary narrows as it leads inland towards the south-east, before dividing to become the Garonne River to the west and the Dordogne to the east. Its banks and islands were home to a number of important oil production and storage sites at Pauillac, Blaye, Bec-d'Ambes and Bassens, the last mentioned on the outskirts of Bordeaux itself, and the region was a frequent destination for gardening activities. Bordeaux was a vitally important port to the enemy, both as a gateway to the Atlantic and as home to U-Boot pens, and consequently was heavily defended along the entire length of the waterway. The targets on this occasion were oil refineries at Pauillac and Bec-d'Ambes, and the attacks were to be carried out for the first time under the umbrella of an escort of twenty-seven "Serrate" Mosquitos provided by 100 Group. "Serrate" was a radar device that enabled the night-fighter variant of the Mosquito to home in on enemy night-fighters to turn the hunters into the hunted, and a spectacularly successful campaign was waged that spread panic through the Luftwaffe Nachtjagd and spawned the term "Moskito Panik" among its crews.

1 Group detailed 169 Lancasters for the Pauillac site, of which fifteen were made ready by 576 Squadron and loaded with nine 1,000 and three 500-pounders each before departing Elsham Wolds between 13.10 and 13.40 with W/C Sellick the senior pilot on duty. In contrast to the previous day, the weather was exceptionally fine, and the bomber stream flew out over Land's End to skirt the Brest peninsula on its way south, before arriving in the target area under clear skies and in good visibility that enabled them to identify ground features on approach. The yellow TIs went down on time and thick black and white smoke began to rise from the moment the first bombs detonated at 18.00, to be followed by those from the Elsham Wolds contingent from 6,500 to 9,000 feet between 18.00 and 18.10. The entire northern half of the complex was left burning and black smoke was rising through 8,000 feet as the last of the bombers turned away.

On the following day, 1 Group issued orders for 176 Lancasters to return to the Gironde estuary, half to attack the southern section of the Pauillac refinery and half to target the oil storage site at Blaye, situated on the East Bank of the estuary further south. 576 Squadron made ready sixteen of its Lancasters for Blaye, loading each with nine 1,000 and three 500-pounders, before dispatching them from Elsham Wolds between 13.55 and 14.45 with S/L Templeman-Rooke the senior pilot on duty. The conditions were as perfect as for the previous day's operation, and all from the squadron arrived safely in the target area drawn on by the smoke still issuing from the site but not impeding identification of the aiming point. The Yellow TIs fell a little to the north-west and the south, but any over and undershooting was quickly rectified by the Master Bomber and a huge fire soon broke out which gradually enveloped the site. The Elsham Wolds participants carried out their attacks from 6,000 to 8,000 feet between 18.59 and 19.07 and witnessed a large orange explosion at 19.10, before setting course for home under the protection of the 100 Group Mosquito escort, which was exchanged at the Brittany coast for one of Spitfires and Mustangs. On return, the Elsham Wolds crews were diverted to Ossington because of fog over northern Lincolnshire.

More than a thousand aircraft were assembled during the course of the 7th to send against five enemy strong points ahead of advancing Allied ground forces in the Normandy battle area. Two of the aiming points were west of the Caen to Falaise road and three to the east, each to be attacked by roughly two hundred aircraft under the control of Master Bombers. 1 Group was assigned to one of the western targets at Fontenay-le-Marmion to the south of the city, for which 204 Lancasters were detailed, seventeen of them provided by 576 Squadron and each carrying eleven 1,000 and four 500-pounders. They departed Elsham Wolds between 20.50 and 21.20 with F/Ls Guilfoyle, Masters and Moss the senior pilots on duty and flew out over Selsey Bill under cloudless skies, which persisted all the way to the target area. P/O Laydon and crew lost their port-outer engine at the English coast but opted to press on and complete the sortie. As the force approached at 23.17, it was greeted by green star-shells fired by the artillery as a guide to the aiming point, and green Path Finder TIs fell beneath them to mark out the area intended for destruction. The bombing began just before H-Hour, and among those delivering an attack were a dozen from 576 Squadron from 7,000 to 7,500 feet between 23.19 and 23.24, the bursts from which were observed to straddle the markers, before they became obscured by smoke and, eventually, obliterated altogether. At 23.25, the Master Bomber reported that no further green TIs were available and issued the code word "Greengage" to signal an end to proceedings, sending home all those with bombs still on board, including the remaining five from 576 Squadron.

Crews at Elsham Wolds were warned of an operation in the early morning of the 8th and again in the afternoon, but both were scrubbed. Elsewhere on that day, the focus returned to oil for 170 Lancaster and ten Mosquito crews of 1, 3 and 8 Groups, who were briefed for attacks on two depots and storage dumps at Aire-sur-la-Lys and Forêt-de-Lucheux, both situated in the Hauts-de-France region in the north-east of the country. 1 Group briefed fifty crews at the 12 and 14 Base stations of Binbrook and Wickenby for the oil tankage depot at the former, and at the target observed little happening on the ground until a large red/orange explosion erupted at 23.34 in the centre of the marked area and emitted a large mushroom of oily smoke. Several fires broke out, the glow from which remained visible for seventy-five miles into the return flight, and all returned safely to their respective stations to report a successful outcome.

On the following night, Elsham Wolds provided two crews from each squadron to lay mines in the Cinnamon garden south of the deep-water ports La Pallice/La Rochelle on the Biscay coast at a location referred to in the 103 Squadron ORB as Pertuis-d'Antioche. The crews of W/O Murray and F/L Guilfoyle took off at 21.25 and 21.30 each with six 1,500lb parachute mines beneath their feet and flew south over the Lincolnshire steel town of Scunthorpe to begin the Channel crossing at Bridport, on course for landfall on the Brittany coast near Treguier. Once establishing their position in the target area, they pinpointed visually on the Ile d'Oleron as the starting point for their timed run and delivered their payloads in a stick by H2S from 11,000 feet at around 01.00, before returning safely from an uneventful night's work.

The 10th brought four flying bomb targets for 1 Group, each assigned to fifteen Lancasters from individual 12 Base squadrons, but the largest operation was against an aviation fuel storage site at Dugny, a north-eastern suburb of Paris around eight miles from the city centre, for which eighty-nine Lancasters were detailed from 13 and 14 Bases. Eighteen 576 Squadron Lancasters received a bomb load of thirteen American-built 1,000-pounders and four 500-pounders and departed Elsham Wolds between 09.00 and 09.50 with F/Ls Bibby, Masters, Moss and Rainey the senior pilots on duty. They climbed into cloud with a base at 2,000 feet, but conditions improved as they headed south, again over Scunthorpe, to exit the English coast over Selsey Bill, and by the time that they made landfall to the north-east of Dieppe, they were benefitting from clear skies and good visibility, which facilitated an accurate attack. The first batch of markers fell short of the aiming point, but the next ones were well placed, and the attack proceeded under the control of a Master Bomber, whose communications were described as indistinct. The 576 Squadron crews bombed from 15,000 feet and above at around noon, and despite the absence of a spectacular explosion and black oily smoke common to most attacks on oil-related objectives, the operation was deemed a success. F/O Mills, the bomb-aimer in the crew of F/O Watts, was severely wounded by a flak splinter over the target, and a landing was carried out at the first suitable station to enable his removal to hospital.

A morning briefing on 1 Group's 12 and 13 Base stations on the 11th informed 120 crews of their part in an attack on marshalling yards that afternoon at Douai, situated ten miles south of Lille in north-eastern France. They were to act as the main force and would be supported by ten Lancasters from 35 (Madras Presidency) Squadron of the Path Finders to provide the marking and Master Bomber. The seventeen-strong 576 Squadron contingent departed Elsham Wolds between 13.30 and 14.10 with F/Ls Bibby, Guilfoyle, Moss and Rainey the senior pilots on duty and each crew sitting on thirteen 1,000 and four 500-pounders. The Channel crossing began at Selsey Bill and ended south of Cayeux-sur-Mer, by which time F/O Durrant and crew had turned back because of intercom failure. On arrival at the target the others found three to four-tenths broken cloud with tops at around 7,000 feet and excellent visibility, which enabled all crews to identify the target visually and the aiming point by the red Oboe TIs in the centre of the yards and to the western edge, which were backed up by yellows. However, these were soon rendered ineffective as they became obscured by smoke, upon which the master Bomber, F/L Forde, instructed the crews to bomb the windward edge of the smoke until he was able to re-mark with yellow TIs. He inadvertently left his transmit button on, which caused some confusion and annoyance, but the bombing went ahead, the 576 Squadron crews delivering their loads from 16,000 feet and above between 16.15 and 16.25. A violent explosion at 16.19 was followed by a column of smoke, and direct hits were observed on rolling stock, engine sheds, depots and also on a road bridge at the northern end of the yards, which left returning crews confident of a successful outcome. This proved to be the final outing for the Special Duties Flight, which performed its final operation in a bombing rather than target-marking role and was disbanded without ceremony a few days later with little recognition for its brief contribution to 1 Group's war effort.

1 Group would be active throughout the 12th, beginning with a late morning take-off for twenty Lancasters from 12 Base to target U-Boot pens at La Pallice on the Biscay coast and thirty from 13 Base assigned to a similar target at Bordeaux further to the south. The seven-strong 576 Squadron element departed Elsham Wolds bound for the latter between 11.15 and 11.30 with S/L Slater the senior pilot on duty and six 2,000-pounders in each bomb bay. They flew out over Bridport and traversed the Brest peninsula, before proceeding south on a course parallel to the coast and arriving at the target under clear skies and good vertical visibility. They delivered their attacks from 11,000 feet and above at around 15.10, complying with the Master Bomber's instruction to slightly overshoot the yellow TIs, and were under fire throughout by heavy flak in barrage form. Once again, a Mosquito escort kept the bombers safe from air attack, and Spitfires were waiting for them at the Finistere coast to shepherd them back across the Channel.

That night was to bring heavy activity, during which the principal operation was the raid by 379 Lancasters and Halifaxes from all but 8 Group on Braunschweig (Brunswick), to ascertain the ability of main force crews to identify and attack a target on the strength of H2s alone without any marking taking place. Meanwhile, a second force of 297 aircraft would attempt to hit the Opel tank works at Rüsselsheim some two hundred miles to the south-south-west, and a rush job added late on would involve 144 aircraft attacking a German troop concentration and a road junction north of Falaise. 1 Group detailed eighty-three Lancasters for Braunschweig, a city known for supporting the German war effort with a particular emphasis on aircraft and automobile component manufacture. 576 Squadron contributed just the crews of F/Ls Guilfoyle, Masters and Moss and F/O Ireland, who departed Elsham Wolds between 21.30 and 21.35, each bearing aloft a 2,000-pounder and twelve 500lb J-Type cluster bombs. They began the North Sea crossing at Mablethorpe and made landfall on the Dutch coast in the region of Harlingen, before heading south-east to cross the German frontier near Nordhorn in excellent weather conditions and continue on a more-or-less easterly course to the target. It was only when some fifty miles short of the destination that the cloud thickened to ten-tenths at around 10,000 feet to obscure the ground. This was an anticipated eventuality and was not critical as the purpose of the operation was to bomb blind on H2S anyway, the 576 Squadron participants complying from 20,000 feet and above between 00.06 and 00.09. Night-fighters had been evident over the target and continued to harry the returning bombers, and were largely responsible for the loss of twenty-seven aircraft, 7.1% of the force, in return for a modestly effective raid, which hit the centre of the city but also other locations up to twenty miles distant. The simultaneous attack on the Opel tank works at Rüsselsheim cost a further twenty aircraft, and the effort and losses were not compensated for with a successful outcome.

As the bombers were turning away from Braunschweig, three Lancasters from each of the Elsham Wolds squadrons were in the process of taking off for Falaise as part of a 1 Group force of thirty-five aircraft. The Falaise area was a bottleneck, through which retreating German ground forces were attempting to escape back to their homeland, while the Allies saw an opportunity to neutralise a substantial threat to its own advance eastwards. The 576 Squadron crews of S/L Slater, S/L Templeman-Rooke and F/L Rainey became airborne at 00.05 and 00.20 and 00.30 respectively with eleven 1,000 and four 500-pounders beneath their feet and flew out over Selsey Bill to make landfall on the Normandy coast. They arrived under a cloudless sky, only for cloud to build as they progressed inland to find the target area concealed beneath a fifteen-hundred-foot layer of ten-tenths with a base at 1,000 feet. Despite this, the plentiful and concentrated red and green TIs could be seen and were bombed by the 576 Squadron trio from 7,000 feet and above at around 02.15, after which, they returned without incident to report a few fires and explosions.

The main activity during the afternoon of the 14th was an operation in support of Canadian divisions in the Falaise area involving 805 aircraft, 130 of them provided by 1 Group. Their targets were seven enemy troop positions, and each attack was to be controlled by a Master Bomber to ensure as far as possible that no "friendly fire" incidents resulted from the close proximity of the opposing forces. One hundred of the 1 Group crews were briefed for aiming point 25, the village of Fontaine-le-Pin, and thirty for 21B, and it was for the former that fifteen 576 Squadron Lancasters departed Elsham Wolds between 13.10 and 13.40 with F/L Bibby the senior pilot on duty and twenty 500-pounders in each bomb bay. P/O Wilson had to feather an engine when it caught fire over Scunthorpe but showed great determination to carry on and complete the sortie. Cloud over England gave way to clear skies over the Channel and French coast, and smoke could be observed in the target area as the 1 Group formations approached. Smoke from Fontaine-le-Pin was rising through 6,000 feet even before some of the force had reached the French coast, and the Master Bomber brought them down to 4,000 feet, before reducing the bombing height still further to 3,000 feet. The smoke rendered map reading difficult and target identification something of a challenge, but 50% of crews were able to see red TIs, and when these disappeared from sight, they were instructed to aim for the northern edge of the smoke. The 576 Squadron crews bombed on the TIs from 2,000 to 3,500 feet between 15.30 and 15.38 and left the scene satisfied that the attack had been concentrated where intended. Aiming point 21B soon became obscured by thick smoke, but the Master Bomber handled the attack expertly, and when two sticks of bombs were seen to undershoot by some three hundred yards, he was quick to admonish the culprits, and no further wayward bombing occurred. Despite the most stringent efforts to avoid friendly fire incidents, about halfway through the sequence of attacks, some bombs did fall into a quarry occupied by Canadian troops, killing thirteen men, injuring fifty-three others, and destroying a large number of vehicles.

In preparation for his new night offensive against Germany, Harris called for operations against enemy night-fighter airfields in Holland and Belgium, in response to which, a list of eight such targets was drawn up. Those at Eindhoven, Soesterberg, Volkel, Melsbroek, St-Trond, Tirlemont-Gossancourt and Le Culot were to be targeted in daylight during the course of the morning and early afternoon of the 15th, and Venlo that night, involving, in all, 1004 aircraft. 1 Group ordered 202 Lancasters to be made ready to be divided equally between Volkel in south-central Holland and Le Culot, situated some ten miles south-south-east of Leuven in north-central Belgium. 576 Squadron loaded each of its nineteen Lancasters with thirteen American-built 1,000 and four 500-pounders and dispatched them from Elsham Wolds between 09.40 and 10.15 bound for Le Culot with F/Ls Bibby, Masters and Rainey the senior pilots on duty. They began the North Sea crossing between Southwold and Orford Ness and made landfall over the Scheldt estuary in perfect conditions, which enabled them to identify the target from many miles away on approach. The Path Finder element carried out its part in the operation in exemplary fashion, dropping TIs close to the runway intersection, but most crews were able to bomb visually, those from 576 Squadron from an unrecorded altitude between 12,000 and 17,000 feet either side of noon. In a short space of time, smoke and dust obliterated the aiming point, but all bombs appeared to fall within the airfield boundaries, and the operation was declared a success. There was some opposition over the target from heavy flak, and on the route between Antwerp and Brussels, but a strong fighter escort kept the Luftwaffe at bay to ensure that there were no losses.

The new offensive began with simultaneous attacks on Stettin and Kiel on the night of the 16/17th, for which 1 Group contributed 134 aircraft to the overall all-Lancaster force of 461 assigned to the former. 576 Squadron made ready nine of its own for the main event, giving each a load of a 2,000-pounder and twelve 500lb J-Type cluster bombs, while five others had six 1,500lb parachute mines winched into their bomb bays for delivery to the Geranium garden off the port of Swinemünde in the Bay of Pomerania. They departed Elsham Wolds together between 21.00 and 21.50 with F/L Rainey the senior pilot on duty among the Stettin-bound element and F/L Bibby leading the gardeners and flew out over Mablethorpe on course for Jutland's western coast. They enjoyed clear skies over the North Sea and Denmark and encountered cloud only when it began to build up over the Baltic to reach ten-tenths with tops at 17,000 feet as they crossed the German coast. It took some three-and-a-half hours to reach the respective target areas, and F/O Stewart and crew were just twenty minutes short when two ailing engines finally compelled them to jettison their load and turn back. The others were greeted by up to nine-tenths high cloud with a base, according to the Master Bomber's broadcast at 00.52½, at 14,000 feet, but with sufficient breaks to enable them to register clear visibility below.

At Stettin, the initial flares and green TIs were observed to be a little north and east of the built-up area, which reduced the effectiveness of the illumination, but this did not prevent the Path Finder primary visual markers from identifying the aiming point and dropping a mix of red and green TIs to form a good concentration that the visual re-centerers maintained throughout. The main force element approached from 16,000 to 20,000 feet and began to bomb the TIs from around 00.56 until 01.21 and reported fires taking hold. The 576 Squadron ORB provides no details of bombing heights and times, but based on the 103 Squadron record, crews carried out their attacks from 17,000 to 18,500 feet between 00.59 and 01.10 in accordance with the Master Bomber's instructions and in the face of a moderate amount of heavy and light flak. Among five missing Lancasters was 576 Squadron's LM133, which was abandoned by its eight occupants over Sweden and crashed some thirty-five miles north-east of Malmo. Seven members of the crew landed safely and were interned for a respectable period before being returned home, but the pilot, F/O Watts RCAF, tragically, landed in a tree and was strangled to death after becoming entangled in his parachute cords.

Meanwhile, the gardeners had planted their vegetables unopposed by H2S from 10,000 to 12,000 feet between 01.11 and 01.25, and F/O Wearmouth and crew were homebound over Denmark when they noticed a single-engine enemy aircraft stalking them. An exchange of fire resulted in the enemy aircraft impacting the ground and exploding. While the above operations were in progress, 190 miles away to the west, severe damage had been inflicted on the docks and shipbuilding yards at Kiel, but much of the bombing had also been wasted outside of the town to the north-west. Not all crews at debriefing were confident about the outcome of the Stettin raid, some suggesting that it had been scattered, when in fact, it had been highly successful and had destroyed fifteen hundred houses, numerous industrial premises, had sunk five ships in the harbour and seriously damaged eight more.

There is confusion concerning an operation late on the 17th against an oil storage depot at Terneuzen, a northern district of the city of Ghent in north-eastern Belgium, sometimes referred to as Ertvelde-Rieme, after a location called Riemer a little to the north of Terneuzen. According to the 1 Group ORB, this operation was cancelled in mid-afternoon and all squadrons stood down for the rest of the day, and there is no mention of it either in Bomber Command War Diaries by Martin Middlebrook and Chris Everitt. However, the 103 and 576 Squadrons' ORBs are adamant that the operation went ahead with a dozen Lancasters from each squadron departing Elsham Wolds between 22.10 and 22.35 with F/Ls Masters and Rainey the senior 576 Squadron pilots on duty and the station commander, G/C Sheen, captaining a 103 Squadron aircraft. Each bore aloft thirteen US-issue 1,000-pounders and four of 500lbs as they flew out over Orford Ness on course for the Scheldt as part of a 1 and 5 Group force of 105 Lancasters and five Mosquitos. Flt/O Sawyer, another former RCAF American now transferred to the USAAF, was forced to drop out because of engine failure, while the others identified the target visually and by TIs under largely clear skies and bombed in accordance with the instructions of the Master Bomber from 10,000 to 12,000 feet between 00.04 and 00.11.

On the following day, 1 Group was handed five daytime targets, beginning, we are informed, with an attack in the early afternoon by thirty aircraft from 14 Base on the Ertvelde-Rieme site. The remaining four targets were all flying-bomb related and involved just four Lancasters each, at Le Nieppe for 103 and 550 Squadrons, Wemars-Cappel for 576 Squadron, Vincly for 625 Squadron and Fromental for 460 Squadron RAAF. The 576 Squadron crews of F/L Bibby and F/Os Durrant, Linklater and Mulrooney departed Elsham Wolds between 19.24 and 19.45, each sitting on twenty

500-pounders, and flew out over Orford Ness under favourable conditions until arriving at the French coast between Calais and Dunkerque. Here, they encountered ten-tenths cloud that forced them to descend to 5,000 feet, at which height they were able to map-read their way to the target, but had to run the gauntlet of intense light flak. This interfered with bombing runs and forced the crews of F/Os Durrant and Mulrooney to make four passes over the aiming point, during the course of which F/O Mulrooney's bomb-aimer, F/O Mortel, sustained a face wound from Perspex splinters. The blood from the wound impaired his vision and the flight engineer, Sgt Beale, was prevailed upon to release the bombs sometime around 21.00. F/L Bibby and crew, four members of which were members of the RCAF, failed to return in LM439 after coming down in the Marquise area between Calais and Boulogne, and only the pilot and navigator survived to fall into enemy hands. That night, major attacks on Bremen and the oil refinery at Sterkrade-Holten involved forces of 288 and 234 aircraft respectively, and by the time that the last aircraft had landed, the twenty-four-hour period had generated 1,069 sorties for the loss of just four aircraft.

Most of Bomber Command's heavy brigade spent the following week in non-operational activity while a few carried out minor and mining operations. Major operations resumed on the 25th, when preparations were put in hand to make ready more than nine hundred aircraft to launch against three major targets, while four hundred others would be engaged in a variety of smaller endeavours. The largest operation was to be the all-Lancaster affair involving 461 aircraft from 1, 3, 6 and 8 Groups in a return to the Opel tank works at Rüsselsheim in southern Germany, while 334 others attended to eight coastal batteries between Brest and the islands to the south of Lorient, leaving 5 Group to focus on Darmstadt, a university city renowned as a centre of scientific research and development, and one of a few almost virgin targets considered to be worthy of attention. The Opel factory had produced motor vehicles up until October 1940 and was a wholly-owned subsidiary of the American General Motors Corporation with a sister plant manufacturing lorries at Brandenburg near Berlin. In 1942, the Rüsselsheim plant was given over to war production and began to manufacture aircraft and tank parts.

1 Group detailed 189 Lancasters, of which fifteen were made ready by 576 Squadron and each loaded with a cookie and twelve 500lb Type-14 cluster bombs, before departing Elsham Wolds between 19.50 and 20.30 with S/L Templeman-Rooke the senior pilot on duty. They flew out over Selsey Bill and made landfall on the Normandy coast to the east of Caen, losing the services of F/O Bell and crew on the way on the failure of their rear turret. Having passed to the west of Paris, the bomber stream headed towards the German frontier in the region of Strasbourg, where patchy cloud gave way to clear skies and good vertical visibility in the target area. The Path Finders opened the attack on time with illuminator flares followed by red and green TIs, which were backed up throughout, and some crews confirmed their positions by H2S before committing themselves to the bombing run. A decoy site some ten miles west-south-west of the target attracted a few bomb loads in the early stages, but the main weight of the attack fell where intended in the face of little effective opposition from the ground. The 576 Squadron crews delivered their loads from 17,000 feet and above between 01.00 and 01.12, aiming at the TIs and fires in the face of numerous searchlights and moderate heavy flak in barrage form. Large explosions were observed at 00.58, 01.02, 01.09 and 01.10, and smoke was seen to be rising through 11,000 feet as the force retreated, leaving a glow from the burning factory visible for eighty miles. Night-fighters were much in evidence and three 103 Squadron crews returned with claims of having each shot one down. Local sources confirmed that parts of the Opel factory had been put out of action for several

weeks, although most of the machine tools escaped damage and production was not badly compromised.

The following night brought an operation by 372 Lancasters and ten Mosquitos from 1, 3 and 8 Groups against Kiel, while 174 Lancasters of 5 Group targeted Königsberg, now Kaliningrad in Russia, at the eastern end of Germany's Baltic coast. 1 Group provided 175 of the Lancasters for Kiel, fifteen of them belonging to 576 squadron, whose crews listened intently at Elsham Wolds to learn of their part in the proceedings. Out on the dispersals, the armourers were busy loading each of their Lancasters with a cookie and eighteen SBCs of incendiaries, which they lifted into the air between 19.40 and 20.20 with F/Ls Bennett and Hague the senior pilots on duty, the latter having arrived from 11 Base on the 12th. The sound of their engines was still heavy in the air when the crews of F/L Masters, F/O Murray, Flt/O Sawyer USAAF and F/O Wearmouth took off in that order between 20.35 and 20.55 bound with eight others from 13 Base for the distant Spinach and Privet gardens located respectively off the ports of Gdynia and Danzig, now Gdansk in Poland, in Danzig Bay. Both Elsham Wolds elements set course via Mablethorpe over thin stratus cloud as far as the west coast of southern Jutland and the bombing brigade arrived in the target area at 23.00 to find eight-tenths thin, low stratus with tops at around 4,000 feet.

Illuminating flares were already falling over the town to the west of the estuary and a very effective smoke screen was in operation over the southern part of the town. Only a few red and green TIs were on the ground, before the rest of the primary visual marker crews were instructed not to release any more, but those already burning proved to be sufficient, and a good concentration of bombing was achieved south of the aiming-point with a very large explosion observed at 23.10. The 576 Squadron crews carried out their assigned tasks from 18,000 feet and above either side of 23.15, and among seventeen Lancasters failing to return from Kiel were five from 1 Group, including 576 Squadron's PB400, which was severely damaged by flak during the bombing run, but pressed on to the aiming point with a burning starboard-outer engine. Once the bomb load had fallen away, F/O Linklater RCAF turned back towards the sea and ordered his predominantly RCAF crew to bale out, which all did successfully and were picked up from the water by the enemy, leaving their captain unaccounted for until his body was recovered for burial. A reconnaissance Mosquito flew over Kiel at 25,000 feet at 00.18 and reported a five-mile arc of fire with a large bank of smoke rising through 15,000 feet.

Meanwhile, some 340 miles to the east, the gardeners had established their positions by H2S on Hel point and delivered five 2,000lb mines each into the briefed locations from 13,000 feet either side of 01.30. Three of those assigned to the Spinach garden failed to return, two belonging to 166 squadron and 576 Squadron's ME792, which disappeared without trace with the experienced crew of P/O Murray, who was on his twenty-ninth sortie and close to the end of his tour.

The final acts of the flying bomb campaign were played out on the 28th, when 150 aircraft were detailed to carry out small "Oboe-leader" raids on a dozen sites, 1 Group assigned to four sites, at Fromental, Wemars-Cappel, Vincly and Chapelle-Notre-Dame, each to be targeted by ten Lancasters. It was for the last-mentioned, located a few miles south-east of Calais, that the Elsham Wolds squadrons were assigned, 576 Squadron providing the crews of F/Os Stedman and Wearmouth and F/Ls Bennett and Masters, whose Lancasters each received a bomb load of thirteen 1,000 and four 500-pounders, before taking off between 18.55 and 19.00. They rendezvoused with the six 103 Squadron Lancasters as they headed south past Reading over patchy medium level cloud, which had dissipated by the time that the Channel crossing began and the skies remained clear for the remainder of the outward flight. Despite ground haze, crews were able to map-read and identify the aiming point visually, confirmed by H2S and also by red TIs dropped by the Oboe Mosquito leaders. Bombing was carried out from 10,000 feet at around 20.45 and appeared to be concentrated, a fact confirmed by bombing photos. The Pas-de-Calais region was captured by Allied ground forces a few days later.

Of 591 Lancasters primed for action in the Baltic region on the 29th, 189 belonged to 5 Group for an attack on the port of Königsberg for the second time in three nights, while 402 Lancasters of 1, 3 and 8 Groups attended to the Baltic port-city of Stettin 260 miles closer to home. The sixteen 576 Squadron participants were part of a 1 Group contribution of 188 Lancasters and each received a bomb load of a cookie and ten assorted SBCs of 4lb and 30lb incendiaries, before departing Elsham Wolds between 20.50 and 21.25 with S/L Slater the senior pilot on duty. They were followed into the air at 21.45 and 21.55 respectively by the crews of F/Sgt Greig and F/O Wearmouth, who were bound, with a load of five 1,500lb mines each, for the waters of the Geranium garden off the Baltic port of Swinemünde. The two elements flew out over Mablethorpe and encountered a layer of low cloud over the North Sea and part of Jutland, which gave way to seven to eight-tenths thin cloud over the target area at between 12,000 and 19,000 feet with good visibility below. At Stettin, the master Bomber called "Basement 12,000", but his signal was weak and not all main force crews heard him as the attack opened with flares. These illuminated the aiming-point and provided the marker crews with a visual reference confirmed by H2S, and when salvoes of red and green TIs fell accurately, they invited the main force bomb loads, which landed squarely and in concentrated fashion where intended. The 576 Squadron crews delivered their payloads from around 02.00, and by 02.08, the whole area had become a sea of flames, spotted by the crew of a reconnaissance Mosquito approaching the target, but still some 250 miles away. They reported a huge explosion at 02.09 and later, a large part of the town burning fiercely with a huge mushroom smoke cloud ascending through 26,000 feet.

F/O Cartwright and crew were first home, landing on three engines at 05.15 to report that they had not reached the target, and must have been deep in enemy territory when turning back as they arrived home only fifteen minutes ahead of the next to land, S/L Slater and crew. Twenty-three Lancasters failed to return and a bad night for 1 Group was reflected in the loss of fifteen, three of them from Elsham Wolds, including 576 Squadron's ME800, which was abandoned by the crew of Thieme, presumably somewhere over Denmark, the pilot and four others to evade capture, while both gunners fell into enemy hands. At debriefing, not all crews were convinced of the effectiveness of the operation, but in fact, it had caused severe damage in parts of the city previously untouched, with more than fifteen hundred houses destroyed, along with thirty-two industrial premises, and besides the industrial and residential damage, a 2,000-ton ship was sunk, and seven others were hit in the docks. Meanwhile, the gardeners had fulfilled their briefs by planting their vegetables in the allotted locations by H2S, but no details were provided in the ORB.

The flying-bomb campaign may have ended on the 28th, but a new one against V-2 rocket storage and launching sites began on the 31st with raids on nine suspected locations at Raimbert, Lumbres North, Lumbres South, Agenville, St Riquier and Pourchinte, all located in the Hauts-de-France region of north-eastern France. 601 aircraft were made ready, 1 Group providing 149 Lancasters in roughly equal numbers for the sites of Raimbert, Agenville and St-Riquier. Fifty-two aircraft from 13 Base were assigned to the Agenville site, located some fifteen miles east-north-east of Abbeville, for which 576 Squadron loaded each of its sixteen Lancasters with thirteen 1,000 and two 500-pounders. They departed Elsham Wolds between 12.45 and 13.15 with F/Ls Hague and Mulrooney the senior pilots on duty and headed south over Scunthorpe and Reading to begin the Channel crossing over cloud at Worthing, having to descend to below the briefed bombing height by the time that the French coast hove into view. They were greeted at the target by intense predicted flak, which may have contributed to the scattered marking, while the Master Bomber's confusing instructions led to a scattering of bombs also. The 576 Squadron crews attacked from 8,000 feet and above between 15.22 and 15.30 and turned for home with the bomb-aimers in the crews of F/Os McDonald and Laydon bearing wounds from flak splinters.

During the course of what had been its busiest month yet, the squadron took part in twenty-four operations and dispatched 262 sorties for the loss of five Lancasters and crews.

September 1944

The destructive power of the Command was now almost beyond belief with each of its heavy bomber groups capable of laying waste to a German city at one go, and, from now until the end of the war, this would be demonstrated in awesome and horrific fashion. Much of the Command's effort during the new month would be directed towards the liberation of the three French ports remaining in enemy hands, but operations began for Elsham Wolds with an attack on Eindhoven aerodrome on the 3rd, one of six Luftwaffe airfields in southern Holland to be targeted in daylight, for which 348 Lancasters, 315 Halifaxes and a dozen Mosquitos were made ready across the Command. 1 Group provided ninety-nine Lancasters from all Bases for Gilze-Rijen and fifty-one from 13 and 14 Bases for Eindhoven, the 576 Squadron element of fifteen taking to the air between 15.20 and 15.45 with F/Ls Bennett, Hague and Mulrooney the senior pilots on duty and each crew sitting on eleven 1,000 and four 500-pounders. The 1 Group squadrons climbed from their north Lincolnshire stations into rain-bearing low cloud, before heading for the Suffolk coast at Southwold on course for Walcheren Island at the mouth of the Scheldt. The poor weather conditions persisted until the targets drew near, at which point the cloud began to dissipate to enable the crews to establish their positions visually. At Eindhoven, the 576 Squadron crews had been given a bombing height of 15,000 feet, from where they aimed at red and Yellow TIs either side of 17.30 in the face of a weak flak defence, and returned safely to report a slightly scattered but successful attack.

A force of 348 aircraft was assembled on the 5th to carry out the first operations against enemy strong points around the port of Le Havre, for which 313 Lancasters from 1, 3 and 8 Groups would be accompanied by thirty Oboe Mosquitos and five Stirlings of 149 Squadron, the last of the type in service with a bomber unit three days ahead of its retirement in favour of Lancasters. 1 Group provided 159 of the Lancasters, which had been assigned to three of six waves, each with a Master Bomber and Deputy to control the attacks and two marker backers-up. 576 Squadron loaded each of its fourteen Lancasters with thirteen 1,000 and four 500-pounders and sent them on their way from Elsham Wolds between 15.55 and 16.55 with W/C Sellick the senior pilot on duty. Nine-tenths cloud lay over England, but as the formations made their way towards the Sussex coast at Worthing, it began to break up and over the target it was no more than three-tenths with tops at around 6,000 feet. The vertical visibility was excellent and the main force crews of the first wave experienced no difficulty in identifying the aiming point visually but were told to orbit until the first red TIs were seen at 18.07. Based on the 103 Squadron record, the first wave Elsham Wolds crews bombed from 11,000 and 12,000 feet between 18.08 and 18.11, and they were followed by those in the third wave from 11,000 to 11,500 feet between 18.24 and 18.26 and the final wave from 11,000 to 12,000 feet between 18.40 and 18.46. The attack appeared to be concentrated where intended, despite smoke enveloping the target from time to time and hiding it from view, while a westerly breeze intermittently blew it away to reveal the TIs again, and a post-raid analysis suggested that around 90% of the bombs had fallen within the six defined target areas.

It was similar fare on the following evening when a force of 344 aircraft was assigned to six aiming-points around Le Havre, at which four Path Finder Lancasters and five Oboe Mosquitos would provide the marking. 1 Group made ready 160 Lancasters assigned to section I, aiming point 4, section II, aiming point 5 and section III, aiming point 6, of which fifteen were provided by 576 Squadron. Each received a bomb load of thirteen 1,000 and four 500-pounders before departing Elsham Wolds in advance of the 103 Squadron element between 17.00 and 17.15 with F/L Masters the senior pilot on duty. They adopted the same route as before and those in section I reached aiming-point 4 to find ten-tenths stratus with a base at around 8,000 feet and fair visibility below. They responded in accordance with the call by the Master Bomber, F/O Mills, to come down to 7,000 feet at 18.57, while he assessed that the green TIs had missed the aiming-point by some fifteen hundred yards. He dropped his own red TIs to within a hundred yards, and these were joined by others from the Deputy Master Bomber and backers-up at 19.00, which fell a little closer and were supplemented later by greens falling closer still. He called in the main force crews, who produced mainly concentrated bombing with a little scatter, thirteen of the 576 Squadron participants delivering an attack, while F/O McDonald and crew were prevented by an unserviceable R/T from picking up the instruction to come below the cloud base and retained their bombs after failing to identify the aiming point. F/O Ridge and crew had a full bomb load on board when instructed by the Master Bomber to go home. The cloud base was sinking gradually and was at 6,000 feet as the section II crews arrived to carry out their attacks, and by the time of the arrival of section III, which included the 103 Squadron contingent, the cloud base had descended to 5,000 feet and the Master Bomber sent a signal at 19.31 and 19.32 to abandon the attack and also take their bombs home.

There was an early start for crews participating in the next round of attacks on five German positions around Le Havre on the 8th, for which 1 Group put up 160 Lancasters in an overall 1, 3 and 8 Group force of 333 aircraft. The four Stirlings would be the very last to conduct a bombing operation, although the type would remain in Bomber Command service for SOE operations from Tempsford. The 576 Squadron element of fifteen Lancasters took off from Elsham Wolds between 06.15 and 07.05 in foul weather conditions with F/Ls Hague and Masters the senior pilots on duty and each crew with thirteen 1,000 and four 500-pounders beneath their feet. They were bound for aiming-point 13 and approached the target area to find ten-tenths cumulus with a base at 10,000 feet and broken cloud at 6,000 feet. The Master Bomber broadcast the cloud base at 6,000 feet at 08.03 and issued instructions for the main force to orbit while he assessed the situation. As they circled, some observed red and green TIs on the ground, which they confirmed to themselves as being accurately placed, and on hearing no further instructions, a number of crews from other squadrons and that of 576 Squadron's F/O Ridge descended to 3,000 feet and bombed, before the order was received by the rest to abandon the attack and take their bombs home. Fourteen 576 Squadron crews and the entire 103 Squadron element complied with the master Bomber's instructions, and in all, only a third of those involved at the various aiming points carried out an attack.

Four aiming-points were earmarked for attention at Le Havre on the morning of the 9th, involving a total of twenty-two 8 Group Lancasters and twenty Oboe Mosquitos marking for 230 Halifaxes of 4 and 6 Groups, but poor visibility intervened again and the operation was abandoned before any bombing took place. The weather over northern France had improved by the following day, and a massive effort involving 992 aircraft was mounted by the Command in the afternoon and evening to deal with eight enemy positions. The aiming-points were given the names of car manufacturers, Buick 1 and 2, Alvis 1, 2, 3 and 4 and Bentley 1 and 2, and 8 Group provided forty Lancasters and forty-one Mosquitos to carry out the marking, with a Master Bomber and Deputy and three backers-up at each. 1 Group detailed two hundred Lancasters for Bentley 1 and 2, twenty of them representing 576 Squadron, each loaded with thirteen 1,000 and four 500-pounders as they departed Elsham Wolds between 16.20 and 16.55 bound for Bentley 1 with S/L Templeman-Rooke the senior pilot on duty. They followed the now familiar route in diminishing cloud conditions to find clear skies and excellent visibility in the target area, and although smoke from the earlier attacks was drifting south-west across the town, it did not compromise the aiming point, which was easily identified. At 18.25, the Master Bomber ordered the main force crews to remain at their briefed height and called them in at 18.40 to bomb on red TIs, those from 576 Squadron complying, according to the 103 Squadron record, from 9,000 to 10,000 feet either side of 18.45. Smoke soon drifted across the aiming point, but its location was maintained with further red TIs throughout the attack, and the Master Bomber was praised for his control and clear instructions. All indications pointed to a concentrated and accurate operation, which achieved its aims.

The morning of the 11th brought the final attacks on the environs of the port, and involved 218 aircraft drawn from 4, 5, 6 and 8 Groups at two aiming-points, Cadillac 1 and 2. 1 Group had been alerted to the possibility of taking part but had been stood down for the day. Photo-reconnaissance confirmed accurate and concentrated bombing, and within hours of this operation, the German garrison surrendered to British forces. Elsewhere that afternoon on 3, 4, 6 and 8 Group stations in a sign of things to come, 379 crews attended briefings to learn of a daunting task facing them a little later, that would require them to present themselves over the heart of the Ruhr in broad daylight. They were told that the targets were synthetic oil refineries, the Nordstern (Gelsenberg A.G) plant at Gelsenkirchen, the Klöckner Werke A.G at Castrop-Rauxel ten miles to the north-east and the Chemischewerke-Essener-Steinkohle A.G fifteen miles further to the east at Bergkamen. As previously mentioned, the German synthetic oil industry relied on two main production methods, the Bergius process for high-grade petroleum products like aviation fuel, and the Fischer-Tropsch process for lower-grade diesel-type fuels. Those mentioned above were all of the Bergius variety and were vital for maintaining a Luftwaffe fighter defence. The bomber force was protected by twenty squadrons of Spitfires and three each of Mustangs and Tempests, and the attacks at Castrop-Rauxel and Bergkamen were concluded successfully in good visibility, while the Nordstern plant was protected by a smoke screen and an assessment of the result was not possible. It mattered little as Germany's oil industry would now face increasing attention right through to the end of the bombing war.

That night, 5 Group delivered a crushing blow on the university city of Darmstadt in southern Germany, destroying the city centre and neighbouring districts and setting off a firestorm in which more than twelve thousand people perished and seventy thousand were rendered homeless out of a total population of 120,000.

The oil offensive continued on the 12th with the briefing of 412 crews on 4, 6 and 8 Group stations for daylight raids on the Hydrierwerke refinery at Scholven-Buer to the north of Gelsenkirchen city centre, the Krupp Treibstoffwerke at Wanne-Eickel to the east and the Hoesch-Benzin plant a dozen miles further east in the Wambel district of Dortmund. Meanwhile, 1, 3 and 8 Groups were busy assembling a force of 378 Lancasters and nine Mosquitos for the final major raid of the war on Frankfurt, while 195 Lancasters and thirteen Mosquitos of 5 Group focussed on Stuttgart with a sprinkling of 101 Squadron ABC Lancasters to provide RCM cover. 1 Group's contribution to the Frankfurt endeavour was two hundred Lancasters, of which nineteen were provided by 576 Squadron, seventeen of them receiving a bomb load of a cookie supplemented with fourteen Type-14 cluster incendiary bombs and two SBCs of 4lb incendiaries, and the remaining two with ten 1,000-pounders and a single long-delay 500-pounder. They departed Elsham Wolds between 18.00 and 18.34 with S/L Slater the senior pilot on duty and proceeded south to begin the Channel crossing at Beachy Head on course for landfall near Dieppe.

The outward flight was conducted at 2,000 feet until 5° East, at which point the bomber stream climbed to 17,000 feet under clear skies, arriving in the target area to find only a little haze between the bomb sights and the aiming point. This was largely negated by the illuminator flares going down at 22.52½ to provide the bomb-aimers with a clear view of the ground. Red and green TIs were cascading as the first main force crews began their bombing runs, and they were seen to settle on the ground just to the south of the marshalling yards. The 576 Squadron crews carried out their attacks from around 17,000 feet either side of 23.00 in the face of an intense searchlight and flak defence, and the bombing generally appeared to be concentrated, eventually drifting towards the more industrialised western districts in the final stages, by which time a dense pall of smoke was rising through 5,000 feet. Night-fighters were out in force and sixteen combats were reported by 1 Group crews, while seventeen Lancasters failed to return, six of them from the ranks of 1 Group. 576 Squadron's ME854 is believed to have crashed some ten miles north-west of the city of Worms, some thirty-five miles south-west of Frankfurt and there were no survivors from the crew of F/O Aldridge. Returning crews reported many explosions and fires, and local sources confirmed the scale of destruction as severe on a night when many firemen were away helping out at Darmstadt. The Stuttgart operation had been equally destructive, and one central district may have suffered a firestorm.

A force of 490 aircraft from 1, 4, 6 and 8 Groups took off to attack the port of Kiel late on the 15th, the 1 Group contribution provided by 101 Squadron in an RCM role. Poor weather conditions improved in the target area on the eastern side of Schleswig-Holstein, where clear skies prevailed and most crews were able to pick out some ground detail, aided by illuminator flares. A smoke screen was activated, but the TIs remained visible throughout, and fires had gained a hold by the time that the force retreated to the west, with the glow from the burning town still visible from Denmark's western coast 120 miles away.

While the above was in progress, nineteen 1 Group Lancasters from 13 and 14 Bases were detailed for mining duties in three gardens, Silverthorn IV in the Kattegat off Anholt island, and the distant Spinach and Tangerine gardens, respectively off the ports of Gdynia and Pillau, the latter, now Baltiysk in Russia, the most distant of all mining locations. Ten 576 Squadron crews were briefed and based on the scant amount of detail provided in the ORB its seems likely that the crews of F/O Bailey and F/Sgt Greig were assigned to Tangerine, F/Os Durrant and Trent to Silverthorn IV and the remaining six to Spinach, led by F/Ls Bennett, Hague and Mulrooney. They departed Elsham Wolds between 21.40 and 22.20 and flew out over Mablethorpe at 1,500 feet on course for Jutland's western coast, and at 7° East, climbed to 11,000 feet, diverging to their respective target areas once over the Baltic. They all arrived at their allotted target areas under clear skies to plant four, five or six vegetables of 1,500lb or 1,800lb weight by H2S without opposition, and arrived home between 04.35 and 08.05, some after more than nine hours aloft.

With Operation Market Garden about to be launched on the 17th, support was requested from Bomber Command to conduct attacks in the early hours by 1 Group on four aerodromes. In roughly equal numbers, 201 Lancasters were detailed to target Rheine and Hopsten, located in the Münsterland to the west of the Dortmund-Ems and Mittelland Canals close to the Dutch frontier, and Leeuwarden and Steenwijk situated in northern Holland. Leeuwarden had earned its "wasps nest" reputation because of the crack fighter units based there, but the area had also gained fame as the birthplace of the infamous and ill-fated WWI spy, Mata Hari. It was for this objective that the Elsham Wolds squadrons made ready thirty-five Lancasters among fifty-one drawn from all three bases, the 14 Base element consisting of 101 Squadron ABC Lancasters to provide RCM cover. The sixteen-strong 576 Squadron element took off between 00.20 and 01.00 with S/L Templeman-Rooke the senior pilot on duty and each bomb bay containing twenty 500-pounders and flew out via Mablethorpe in excellent conditions to make landfall on the northern tip of Texel. Clear skies and good visibility prevailed in the target area and the marking with red TIs was punctual and concentrated, providing the bomb-aimers with a clear reference for bombing from 11,000 and 11,500 feet between 02.25 and 02.30. The night was very dark, which made it difficult to assess what was happening on the ground, and it was only in the light from photo flashes that any detail was discernible. The consensus was that the success of the operation depended upon the accuracy of the TIs, which had been peppered with bomb bursts, and post-raid reconnaissance confirmed that all four aerodromes had sustained extensive damage.

Early briefings across the Command on the 17th prepared 762 crews for operations against enemy troop positions at seven locations around the port of Boulogne, the raids staggered over a four-hour period and benefitting from an 8 Group contribution of five Lancasters and five Oboe Mosquito at each aiming-point. Three thousand tons of bombs was sufficient to persuade the German garrison that their time was up, and the port was returned to Allied control soon afterwards. Having already operated during the night, 1 Group was not invited to take part, but made ready 104 Lancasters to send against three coastal batteries on Walcheren Island and an ammunition dump or possibly V-1 storage depot at Eikenhorst, near Castricum on the Dutch coast, later in the day. 576 Squadron detailed ten Lancasters for Eikenhorst, loading each with thirteen 1,000 and four 500-pounders, before dispatching them from Elsham Wolds from 16.20 with F/Ls Bennett, Leyton-Brown and Mulrooney the senior pilots on duty. They began the North Sea crossing at Orford Ness and arrived in the target area to find it well marked with green TIs backed up by reds, the excellent conditions enabling them to bomb visually from 11,000 feet and above from around 18.45, with all the indications pointing to a successful operation.

Most of 1 Group was stood down, thereafter, and it was left to 101 Squadron to support a 5 Group operation against the twin towns of Mönchengladbach and Rheydt on the 19th, for which the now famous W/C Guy Gibson VC was selected for the role of Master Bomber. It was not a role for which he was experienced, particularly in view of the complexity of the marking required on this night, and his familiarity with the Mosquito was questionable, which may have led to his failure to return after what was a largely successful operation. His Mosquito crashed on the outskirts of the Dutch town of Steenbergen, probably as the result of fuel starvation caused by Gibson's unfamiliarity with the fuel transfer taps, and it was only after the war that his identity was confirmed and a headstone erected next to that of his navigator, S/L Warwick, in the town's Catholic cemetery.

The time had now arrived to turn attention upon Calais as the final French port still under enemy occupation and 646 crews attended briefings across the Command on the 20th, among them seventy Lancaster and forty Mosquito crews of 8 Group, who would lead attacks on five aiming-points, three of them receiving two visits. 1 Group assembled 184 Lancasters, sixty-three from 12 Base, sixty-five from 13 Base and fifty-two from 14 Base, and they were divided between two aiming points, 6C and 6D, which were heavy gun emplacements at Sangatte, located to the west of the main town and port area. 576 Squadron loaded each of its fourteen participating Lancasters with thirteen 1,000 and four 500-pounders and sent them on their way from Elsham Wolds between 14.50 and 15.10 with F/Ls Bennett, Leyton-Brown, Masters and Mulrooney the senior pilots on duty. They climbed away into poor weather conditions, which would persist throughout the operation, and flew out over the Kent coast to find the cloud dispersing somewhat over the sea and leave a thin layer of stratus at the target with a base at 3,000 to 4,000 feet. The master Bomber called the main force elements down to 3,000 feet to carry out their attacks, and those assigned to 6C were able to observe red TIs on the aiming point as they approached in good visibility with ground features identifiable. At 6D, cloud and haze made it more difficult to identify the aiming point, and communications problems between the Master Bomber and main force added to the difficulties. After releasing their bombs from 3,000 feet between 16.40 and 16.49, some crews were of the opinion that the attack had overshot to some extent but commented on the helpfulness of the Master Bomber in trying to ensure a successful outcome. The master Bomber called a halt at 16.50 after the target area became concealed beneath smoke and debris, but the bombing appeared to have fallen within the marked area and was deemed successful. Frustratingly for F/L Bennett and crew, the bomb-aimer found his bomb sight to be unserviceable at the last minute, and they were unable to deliver an attack.

Earlier on the 20th, F/L Peter Hague had been posted across the tarmac to 103 Squadron on promotion to acting squadron leader rank to fulfil the role of flight commander, having undertaken ten sorties with 576 Squadron. His was one of a number of departures of experienced crews from 576 Squadron during the month, compensated for by an influx of new crews from 11 Base. F/L Rainey and F/O Wearmouth had moved on to 1667 Conversion Unit on the 9th and 13th respectively at the completion of their tours, Flt/O Sawyer went to the Aircrew Repatriation Centre on the 15th for transit back to the United States, and the squadron's bombing leader since the start, F/L Jenkinson, arrived there also on the 21st for dispatch back home to Canada. P/O Stedman and F/O

Cartwright concluded their tours also at this time and P/O Wilson and crew were posted to 156 Squadron for Path Finder duties.

The weather remained unfavourable over the ensuing days, keeping most squadrons on the ground or restricted to training flights until the 23rd, when the lull in operations ended with a call to arms. The target for the night's main operation was Neuss, a city situated on the western bank of the Rhine opposite Düsseldorf, for which a force of 549 aircraft was drawn from 1, 3, 4 and 8 Groups. While this was in progress, seventy miles to the north-east, 5 Group would be engaged at two targets, the twin aqueduct section of the Dortmund-Ems Canal near Ladbergen and the nearby Handorf Luftwaffe aerodrome, for which a total of 243 Lancasters and ten Mosquitos was detailed. 1 Group contributed 204 Lancasters to the Neuss endeavour, nineteen of them belonging to 576 Squadron, each of which received a bomb load of a dozen 1,000 and four 500-pounders, before departing Elsham Wolds between 18.20 and 19.05. The senior pilot on duty was S/L Slater, undertaking, according to the squadron ORB, the twenty-ninth and final sortie of his second tour, for which he would shortly receive the award of a DSO. They exited the English coast at Clacton, unaware that the sensitivity of the Oboe equipment would lead to the early return of ten Mosquitos, leaving the others to drop their red TIs into the tops of the ten-tenths cloud that lay over the target at up to 10,000 feet. All but one of the 576 Squadron crews picked up the red TIs or their glow and delivered their bombs from 17,000 feet and above from around 21.20, while F/O Smith and crew were chased across the target by a night-fighter and missed the aiming point, eventually jettisoning the bomb load over the sea. It was not possible to form an impression of what was happening on the ground, and Bomber Command claimed that the main weight of bombs had fallen into the Rhine docks and industrial areas, while local sources reported 617 houses and fourteen public buildings destroyed. Five Lancasters and two Halifaxes failed to return, 576 Squadron represented by NN711, which had been assigned to an early wave and crashed on the western bank of the Rhine in the southern outskirts of Moers at 20.20 with no survivors from the experienced crew of F/O Durrant.

The assault on enemy positions around Calais resumed on the 24th, when five aiming-points were briefed out, the attacks upon which would follow a sequence beginning at aiming point 8, and continuing through 10, 11 and 9 before ending at 12. 1 Group's contribution amounted to just twenty-five Lancasters from Elsham Wolds, which were called to arms at such short notice, that 103 Squadron had time only to load eleven of its intended fifteen participating Lancasters with thirteen 1,000 and four 500-pounders. The fourteen 576 Squadron participants took off between 15.55 and 16.50 with F/Ls Bennett, Leyton-Brown and Mulrooney the senior pilots on duty and soon disappeared into the low rain-bearing cloud base as they made their way south to begin the Channel crossing in the region of Dover. Conditions were no better in the target area, where bombing had to take place either visually or on Oboe skymarkers, by the 576 Squadron crews visually from 2,000 feet either side of 17.30. At such a low altitude, most were lucky to collect only shrapnel damage from the lethal light flak, F/O Crowther and crew returning on three engines having lost the starboard-outer. Seven Lancasters and a Halifax were less fortunate and failed to return, and among the former was PD235, in which F/L Bennett and all but his evading flight engineer lost their lives.

A further attempt on enemy strong points around Calais was made on the following morning involving 872 aircraft, 201 of them provided by 1 Group and divided between two aiming points.

576 Squadron contributed just four of its Lancasters, which departed Elsham Wolds between 07.15 and 07.20 bearing aloft the crews of F/Os McDonald, Mills, Pegg and Smith and bomb loads of thirteen 1,000 and four 500-pounders. They headed south in perfect weather conditions, only for them to deteriorate dramatically over the Channel and French coast to leave a blanket of low cloud with a base at 2,000 feet, which would result in only 287 aircraft bombing. At 08.38, the master bomber for aiming point 2A abandoned the operation and sent the crews home with their bombs, and the Master Bomber at aiming point 1B followed suit at 09.02. Despite the huge effort involved in launching so many aircraft, the 1 Group A-O-C decreed that the sorties would not count towards the completion of a tour.

Nine separate attacks were briefed out to 722 crews across the Command during the early morning of the 26th, 531 to target four coastal batteries at Cap Gris-Nez, situated some ten miles along the coast to the west of Calais, and 191 to attack enemy positions closer to the port. 1 Group supported the operation with seventy-seven Lancasters for aiming point 7A, seventy-eight for 7B and fifty-three for 7C, and while neither the 1 Group nor station and squadron records inform us as to which the 576 Squadron element of nine was assigned, there are clues which suggest that it was 7A. They departed Elsham Wolds between 10.55 and 11.25 with F/L Leyton-Brown the senior pilot on duty, and F/L Hague on the same operation in a 103 Squadron Lancaster, each bomb bay replete with thirteen 1,000 and four 500-pounders. They headed south, adopting a similar route to that of the previous day, and began the Channel crossing over six to eight-tenths cloud, which gave way to clearing skies in the target area, where the smoke from earlier attacks had drifted away to enable crews to establish their positions visually. The 576 Squadron crews complied with the Master Bomber's instruction to descend to 3,000 feet and delivered their attacks from that altitude onto red TIs, before all returned safely.

Crews were roused early from their beds on the 27th, and no doubt expected to be briefed for the next round of attacks on enemy positions around Calais, 341 crews from 1, 3, 4 and 8 Groups having their expectations fulfilled. The remaining 346 from 6 and 8 Groups discovered that they would be divided more-or-less equally between the destinations of Bottrop and Sterkrade-Holten, situated within six miles of each other on the northern edge of the Ruhr to the north of Duisburg and Essen. In all, seven aiming-points around Calais were to be targeted in the presence of twenty-four 8 Group Lancasters and thirty-five Oboe Mosquitos, and three aiming points, 12, 17 and 16, were assigned to 1 Group forces respectively of thirty-nine, forty-one and forty Lancasters. The fifteen-strong 576 Squadron element departed Elsham Wolds between 08.45 and 09.15 with F/Ls Masters and Mulrooney the senior pilots on duty, the former having stepped into S/L Slater's shoes as B Flight commander, and climbed out through the ten-tenths cloud that lay over the entire route with tops at 6,000 feet. As they crossed the Kent coast, the Master Bomber issued instructions to descend to the cloud base at 5,000 feet, and they actually broke cloud at 5,500 feet, where visibility was excellent. This allowed ample opportunity to prepare for the bombing run at aiming point 16, which, like the others, was identified visually, before being marked with green and red TIs. The greens were observed to have fallen to the north-west of the aiming point and the reds to the west, but the 576 Squadron crews ignored both and bombed visually from around 5,500 feet either side of 10.30. The bombing was both accurate and concentrated, and by the end of the attack, the target was concealed by rising smoke and dust.

The final operations to clear the enemy from the Calais area took place on the 28th, and involved 494 aircraft from 1, 3, 6 and 8 Groups, which were assigned to four positions around the port and six coastal batteries at Cap Gris-Nez. 1 Group contributed eighty Lancasters, forty each from 12 and 13 Bases to target aiming points 18 and 8, the eight representing 576 Squadron loaded with the usual thirteen 1,000 and four 500-pounders, before departing Elsham Wolds between 07.50 and 08.10 with each crew captained by a pilot of flying officer rank. They flew out under clear skies until some five miles short of the French coast, where they were greeted by nine to ten-tenths cloud with tops at between 3,000 and 8,000 feet. Both 1 Group elements were instructed to orbit out to sea while the Master Bombers assessed the situation, and orders were issued at 09.36 and 09.48 to go home. At least, this time, the A-O-C decreed that the sorties should stand as completed. The final attacks on enemy positions took place that evening, some of them successfully, and the German garrison surrendered to Canadian ground forces soon afterwards. There was much to do to clear and repair the ports at Le Havre, Boulogne and Calais, and the port of Antwerp also needed to be liberated to speed up the supply of equipment to the front for the push into Germany.

During the course of another hectic month, the squadron took part in sixteen operations and launched 217 sorties for the loss of three Lancasters and crews.

October 1944

Having discharged his primary obligation to SHAEF, Harris could now turn his attention once more fully upon industrial Germany, with a particular emphasis on oil production and was about to launch a second Ruhr offensive to exploit the massive force at his disposal, in which each individual group had the potential to lay waste to an entire city in one attack. The independent 5 Group had been delivering hammer blows for months and soon, in mid-month, 3 Group would be handed a measure of autonomy in the form of the G-H bombing system, which it would employ to great effect for the remainder of the war, principally against oil and communications targets. A theme running throughout October was a campaign against the island of Walcheren in the Scheldt estuary, where heavy gun emplacements were barring the approaches to the much-needed port of Antwerp some forty miles upstream. Attempts to bomb these positions in September had proved unsuccessful, and it was decided to flood the land, both to inundate the batteries, and to render the terrain difficult to defend when the ground forces moved in.

A force of 252 Lancasters was assembled from the ranks of 1, 5 and 8 Groups and made ready on the 3rd to attack the seawalls at Westkapelle, the most westerly point of the island. Eight waves of thirty aircraft each were to attack at fifteen-minute intervals, with the Tallboy-carrying Lancasters of 617 Squadron standing off to be called in only if required. 1 Group contributed 120 Lancasters, which were to form waves five to eight, 12 and 14 Bases constituting one wave each and 13 Base two. 576 Squadron loaded each of its thirteen Lancasters with a cookie, eight 1,000-pounders and a single 500-pounder and sent them on their way from Elsham Wolds between 13.00 and 13.15 with a dozen crews captained by a pilot of flying officer rank and one of pilot officer. They passed over Scunthorpe as they made their way towards The Wash, where they encountered layers of up to eight-tenths cloud at between 4,000 and 9,000 feet, and this persisted from the exit point over Aldeburgh all the way to the target and prompted the Master Bomber to bring the force down to 5,000 feet, where the visibility was good. The target was clearly visible on approach and the marking punctual but required corrections from the Master Bomber, and within two minutes of the start of the 12 Base attack at 14.00, water was observed to be seeping through the dike. By 14.10, a clear breach had opened, and the water was spreading into the outskirts of Westkapelle village as the 576 Squadron element carried out its part in the plan from around 14.16, leaving a hole in the wall that would be extended to a width of some one hundred yards by those following behind. In the event, 617 Squadron was not required and was able to take its precious and very expensive Tallboys home.

While a 5 Group force carried out a scattered attack on Wilhelmshaven on the morning of the 5th, 531 other aircraft of 1, 3 and 8 Groups were being prepared for a two-phase operation that night against Saarbrücken, the capital of the coal-producing Saarland region of south-west-central Germany, which had not been attacked since September 1942. It was in response to a request from the American Third Army, which was advancing towards the German frontier in that region. The purpose of the first phase, to be delivered by 184 Lancasters of 3 Group and a sprinkling of 101 Squadron ABC Lancasters, was to hit the marshalling yards to cut enemy rail communications, while the second phase, by 239 Lancasters of 1 Group two hours later, was to be directed at the city, with 8 Group's ninety-six Lancasters and twenty Mosquitos divided equally between the two phases to establish and maintain the aiming-points. Each of 576 Squadron's twenty-two Lancasters received a bomb load of a cookie and fourteen Type-14 cluster bombs, before departing Elsham Wolds between 18.05 and 18.45 with W/C Sellick the senior pilot on duty. They began the Channel crossing at Worthing and made landfall on the French coast at Le Treport, having lost the services of F/O Thompson and crew to Gee failure. The outward route was characterised by eight-tenths low cloud as far as 6° East, at which point it dissipated to leave a thin veil over the target area with haze below. Illuminating flares at 22.23 were followed by cascading red and green TIs, at which the 576 Squadron crews aimed their bombs from 14,000 feet and above between 22.30 and 22.50. Several large explosions were witnessed, a particularly large one occurring at 22.45, from which smoke rose to 12,000 feet, and the city was well alight as the last of the bombers turned away to leave a glow in the sky visible for a hundred miles. Local reports revealed that the railway lines had been cut to stop all through traffic, and 5,882 houses had been destroyed, largely in the Altstadt and Malstatt districts, but the relatively modest death toll of 344 people suggested that what was now a front-line city had been partially evacuated.

From this point until the end of the war, German towns and cities were to be subjected to a new and terrible bomber offensive, and the opening rounds of a new Ruhr offensive began on the 6th with daylight attacks on the Ruhr-Benzin A.G and Hydrierwerke-Scholven oil plants at Sterkrade-Holten and Scholven-Buer respectively by a combined 4 Group Halifax force of 254 aircraft. Later, 3, 6 and 8 Groups assembled a force of 523 aircraft to attack Dortmund, while 5 Group had its own non-Ruhr target and prepared 237 Lancasters and seven Mosquitos for what would prove to be the thirty-second and final raid of the war on the city of Bremen. A signal to all stations from Bomber Command HQ on this day brought the news of a reduction in the length of a tour from thirty-five to thirty-three sorties, and this would be an unexpected bonus for some crews, who could spend the evening celebrating in the mess rather than exposing themselves to risk over Germany. However, this was not the final word on the length of a tour, which would take on the characteristics of an elastic band.

1 Group was fully rested when orders were received on the 7th to prepare for daylight attacks on the German frontier towns of Cleves (Kleve) and Emmerich. These were prompted by the failure

of Operation Market Garden, which had left the Allied right flank exposed and vulnerable to a German counter-attack. Five miles apart and separated by the Rhine, both towns would face large forces, Cleves of 351 Halifaxes and Lancasters from 3, 4 and 8 Groups and Emmerich of 340 Lancasters and ten Mosquitos from 1, 3 and 8 Groups. 1 Group contributed 254 Lancasters, among them the first to represent the recently-formed 153 Squadron, while nineteen 576 Squadron aircraft were each loaded with a cookie and sixteen deep SBCs, each containing 150 rather than the standard 90 x 4lb incendiaries. They departed Elsham Wolds between 11.40 and 12.25 with F/L Masters the senior squadron pilot on duty and station commander, G/C Sheen, having commandeered the crew of F/O Thompson. They flew out over Cromer with eight to ten-tenths cloud beneath, which lifted at the Dutch coast to allow them to map-read from the Hague area to the target, following the course of the Rhine into the built-up area of the town, where the inland docks were clearly visible. Red and Green TIs marked out the aiming point, and the 576 Squadron crews carried out their attacks visually in accordance with the Master Bomber's instructions from 10,000 to 13,000 feet between 14.19 and 14.30. Many explosions were observed, one at 14.28 sending a pall of black smoke skyward, probably from one of the oil storage facilities located in the town, and with TIs no longer visible, crews were instructed to aim at the smoke, which had reached 12,000 feet as the last of the bombers turned away. The defenders responded with accurate predicted flak, and three aircraft were seen to go down during the course of the attack, while F/L Mulrooney's PB467 sustained considerable damage but made it home safely. Reconnaissance confirmed the outstanding success of the operation, which destroyed more than 2,400 buildings and damaged nearly seven hundred others and local sources reported a civilian death toll of 641 along with ninety-six military personnel.

It was on this day that 15 Base came into being with the re-opening for business of its main station at Scampton, now famous as the launch pad for 617 Squadron's Operation Chastise carried out against the Ruhr Dams in May 1943. Then a 5 Group station, it had closed in August 1943 for the laying of concrete runways and had since been transferred to 1 Group. 153 Squadron would transfer there from Kirmington eight days hence, and satellite stations at Dunholme Lodge, Fiskerton and Hemswell would also welcome further new squadrons before the end of the month as 1 Group expanded again.

The 11th brought operations by 1 and 5 Groups against coastal batteries in the Scheldt estuary, at Fort Fredrick Hendrik at Breskens on the southern bank of the Western Schelde for 1 Group and at Flushing across the water on Walcheren for 5 Group. There were two aiming points for 1 Group, divided equally between 150 Lancasters, forty provided by 12 Base, sixty-two by 13 Base and forty-eight by 14 Base. It was a day of low cloud and drizzle as the twelve 576 Squadron Lancasters departed Elsham Wolds in two elements of eight and five between 14.30 and 15.25 with F/Ls Dutton and Green the senior pilots on duty and each Lancaster carrying thirteen 1,000 and four 500-pounders. As they approached the target area, the Master Bomber was contending with a wedge of cloud over aiming point A at between 2,500 and 6,000 feet, and at 15.59, he instructed the crews to orbit over the sea and await instructions. At 16.35 he abandoned the attack and instructed crews to take the bombs home, by which time one from another squadron, hearing no instructions and finding a gap in the clouds, had released their load. Conditions were more favourable at aiming point B, where the Master Bomber called the bombers down to 4,000 feet and the five representing 576 Squadron bombed on red TIs between 16.51 and 16.54. The 5 Group effort across the water to the north was also concluded without problem. Those whose sorties had to be aborted were allowed to count them towards the completion of a tour.

The operation was repeated on the following morning in two phases involving forty and thirty-seven Lancasters, eight of them provided by 576 Squadron, and as usual for daylight operations, they would be well protected by a strong fighter escort of Spitfires and Mustangs. They departed Elsham Wolds between 06.25 and 06.40 with F/Ls Leyton-Brown and Mulrooney the senior pilots on duty and flew out over cloud that gradually gave way to clear skies in the target area. Oboe Mosquitos dropped green TIs to mark out the aiming point and these were backed up by reds, at which point the Master Bomber called in the heavy brigade to deliver their attacks, the 576 Squadron crews complying and releasing their thirteen 1,000 and four 500-pounders each visually from 9,000 feet and above either side of 08.15. It was difficult to assess the outcome through the inevitable smoke and dust, and it was left to post-raid reconnaissance to confirm that two of the four gun positions had been destroyed.

The 14th was the day on which were fired the opening salvoes of Operation Hurricane, a terrifying demonstration to the enemy of the overwhelming superiority of the Allied air forces ranged against it. Bomber Command ordered a maximum effort from all but 5 Group to attack Duisburg, for which 1,013 Lancasters, Halifaxes and Mosquitos answered the call. The American 8th Air Force would also be in business on this day, targeting the Cologne area further south with 1,250 bombers escorted by 749 fighters. 1 Group briefed 245 crews for three of five aiming points, 183 for aiming point P, twelve for aiming point Q and fifty to attack the Thyssen steel works. 576 Squadron filled the bomb bays of its twenty-two Lancasters with a variety of bomb loads, thirteen with a cookie and eighteen SBCs of 4lb and 30lb incendiaries and five with a cookie and fourteen Type-14 cluster bombs destined for aiming points P and Q, and three with thirteen 1,000-pounders and four long-delay 500-pounders to employ against the steelworks. They departed Elsham Wolds between 06.00 and 06.45 with S/L Templeman-Rooke the senior pilot on duty and flew out over the English coast from Cromer to Orford Ness on course for the Belgian coast near Zeebrugge. The giant force picked up an RAF fighter escort as it made its way to the target, and the vanguard arrived over the western edge of the Ruhr to find drifting cloud in layers at between 8,000 and 14,000 feet, which prevented the Master Bomber from identifying aiming-point P. He instructed the main force crews at 08.42 to bomb the built-up area generally, only for the cloud to part briefly five minutes later for one minute only and allow him to redirect them to the planned aiming-point. The 576 Squadron crews carried out their respective attacks visually from around 18,000 to 19,000 feet between 08.45 and 08.53 in accordance with the Master Bomber's instructions and contributed to the 4,500 tons of high-explosive bombs and incendiaries that fell into the city to cause unimaginable destruction, to which would be added that night.

A force of 1,005 aircraft was assembled during the day to continue Duisburg's ordeal that night, and 576 Squadron weighed in with twenty Lancasters in an overall 1 Group contribution of 217, 118 assigned to aiming-point Q, sixty-two to aiming point R and thirty-seven to aiming point S. Seventeen of the 576 Squadron aircraft received a bomb load of a dozen 1,000-pounders and four long-delay-fused 500-pounders, while three others carried a cookie supplemented with seven Type-14 and five Type-15 cluster bombs, all of which was lifted into the air between 21.45 and 22.45 with F/Ls Green and Leyton-Brown the senior pilots on duty. They flew out in fine conditions via a somewhat circuitous route, according to the ORB, that took them over Scunthorpe and Reading on their way to Beachy Head, before turning sharply towards the French coast to make landfall at Cayeux-sur-Mer. F/O McDonald and crew dropped out with engine issues, leaving the others to arrive at the target under almost clear skies and find it still burning from the morning attack. They aimed at the plentiful red TIs from 19,000 feet and above either side of 01.30 and observed a large red explosion at 01.34, before turning away to leave a beacon visible from 150 miles away. The total weight of high explosives and incendiaries delivered in the two raids by the 2,018 participating aircraft amounted to 9,000 tons, and this massive effort in fewer than twenty-four hours was achieved without a contribution from 5 Group, which took advantage of the activity over the Ruhr to finally deliver a devastating attack on the northern city of Braunschweig.

There was no immediate respite from operations as preparations were put in hand on the 15th to attack Wilhelmshaven that night for what would prove to be the last of fourteen major raids on this naval and ship-building port, which was home to the Kriegsmarinewerft. Prior to 1935 it had been the Reichsmarinewerft and had built the "pocket" battleships Admiral Scheer and Admiral Graf Spee in 1934 and 1936 respectively, the Scharnhorst heavy cruiser in 1939 and the Bismarck Class Tirpitz battleship in 1941, before production was turned over largely to U Boots, twenty-seven of which had been launched down the slipways up to this night. The bomber crews would have done their best to catch up on sleep as the work of the day went on around them, and some of those who had landed at dawn were up, briefed and fed in time to join others for an early evening take-off in an overall force of 506 aircraft drawn from all but 5 Group. 1 Group contributed seventy Lancasters from 12, 13 and 14 Bases to the main event, nine belonging to 576 Squadron, six of which were loaded with a dozen 1,000-pounders and four long-delay-fused 500-pounders and the others with a cookie and an assortment of cluster bombs and incendiaries. They departed Elsham Wolds between 17.20 and 17.35 with S/L Templeman-Rooke the senior pilot on duty and flew out over Mablethorpe under clear skies until the midpoint of the North-Sea crossing, when, according to some, cloud gradually built-up to ten-tenths thin stuff with a base at around 12,000 feet. Typically, there was no agreement as to the conditions, and some crews reported clear skies with haze or cirrus cloud at between 16,000 and 19,000 feet, through which the red and green TIs could be seen and their accuracy confirmed by H2S, while the 8 Group ORB recorded that it was impossible to make out ground features from above 12,000 feet. What may have been spoof green TIs were reported some five miles to the west and north-west of the target, and these attracted some bomb loads. The 576 Squadron crews delivered their payloads on red and/or green TIs from below the cloud base at around 12,000 feet between 19.40 and 20.00 and observed little of the outcome. The bombing appeared to be scattered, and this was largely confirmed by local sources, which named only the Rathaus (Town Council offices) as completely destroyed.

A major step forward in Bomber Command operations came with the virtual independence of 3 Group, beginning on the morning of the 18th after a year of trials with the G-H bombing system. This mirrored to an extent the American method of releasing bombs on observing the leader's fall away, but the RAF system was equally effective at night. The first massed live trial took place against the small city of Bonn, situated some twenty miles to the south-east of Cologne, which had little previous damage to cloud the assessment of the G-H performance. The operation was not entirely successful, but time and practice would lead to a highly effective means of attacking precision targets like oil refineries and marshalling yards in particular, and this would ease the pressure on 8 Group.

There were two major operations on the night of the 19/20th, both over southern Germany, one by 5 Group on Nuremberg, and the other by 565 aircraft of 1, 3, 6 and 8 Groups, on Stuttgart. The latter was to be a standard city-busting raid to be conducted in two waves, separated by four-and-a-half hours, for which 1 Group detailed 251 Lancasters, 134 to attack aiming point D and 117 to target aiming point E. 576 Squadron loaded seven of its twenty-one Lancasters with a cookie and twelve deep SBCs of 4lb incendiaries each and sent them on their way from Elsham Wolds between 16.55 and 17.20 with F/Ls Campbell, Dutton and Green the senior pilots on duty. The Channel crossing began at Beachy Head and terminated on the other side at Cayeux-sur-Mer over cloud, which persisted all the way across France as far as the target, where it topped out at up to 12,000 feet and required the Path Finder crews to employ H2S to establish their positions. The red and green TIs disappeared quickly into the white stuff to leave a faint, reflected glow, forcing the Master Bomber to call for skymarking. The red Wanganui flares with yellow stars fell with a reasonable degree of concentration and continuity from 20.28, and the 576 Squadron crews delivered their attacks thereafter from 14,000 feet and above after confirming their positions by H2S. A 3 Group crew described the target area as glowing as bright as day, and reported a white explosion at 20.44, while others observed black smoke emerging through the cloud tops and the glow of fires below.

The second wave element of fourteen 576 Squadron Lancasters took off between 21.02 and 21.40 with F/L Leyton-Brown the senior pilot on duty and each crew sitting on nine 1,000 and four 500-pounders, two of the latter with long-delay fuses. The effort was reduced by one, when an engine fire forced F/L Leyton-Brown and crew to abandon their sortie, leaving the others to follow the same route as the first wave, drawn on to the aiming point by the glow of fires beneath the ten-tenths cloud topping out at 12,000 feet. Time-on-target was 00.52 to 01.10, and the attack proceeded much as that delivered earlier, the 576 Squadron crews aiming at TIs from 14,000 feet and above either side of 01.00. It was not possible to assess what was happening on the ground, but clear evidence of fire and a large explosion at 01.05 indicated a successful outcome, which local sources confirmed. The bombing had been scattered across the city and outlying communities and had caused widespread damage, with the important Bosch factory mentioned among industrial concerns to sustain damage.

The Hurricane force had lain dormant since Duisburg, but was roused from its slumber on the 23rd, when Essen was posted as the target that evening for a record 1,055 aircraft carrying 4,538 tons of bombs, more than 90% of which was high explosive. Once again, this massive effort would be achieved without the involvement of 5 Group, which had been given the night off. 1 Group detailed 237 Lancasters, of which eighteen were made ready by 576 Squadron, each having a cookie winched into its bomb bay, to be supplemented in thirteen aircraft with six 1,000 and seven 500-pounders and in five others with sixteen assorted SBCs of incendiaries. They departed Elsham Wolds between 15.50 and 16.30 with W/C Sellick the senior pilot on duty and climbed out into scattered cloud before heading south to exit the English coast between Beachy Head and Hastings on course for the French coast at Cayeux-sur-Mer, from where they were to thread their way between the flak hotspots of Cologne and Mönchengladbach. The cloud thickened over the Channel until the tops were at 23,000 feet, and, by the time that the target hove into view, the cloud had become ten-tenths up to 14,000 feet. The Path Finders had prepared a ground and skymarking plan, and after the Oboe TIs had been swallowed up by the cloud, red skymarker flares were released at 19.28 to be followed by greens three minutes later. The 576 Squadron crews carried out their attacks on both red and green skymarkers from around 18,000 to 20,500 feet between 19.29 and 19.52 and found it impossible to observe the fall of the bombs, but an intense glow on the cloud told its own story that there was still plenty of combustible material in the tortured city. All five missing Lancasters were from the ranks of 1 Group and among them was 576 Squadron's PB467, which disappeared without trace with the crew of F/O Dawson. Local reports from Essen confirmed the destruction of 607 buildings and a further eight hundred seriously damaged along with a death toll of 667 people.

Harris had not yet done with his old enemy, and ordered another attack, this time by daylight on the 25th, for which 771 aircraft were made ready, including a 1 Group contribution of 229 Lancasters for aiming points J, the Krupp district, and G, the general built-up area. 576 Squadron made ready nineteen Lancasters, fifteen loaded with eleven 1,000 and four 500-pounders and the rest with a cookie and incendiaries before departing Elsham Wolds between 12.30 and 13.05. F/L Masters was the senior pilot on duty among those of flight lieutenant rank, although he should, perhaps by now, be recorded as an acting squadron leader to reflect his status as B Flight commander. After climbing out they headed for Bradwell Bay on the Essex coast and made landfall on the other side over the seaside resort of Knokke, before traversing Belgium to enter Germany near Aachen and proceed to the target in cloudy, but quite favourable weather conditions. The bomber stream encountered ten-tenths cloud with tops at between 6,000 and 12,000 feet during the run-up to the target, but isolated breaks appeared, one a mile wide, which allowed crews to assess the accuracy of the red and yellow TIs in relation to the Krupp complex. The master Bomber ordered the red TIs to be ignored in favour of the yellows, which appeared to be two thousand yards north of the Krupp complex aiming-point, before a massive explosion close by at 15.29 created a pall of smoke, which the Master Bomber was then able to employ as the focus for the rest of the bombing. Some crews bombed visually through gaps in the cloud, while the remainder aimed at the skymarkers, those representing 576 Squadron from an undisclosed height at some time between 15.30 and 15.55, and all returned safely to make their reports. Many bomb bursts and volumes of smoke were evident through the clouds, and it was clear to all that another devastating blow had been visited upon the city, which had, by now, lost its status as a major centre of war production. Local reports confirmed the destruction of 1,163 buildings, almost twice the number resulting from the larger attack thirty-six hours earlier, and the death toll was also greater at 820 people. The Krupp complex was in a state of paralysis, and other than steelworks and coal mines, the majority of industry had been dispersed to other regions of Germany.

On the following evening, the crews of F/O Mulrooney and F/L Leyton-Brown were among ten from 13 Base assigned to mining duties in the Rosemary garden in Heligoland Bight and departed Elsham Wolds at 17.20 and 17.25 respectively, each with six 1,800lb mines beneath their feet. They flew out over Mablethorpe and found the garden area under ten-tenths cloud with a base at 3,000 feet and delivered their mines by H2S from around 11,500 feet sometime between 19.35 and 19.50. F/L Leyton-Brown and crew were pursued out of the target area by a Ju88, with which fire was exchanged, but the encounter soon came to an end with neither party sustaining damage.

On the morning of the 28th, 4 Group dispatched a main force of 155 Halifaxes to join forces with eighty-six Lancasters and thirty-six Mosquitos of 8 Group to continue the assault on the defences on the island of Walcheren, and while that operation was in progress, preparations for the first of a three-raid mini-campaign against Cologne were already in hand. The last time that the Command had targeted Cologne in such a way was in June/July 1943, when three raids had been mounted over the course of ten nights, resulting in the destruction of 11,000 buildings, 5,500 fatalities and 350,000 people rendered homeless. The operation was to be conducted in two phases, with one aiming-point in the district of Müllheim, to the north-east of the city centre, and the other in Zollstock to the south-west. A force of 733 aircraft included a 1 Group contribution of 249 Lancasters for aiming points G and H, 576 Squadron supporting the operation with eighteen aircraft, each of which had a cookie in the bomb bay, six supplemented with cluster bombs and standard incendiaries, and the rest with five 1,000 and six 500-pounders. They departed Elsham Wolds between 13.05 and 13.40 with S/L Templeman-Rooke the senior pilot on duty, and headed for Orford Ness, encountering a weather front over the North Sea on their way to making landfall on the French coast in the Dunkerque region.

The cloud built and diminished in turns, and at the target was at six-tenths, topping out at around 10,000 feet, which allowed some crews to bomb visually and others on red, green and yellow TIs, those of 576 Squadron from an undisclosed altitude between 10,500 to 19,500 feet either side of 16.00 in the face of an accurate flak barrage that caused damage to a number of aircraft. Fires and copious amounts of smoke followed the bombing, and a suspension bridge over the Rhine collapsed after receiving direct hits. No great concentration of marking was achieved, and there were periods when no flares were visible, during which time, the main force crews targeted the built-up area generally. A few red and green TIs were spotted intermittently, but they were of little use, and the bombing was scattered across the south-western districts of the city. A large explosion was reported at 16.04 following a direct hit on a factory, and smoke was rising through 15,000 feet from the other aiming point as the bombers turned away. Despite reservations concerning the quality of some of the bombing, both aiming-points had been devastated, local reports confirming the destruction of 2,239 blocks of flats and fifteen industrial premises, along with many other buildings of a public nature. Severe damage had also been inflicted upon power stations, transportation and railway and river docks installations.

The main theme on the 29th was the push to wrest Walcheren from the hands of the enemy, and 358 aircraft were drawn from 1, 3, 4 and 8 Groups to target eleven aiming-points during the morning. 1 Group put up seventy-five Lancasters, twenty-five for each of three aiming points at Domburg on the north-western coast, the five 576 Squadron crews of F/Ls Arthur and Dutton and F/Os Boggiano, Hardman and Stewart departing Elsham Wolds between 11.25 and 11.30 and each Lancaster carrying thirteen 1,000 and four 500-pounders. They crossed the English coast at Orford Ness over ten-tenths cloud, which persisted over the North Sea with tops at around 10,000 feet, but convenient gaps over the target allowed most crews to make a visual identification of their respective aiming point. The 12 Base crews were able initially to make a visual identification of their aiming point, where a red TI was observed to go down at 12.59 and fall into the sea some four hundred yards short. The Master Bomber called the main force in to bomb with a three-second overshoot, but only a proportion of the force had complied before the Master Bomber called a halt and ordered those still carrying bombs to orbit. At this point the cloud rolled in to conceal the ground and the Master Bomber decided to abandon the operation, possibly believing the task had been accomplished.

Fewer difficulties at the 13 and 14 Base aiming points allowed the bombing to go ahead unhindered, the 576 Squadron crews complying with the Master Bomber's instructions and bombing on red and later green TIs from 7,000 feet and above between 13.15 and 13.19. The operation was deemed to be a success, and the final operations against Walcheren were undertaken by 5 Group on the 30th, when two forces of fifty-one Lancasters and four Mosquitos each were sent against coastal batteries at Westkapelle and Flushing. Canadian and Scottish ground forces went in on the following day, and a week of heavy fighting preceded the island's capture. Even then, the clearing of mines from the approaches to Antwerp kept the port out of commission for a further three weeks and the first convoy arrived for unloading on the 28th of November.

A force of 905 aircraft was made ready for another massive assault on Cologne on the 30th, for which 1 Group detailed 251 Lancasters, nineteen of them representing 576 Squadron, each loaded with a cookie, thirteen supplemented with six 1,000 and five 500-pounders and six with incendiaries. They departed Elsham Wolds between 17.15 and 17.50 with F/Ls Brown, Campbell and Green the senior pilots on duty, and climbed away into ten-tenths cloud, which persisted for most of the outward flight via Beachy Head. F/O Wright and crew lost the use of their navigation equipment and turned back, leaving the others to press on over the Channel, where the cloud tops reached 20,000 feet with a bright, full moon above. As the target drew near, the cloud tops lowered to 10,000 to 15,000 feet, into which the red and white marker flares delivered by nine of the Oboe Mosquitos drifted in concentrated fashion. The main force crews confirmed their accuracy by Gee and H2S, before carrying out their attacks, those from 576 Squadron delivering their bomb loads, based on the 103 Squadron record, from 16,500 to 18,500 feet between 20.58 and 21.22, and although the ground was obscured, the glow in the clouds suggested a successful outcome. A post-raid analysis suspected a scattered attack, but local reports confirmed heavy damage in south-western suburbs, where housing, communications and utilities were the principal casualties.

A force of 493 aircraft from 1, 3, 4 and 8 Groups was made ready on the 31st to complete the series of raids on Cologne, 1 Group providing 219 Lancasters with 103 Squadron representing Elsham Wolds. 576 Squadron, meanwhile, was in the process of moving to a new home at the former 5 Group station at Fiskerton, near Lincoln. The bomber stream began the Channel crossing at Beachy Head and made its way to the target under another full moon with cloud below topping out at 12,000 feet. The cloud persisted to the target where tops were at 6,000 to 10,000 feet and the attack opened with red and white flares delivered by Oboe Mosquitos at 20.56, which were backed up in what appeared to be concentrated fashion by greens from the heavy marker element. Crews established their positions by Gee and H2S-fix before carrying out their assigned roles, and returning crews reported concentrated bombing and a large red glow beneath the clouds as they turned for home. Local reports confirmed that the southern districts had received the main weight of bombs, but the reporting system was breaking down and precise details were not forthcoming. It is likely, that the city had been largely evacuated by this stage, and all future operations would be directed at its numerous and extensive marshalling yards.

During the course of the month, 576 Squadron carried out fifteen operations and dispatched 227 sorties for the loss of a single Lancaster and crew.

November 1944

As worthwhile targets became increasingly difficult to find in a country so thoroughly destroyed by bombing, smaller, seemingly irrelevant towns and cities began to find themselves in the bomb sights, particularly if they happened to lie in the path of the retreating enemy forces or on a main railway line. Oil was now the overriding priority, and November began with a daylight attack by 5 Group and 8 Group Mosquitos on the Gewerkschaft Rheinpreussen A.G plant, located on the west bank of the Rhine opposite Duisburg on the western edge of the Ruhr. The name of this target would strike fear into the hearts of 3 Group crews, who had suffered heavy casualties while attacking the plant during the summer, but it meant nothing to 5 Group crews, who were less familiar with it and would have found the name of Wesseling far more unsettling.

Düsseldorf's turn to face a massive force came on the 2nd, when 992 aircraft were made ready for what would prove to be the final major raid of the war on this much-bombed city, and it was one of those rare occasions when 5 Group, the "Lincolnshire Poachers", were invited to operate with the rest of the Command. 1 Group detailed 252 Lancasters, nineteen of them made ready by 576 Squadron and each loaded with a cookie supplemented with six American-built 1,000 and six 500-pounders, before departing Fiskerton for the first time in anger between 16.00 and 16.30 with F/Ls Arthur, Campbell, Dutton and Green the senior pilots on duty. They adopted the circuitous route to the southern Ruhr via Beachy Head and Cayeux-sur-Mer, losing the services of F/O Button and crew to an engine issue on the way, and arriving at the target to encounter clear skies, moonlight and only ground haze to slightly mar the vertical visibility. The moonlight nullified the glare of the searchlights ringing the city, but of greater concern was the heavy flak bursting at 17,000 to 20,000 feet as they ran across the city towards the aiming-point. The attack opened early with red flares and TIs dropped by eight Oboe Mosquitos at 19.05, which enabled the crews to identify the river, railway tracks and built-up area visually, and the heavy marker element maintained the aiming-point throughout the raid with mostly well-placed green TIs. The Fiskerton crews carried out their bombing runs, we must assume from the records of other units, from around 18,000 feet either side of 19.30, and by 19.20 it was clear that fires were gaining a hold. Smoke was rising through 10,000 feet as the last crews headed for home with the glow from the burning city remaining visible as far away as Charleroi in Belgium, some 115 miles away.

It was established later that five thousand houses had been destroyed, along with many important war-industry factories, but night-fighters had been active and the operation cost eleven Halifaxes and eight Lancasters, two of the later belonging to 576 Squadron. It is believed that LM122 was hit by a falling bomb over the target but struggled away and came down west of the Rhine with fatal consequences for P/O Hepburn and three of his crew, while two of the three survivors evaded capture and only the wireless operator ended up in enemy hands. NE115 went down in the target area, and only F/O Mulrooney escaped with his life, suggesting that the Lancaster broke up in the air and cast him into space. His mixed RAF/RAAF crew included mid-upper gunner, P/O Parker DFM, who had served a first tour with 101 Squadron, while the flight engineer and bomb-aimer were in their late thirties and among the more mature airmen to give their lives.

The continuing campaign against Ruhr cities brought Bochum into the spotlight on the 4th, when a force of 749 aircraft was drawn from 1, 4, 6 and 8 Groups, while 5 Group renewed its acquaintance with the Dortmund-Ems Canal, which had been repaired following the successful breaching of its banks near Ladbergen in September. 1 Group detailed 235 Lancasters, the seventeen representing 576 Squadron each receiving the same bomb load as for the previous operation, before departing Fiskerton between 17.15 and 17.35 with pilots of flight lieutenant rank leading the way. They flew out over Orford Ness on course to make landfall on the Dutch coast in the vicinity of The Hague, where they invited the attention of the local flak as they passed by with 130 miles still to travel to the target. They found the central Ruhr to be under a veil of very thin cloud of up to three-tenths at 5,000 feet, through which red Oboe TIs were seen to cascade at 19.26, to be followed over the ensuing minutes by greens to maintain the aiming-point for the duration of the attack. The 576 Squadron crews carried out their attacks with the rest of the main force from 16,000 to 18,500 feet between 19.30 and 19.50, witnessing a number of large explosions, one throwing flame a thousand feet into the air, while a reconnaissance Mosquito crew reported a circular patch of fire and one particularly intense conflagration visible from one hundred miles away. At debriefings, there were reports of a heavy flak barrage and many night-fighters, including jets, and F/O Paley and crew were among those from Fiskerton to report coming under attack, in their case from a Ju88 just short of the bombing run. The assailant was eventually shaken off through evasive action, but not before PA173 had sustained extensive damage, and we are not told whether or not they were able to bomb the target or jettisoned their bombs during the engagement. The success of the operation was confirmed by post-raid reconnaissance and local reports, which confirmed that the city centre and industrial districts had borne the brunt of the attack, with four thousand buildings destroyed or seriously damaged, and almost a thousand people killed. However, the defences demonstrated that they were not yet spent, and brought down twenty-eight aircraft, twenty-three of them Halifaxes.

Bochum's neighbour, Gelsenkirchen, was posted as the target for a two-phase daylight operation on the 6th, for which a force of 738 aircraft was assembled. In the past, it had been the synthetic oil plants that had drawn the bombers on, but this time, part of the force was to attack the built-up area as well as the Nordstern refinery. 1 Group detailed 221 Lancasters, seventeen representing 576 Squadron, which departed Fiskerton between 11.40 and 12.05 with S/L Templeman-Rooke the senior pilot on duty and an extra 500-pounder added to the standard high-explosive bomb load. The crews of S/L Templeman-Rooke, F/Ls Acheson and Dutton and F/O Mills were the designated leaders of the forty-three-strong 15 Base contingent as they adopted a route similar to that for the previous operation, passing over the cathedral city of Lincoln on their way to Orford Ness to begin the North Sea crossing. After losing the services of F/O Leydon and crew to engine failure, the formation flew into cloud that increased to almost ten-tenths at the Dutch coast, breaking up, thereafter, to six to eight-tenths at 9,000 feet. As if by magic a gap appeared right over the target, which enabled the early arrivals to pick out the distinctive L-shaped docks in the Schalke-Nord district to the north-west of the aiming point. Bombing commenced a few minutes early on red and green TIs, the latter assessed by the 35 Squadron Master Bomber, S/L Leicester, as more accurate and he directed the crews towards them at 14.01. However, it wasn't long before thick smoke spread across the area to obscure any sight of the ground, and at 14.06 he instructed the crews to focus on the built-up area generally. The 576 Squadron crews delivered their payloads either visually or on red TIs from 17,000 to 20,000 feet either side of 14.00 in the face of accurate heavy flak, which inflicted damage on a number of aircraft and was probably responsible for the failure to return of three Lancasters and two Halifaxes. Many explosions were witnessed, and the presence of a column of black, oily smoke rising through the cloud tops through 10,000 feet suggested that the Nordstern plant had been hit. The consensus among the crews at debriefing was of a concentrated attack, although it was impossible to make an accurate assessment. Local reports confirmed that a "catastrophe" had befallen the city, and that more than five hundred people had lost their lives.

The Ruhr oil industry continued to hold the Command's attention on the morning of the 9th, when the target was the Krupp Treibstoffwerke synthetic oil plant at Wanne-Eickel, situated no more than three miles east-north-east of Gelsenkirchen, for which a heavy force of 256 Lancasters was made ready. 1 Group was responsible for 226 of them and 576 Squadron fifteen, which all received the same bomb load of a cookie and sixteen 500-pounders, before departing Fiskerton between 08.05 and 08.35 with F/Ls Acheson, Leyton-Brown and Masters the designated 15 Base leaders. They climbed into clear skies and formed into a vic at the head of the formation as it headed for Orford Ness, finding cloud building over the North Sea to ten-tenths with tops at 20,000 feet and persisting all the way to the eastern Ruhr with tops in places as high as 21,500 feet. There was a gap of clear air between 10,000 and 17,000 feet, but this was of no help, and the conditions prevented the Path Finders from delivering markers, in response to which, ten minutes before H-Hour, the Master Bomber ordered the crews to bomb on H2S, Gee or e.t.a. The 576 Squadron crews complied from around 17,000 to 21,000 feet between 10.40 and 10.50 and found it impossible to assess the outcome, but a local report suggested that the bombing almost entirely missed the town.

Attention turned to the Hoesch-Benzin oil plant in the Wambel district of Dortmund on the 11th, for which 1 Group assembled a main force of 183 Lancasters, including seventeen provided by 576 Squadron, which each reverted to the standard bomb load of a cookie supplemented with six 1,000 and six 500-pounders. They departed Fiskerton between 15.45 and 16.20 with F/Ls Acheson, Arthur, Leyton-Brown and Living the senior pilots on duty and joined up with the rest of the bomber stream on the flight via Hastings to Berck-sur-Mer for the southern approach to the target area. F/O Stewart had to shut down his port-outer engine, which left his rear turret without power, but he and his crew pressed on as the cloud thickened from 4° East to become ten-tenths by the time that the Ruhr drew near and remain so over the target with tops at 10,000 to 15,000 feet. This provided most unfavourable conditions for the Path Finder marker crews, and those of the main force were left to try to seek out the glow of red and green markers through the cloud or simply bomb on H2S and Gee. Based on the records of other units, the 576 Squadron crews carried out their attacks from 16,500 to 19,500 feet between 19.00 and 19.10, before returning with little idea of where their bombs had fallen. Remarkably, despite the challenges, it seems that the attack was accurate, and local sources confirmed that the oil plant had been severely damaged along with housing and a nearby aerodrome.

The 16th was devoted to the destruction of the three small towns of Heinsberg, Jülich and Düren, located respectively in an arc from north to east of Aachen, and close to the German lines upon which American ground forces were advancing. Forces totalling 1,188 aircraft were assembled, with 1 and 5 Groups providing the main force of 452 Lancasters for the last-mentioned with thirty-three Lancasters and thirteen Mosquitos of 8 Group to provide the marking, while 4 and 6 Groups were to contribute 254 Halifaxes and forty-five Lancasters between them as the main force at Jülich, supported by thirty-three Lancasters and seventeen Mosquitos of 8 Group. This left Heinsberg as the objective for a G-H raid by 182 Lancasters of 3 Group. Fifteen of 1 Group's 238 Lancasters were provided by 576 Squadron and given a bomb load each of a cookie, six 1,000 and seven 500-pounders, before departing Fiskerton between 12.40 and 13.05 with F/Ls Arthur, Dotten, Leyton-Brown and Living the senior pilots on duty. They flew out over Bradwell Bay and made landfall on the Belgian coast over ten-tenths cloud, which cleared to three-tenths stratus above 6,000 feet as they approached the aiming-point. A red Oboe TI was dropped right on the mark at 15.26, after which the Master Bomber repeatedly called the main force crews down to 10,000 feet and instructed them to aim for this and, later, red and green TIs, which fell with similar accuracy. Not all complied with the Master Bomber's height instructions as bombing took place either side of 15.30, but smoke was observed to be rising through 9,000 feet and drifting across the target area as the last of the bombers turned for home. Most were confident in the success of the attack, and although the majority of photos were unplottable, it was established soon afterwards that the operation had been a complete success at a cost of just three aircraft, and post-raid reconnaissance confirmed that the town had been all-but erased from the map. Local sources provided a death toll in excess of three thousand inhabitants, which proved to be an unnecessary loss of life when unfavourable ground conditions prevented the American advance from succeeding. The other operations were equally effective, although no report emerged from Jülich to provide details.

Briefings took place on 4, 6 and 8 Group stations on the morning of the 18th to inform 479 crews of the details for an attack on the city of Münster, situated some twenty-five miles from the north-eastern edge of the Ruhr. The operation failed to achieve concentration, and few details emerged locally to shed light on the outcome. By the time that this force landed, preparations were already well in hand for a return that evening to the Krupp Treibstoffwerke (fuel works) at Wanne-Eickel, for which a 1 Group main force of 253 Lancasters was assembled along with an 8 Group marker element of thirty-two Lancasters and twenty-four Mosquitos. The eighteen 576 Squadron participants each received a bomb load of a cookie and sixteen 500-pounders and departed Fiskerton between 15.35 and 16.15 with F/Ls Acheson, Arthur, Dotten, Leyton-Brown and Masters the senior pilots on duty. They climbed away through poor weather conditions of low cloud and mist and headed south to Beachy Head to begin the Channel crossing, which ended on the French coast south of Berck-sur-Mer under clearing skies. Shortly after crossing the Rhine, a thin layer of stratus slid in at 8,000 feet and remained in place with occasional breaks over the target. Seven of the Mosquitos had laid a "window" screen ahead of the bombers, and four of the Oboe variety delivered red TIs, which were seen to cascade at 18.55 and were followed by others three minutes later and greens at 18.59. Few crews could pick out ground detail, but the red and green TIs were visible through the clouds, and apart from one group of greens, were well placed on the aiming-point. The bombing was focused on the main group of reds and greens, and very soon a large fire developed, which emitted a column of black smoke seemingly from the refinery. The bombers were met by heavy flak in barrage and predicted form as they carried out their attacks, the 576 Squadron crews crossing the aiming-point with the rest of the 1 Group contingent at 16,000 to 18,500 feet between 19.00 and 19.10. The consensus among returning crews was of a successful operation, photo-reconnaissance revealing fresh damage to the oil plant, and according to local reports, the nearby Hannibal coal mine was destroyed.

The night of the 21/22nd would be one of large-scale activity at numerous locations involving 1,345 sorties. 1 Group assembled a main force of 238 Lancasters to attack the railway yards at Aschaffenburg, situated some twenty miles south-east of Frankfurt, and they would be supported by thirty-six Lancasters and nine Mosquitos of 8 Group. In addition, a dozen 13 Base Lancasters were assigned to mining duties in the Onion garden in Oslo harbour. Elsewhere, 273 aircraft with a predominantly 6 Group main force were assigned to an oil refinery at Castrop-Rauxel in the Ruhr, while 4 Group focused on a similar target at nearby Sterkrade-Holten as part of an overall force of 270 aircraft. 5 Group would be targeting the Dortmund-Ems and Mittelland Canals further north at Ladbergen and Gravenhorst in two forces with a combined total of 260 aircraft, while small-scale and mining operations took place at a variety of other locations.

576 Squadron made ready sixteen Lancasters for the main event, loading each with a cookie and sixteen 500-pounders, but one became unserviceable late on and two burst a tyre while taxiing to the runway, forcing their withdrawal. The thirteen remaining Lancasters took to the air from Fiskerton between 15.30 and 16.05 with S/L Templeman-Rooke the senior pilot on duty, and after climbing out, pointed their snouts towards the south to begin the Channel crossing at Beachy Head. Cloud began to build over France and was at ten-tenths with tops at 8,000 to 10,000 feet as the bomber stream reached the target area shortly after 19.00, prompting the Deputy Master Bomber to descend to 7,000 feet, where he continued to be thwarted by the conditions. The Master Bomber issued instructions for the main force crews to bomb on navigational aids, and while red, green and yellow TIs were spotted by a few main force crews, the majority aimed at the glow beneath the clouds from 12,500 to 13,500 feet between 19.15 and 19.23. It was impossible to assess the outcome, and it was left to local sources to confirm that fifty bombs had hit the railway yards but had not severed the main access line in and out, while the main weight of the attack had fallen into the central and northern districts of the town, destroying five hundred houses and seriously damaging three times that number.

There would be no further operations for the majority of the heavy squadrons over the ensuing six days, despite a number being announced, but then scrubbed, while 3 and 5 Groups went about their business independently. On the 22nd, the newly reformed 150 Squadron left Fiskerton for Hemswell, where it would be joined a week hence by 170 Squadron, and both would feature in the excellent colour documentary film, Night Bombers, produced by the then Base commander A/C Cozens.

Some seemingly strategically insignificant towns and cities now began to find themselves in the bomb-sights, among them the university city of Freiburg, situated in the south-western corner of Germany with the French and Swiss frontiers to west and south. It was believed to be inhabited by German troops preparing to resist the approaching American and French forces some thirty-five miles away, and found itself a target on the night of the 27/28th. 1 Group was now able to call upon the resources of fourteen squadrons with the recent addition of 150 and 170 Squadrons, and this enabled a record 292 Lancasters to be assembled in an overall force with 8 Group Lancasters and Mosquitos of 341 aircraft, 576 Squadron contributing eighteen Lancasters, each of which received a bomb load of a cookie, thirteen supplemented with five 1,000 and seven 500-pounders, and five with cluster bombs and incendiaries. They departed Fiskerton between 15.55 and 16.20 with no fewer than five pilots of flight lieutenant rank leading the way and set course in clear skies for Orford Ness. Cloud began to build over the French coast, and increased to full cover by the German frontier, but dispersed to five to six-tenths, thin and low over the target. The first flares were released at 19.55, and thanks to mobile Oboe stations operating from the liberated countries, Mosquitos were able to deliver red TIs a minute later, which were soon backed up by greens. The Master Bomber's instructions were loud and clear, and, once he had directed the main force crews to aim for the red and green TIs around the aiming-point, 1,900 tons of bombs fell in an orgy of destruction lasting twenty-five minutes. The 576 Squadron crews carried out their attacks almost totally unopposed from 12,000 to 14,500 feet between 20.00 and 20.15, and a reconnaissance Mosquito crew reported a city on fire with smoke rising through 8,000 feet. Local sources would confirm the destruction of two thousand houses and severe damage to 450 others, and a death toll of more than two thousand people with a further four thousand injured and almost nine hundred registered as missing. In contrast, the Bomber Command losses amounted to a single Lancaster.

The final major operation of the month brought a return to the Ruhr, to Dortmund at the eastern end, for which 1 Group put together a main force of 262 Lancasters, eighteen of them provided by 576 Squadron, with 8 Group adding thirty-two Lancasters and seventeen Mosquitos to take care of the marking. Thirteen of the Fiskerton contingent had their cookie supplemented with six 1,000 and eight 500-pounders, and the rest cluster bombs and standard incendiaries as they took off between 11.55 and 12.25 with F/Ls Acheson, Arthur, Dotten and Dutton the senior pilots on duty. They climbed into five-tenths cloud, which had dispersed completely by the time that they exited the English coast at Orford Ness, and lost the services of F/O Crowther and crew to engine failure, while the rest formed into a loose "gaggle" with the crews of F/Ls Acheson, Arthur and Living up-front supporting the lead vic. The cloud built-up again at the enemy coast to become six to eight-tenths over the Ruhr with tops at anywhere from 2,000 to 8,000 feet, and it was on approach to the target that F/O Bastick lost his port-inner engine to flak but pressed on to complete the bombing run. The conditions prevented the Master Bomber from identifying the aiming-point and the combination of sky and ground marking became scattered and sparse, if well-placed, to the extent that it could only be seen from directly above. The Master Bomber was left with no choice but to instruct the crews to bomb visually or on navigational aids, the Fiskerton crews complying from an average 20,000 feet either side of 15.00 in the face of a hostile flak defence, which inflicted shrapnel damage on nine 576 Squadron aircraft. At debriefings some crews commented on the destruction of a Lancaster, which was seen to explode over the target after being hit by a mythical "scarecrow", and this was identified later as a 153 Squadron aircraft, one of five lost from the ranks of 1 Group. The operation was thought to have been scattered, despite which, local sources confirmed that some fresh damage had occurred.

During the course of the month, the squadron carried out ten operations and dispatched 167 sorties for the loss of two Lancasters and crews.

'Siemensstadt' on the Elmowerk, framed by the SSW logo (left) and the S&H logo (right), 1936.

Housing built for Siemensstadt workers.

The Wernerwerk M production facility in Siemensstadt in Berlin, 1944
(All Siemens photographs by kind permission of "Siemens Historical Institute". The copyrights to which remain with Siemens AG, Munich/Berlin).

A 150cm Flakscheinwerfer 34 searchlight

F/O David Crofts RAAF (AWM)

P/O John Musgrove RAAF (AWM)

F/Sgt Reginald Begg RAAF was killed on 25th June 1944. He was 22 years old. (AWM)

F/Sgt Brian Wicks RAAF was killed 16th December 1943 aged 20 years. (AWM)

Devastation in Dijon

The Crofts Crew
Donald Tyshing (Nav); Bert Roberts (FE); Roy Vesperman (MUG); David Crofts (Pilot); John Musgrove (BA); Harry Dale (W.Op); Dave "Titch" Fowkes (RG). (AWM)

Lancaster RA594 UL-V, Dave Crofts with air & ground crew (Harry Holmes)

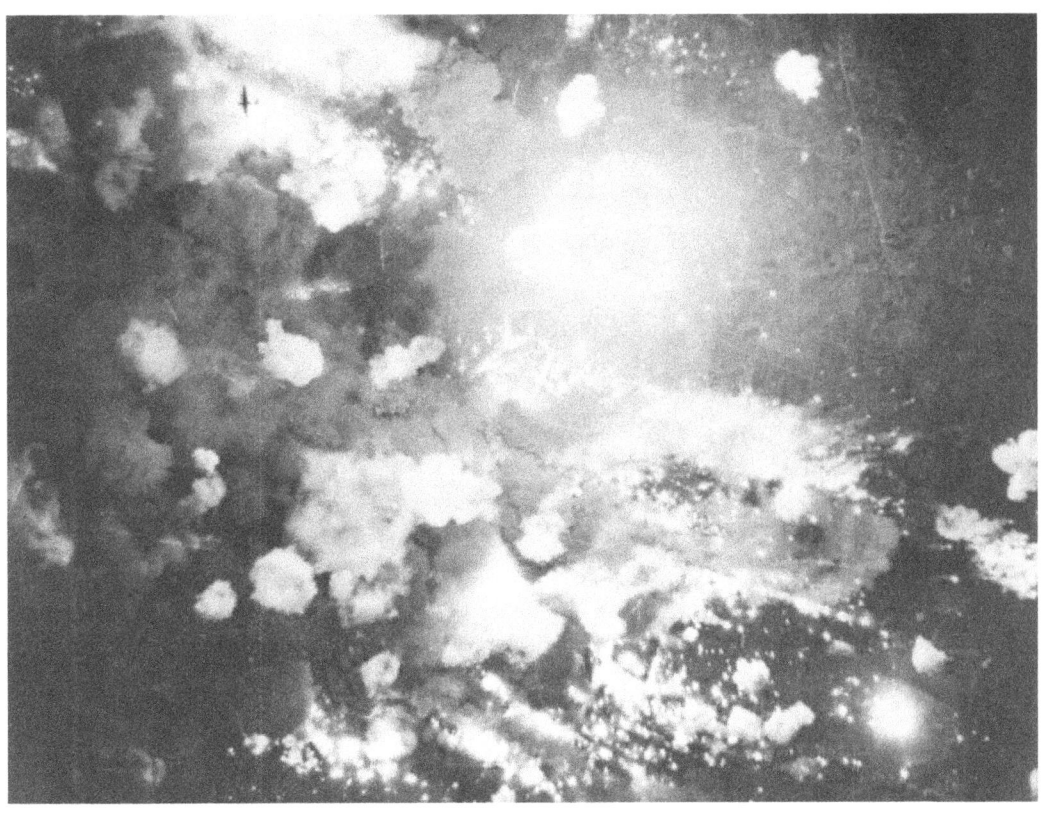

Bombing Duisburg

A wrecked locomotive framed in the broken structure of the ruined buildings at the railway centre at Hasselt, following attacks by Allied bombers which included some from 576 Squadron in May 1944.

Schrage Musik - was a common name for the fitting of an upward-firing autocannon or machine gun, to an interceptor aircraft, such as a night fighter. It caused devastation to Bomber Command crews as the fighters positioned themselves unseen under Lancasters in particular. The aircraft would suddenly explode and if witnessed by other crews, their reports were explained erroneously as being 'scarecrows' – German shells.

Captured Messerschmitt Bf 10G-4 fuselage showing the twin MG FF/M Schräge Musik installation with the cannon muzzles just protruding from each side of the top of the rear cockpit, France c. 1944.

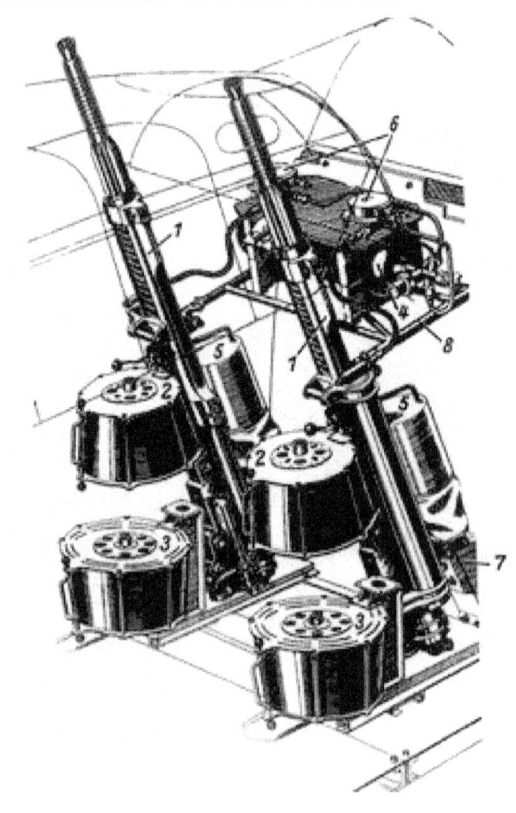

Interior view of Messerschmitt Bf 110G-4 Schräge Musik installation: 1. MG FF/M 2. Main drums 3. Reserve drums 4. Pressurized container with pressure-reducing gear and stop valve 5. Spent cases container 6. FPD and FF (Radio installation) 7. Weapon mount 8. Weapon recoil dampener

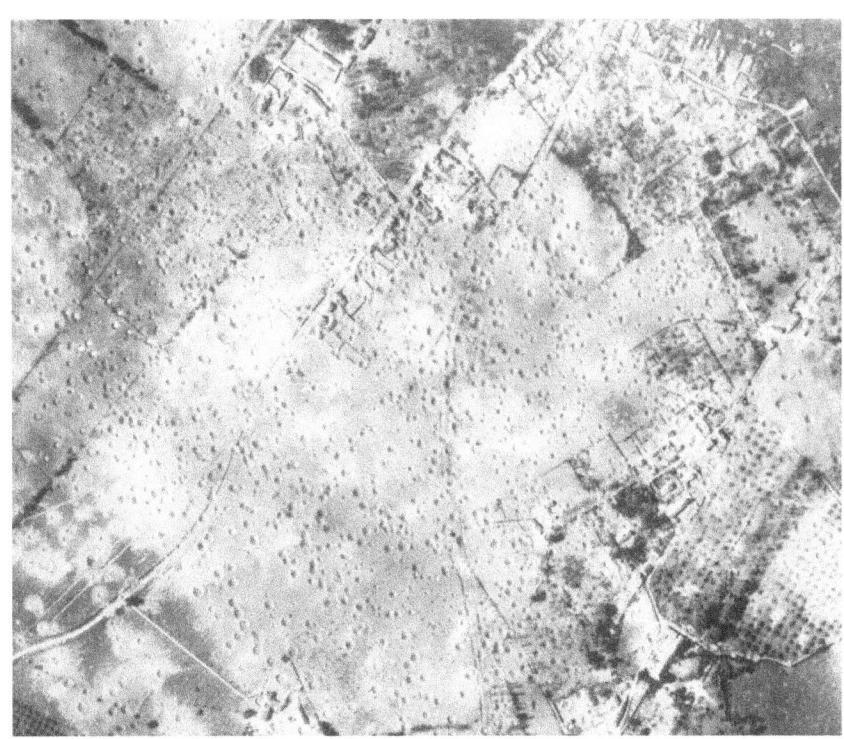

Damage to German fortified positions in the Sannerville area south of Caen after the attack by Lancasters and Halifaxes of RAF Bomber Command on the morning of 18th July 1944. The whole area around the aiming point is covered with a dense concentration of deep craters.

Russelsheim

Damage to Kiel Harbour

The German heavy cruiser Admiral Scheer capsized in the docks at Kiel after being hit by bombs during a raid by Avro Lancasters of Nos 1 and 3 Groups on the night of 9/10th April 1945.

S/L Douglas Haig
576 Squadron "A" Flight Commander
(J. Albrecht 625 Squadron Historian)

P/O Neil Lambell DFC (AWM)

Stuttgart

Target photo of attack on Gelsenkirchen

Tackling the devastation in Leipzig 1948.

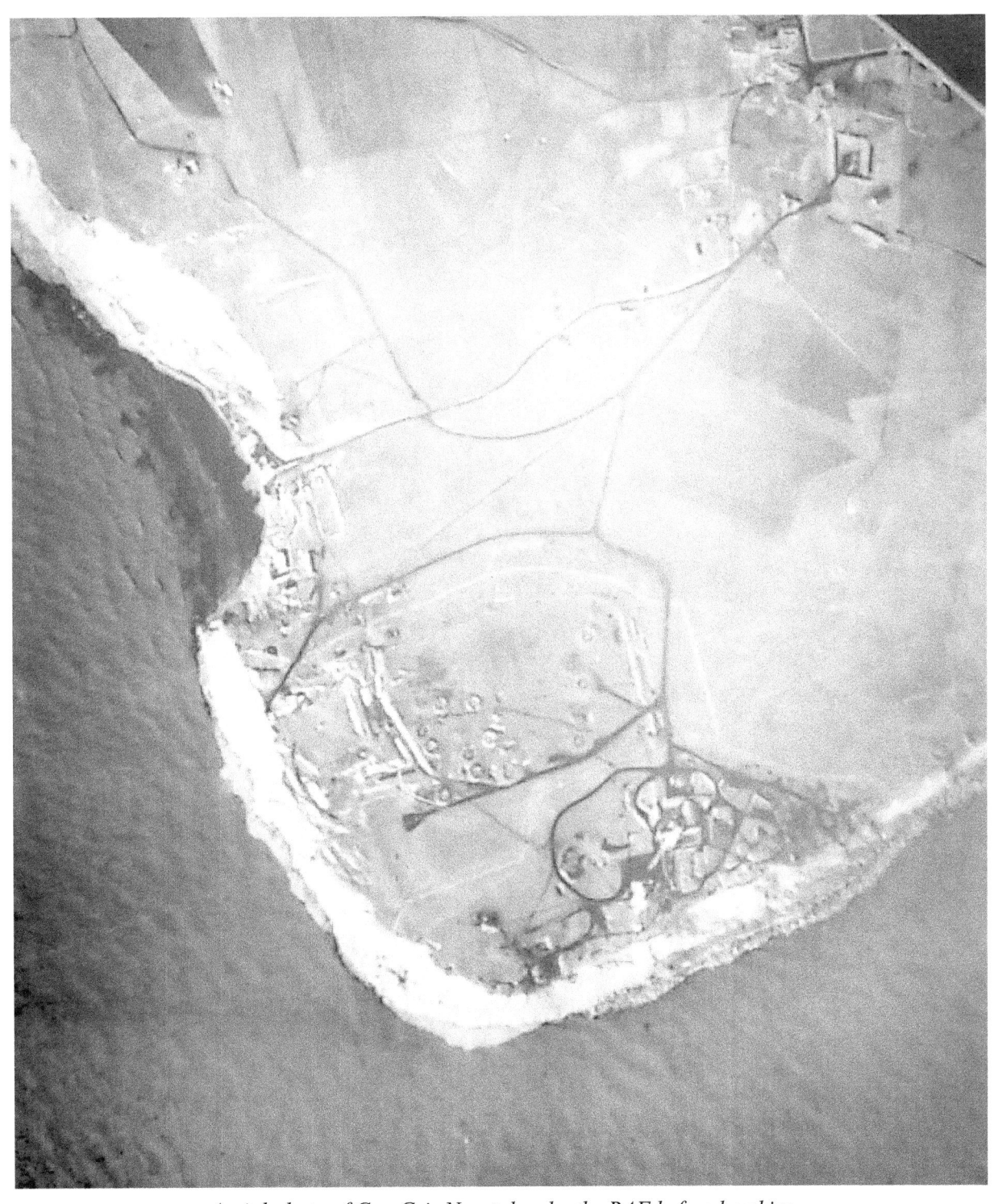

Aerial photo of Cap Gris Nez, taken by the RAF before bombing

Part of the locomotive shop of the Krupps AG works at Essen, Germany, seriously damaged in numerous raids in 1943-44, and further wrecked in the daylight raid of 11th March 1945.

Before and after bombing - Frankfurt

F/O C R Pegg & crew.
Shot down 16th January 1945 in Lancaster PD309 UL-W2. Crew all safe.

HM Queen Elizabeth II unveiling the Runnymede Memorial 17th October 1953.

Runnymede Memorial
The Air Forces Memorial at Runnymede commemorates by name 20,263 men and women of the air forces, who were lost in the Second World War during operations from bases in the United Kingdom and North and Western Europe, and who have no known graves.

RAF Fiskerton Lincolnshire, 1945 Allied Air Force members shovelling snow off a runway in front of a Lancaster bomber. (AWM)

F/L McPhail & crew with Lancaster RF213 UL-B2 (Harry Holmes)

F/L C H Living & crew all KIA 22nd February 1945 in Lancaster ME735 UL-P2. Crew: F/L Charles Living RCAF, Sgt John Mooney, F/O John Russell RCAF, F/O Raymond Hill, F/Sgt Geoffrey Tabor, Sgt Harold Peach and Sgt Harry Burrows.

F/L Drew with air & ground crews with Lancaster PB753 UL-X2   (Harry Holmes)

F/Sgt John Ryan RAAF, KIA on 17th March 1945, aged 20, when his Lancaster failed to return from a raid on Nuremberg, Germany. (AWM)

F/L Don Thieme. Evaded when his Lancaster crashed in the Netherlands on the 21st February 1945. (Aircrew Remembered).

L – R: F/L E G Robinson RAAF, Sgt W Collet, Sgt W McLachlan, S/L A H Dutton, F/O W F Whitehead, F/O J M Moir RAAF, Sgt J N McCullie in rear turret. The Lancaster is PA265 which crashed 17th March 1945 with the loss of all the Ryan Crew.   (Harry Holmes)

F/L R F Wordsell and Crew

A 576 Squadron Lancaster preparing for take-off at Fiskerton 1945. (AWM)

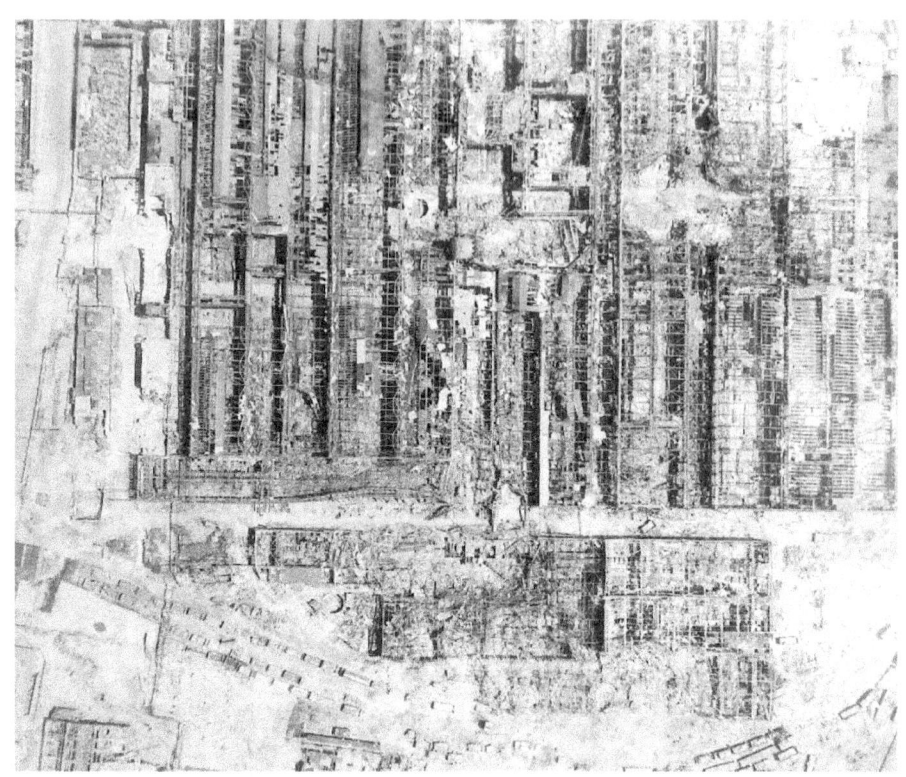
What remained of the Krupp Factory Essen 1945

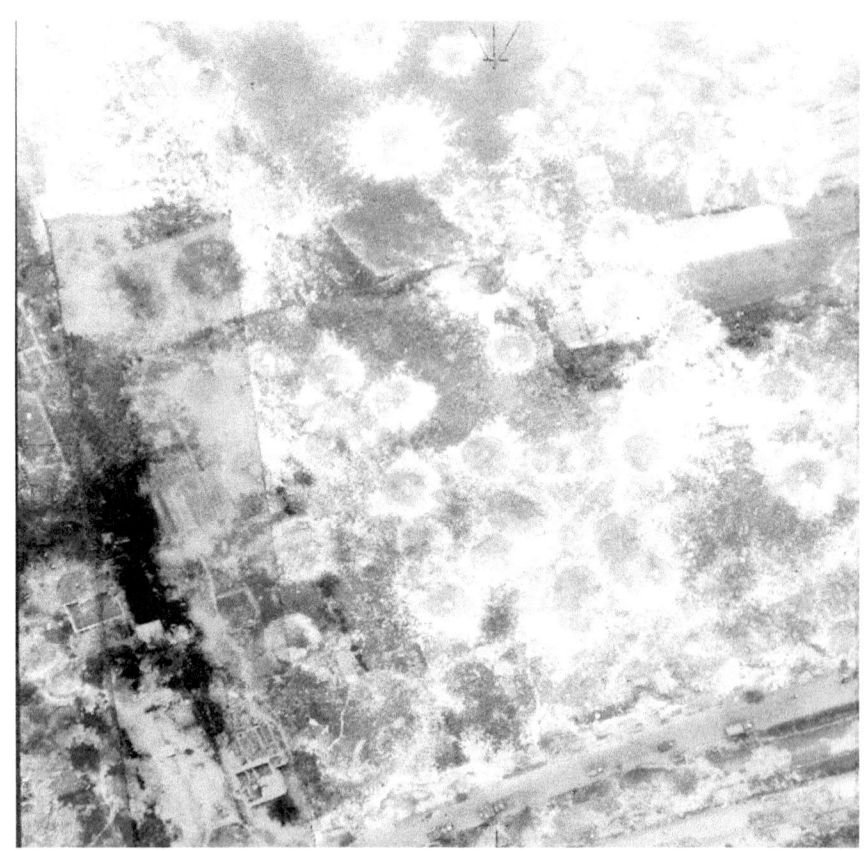
Dortmund

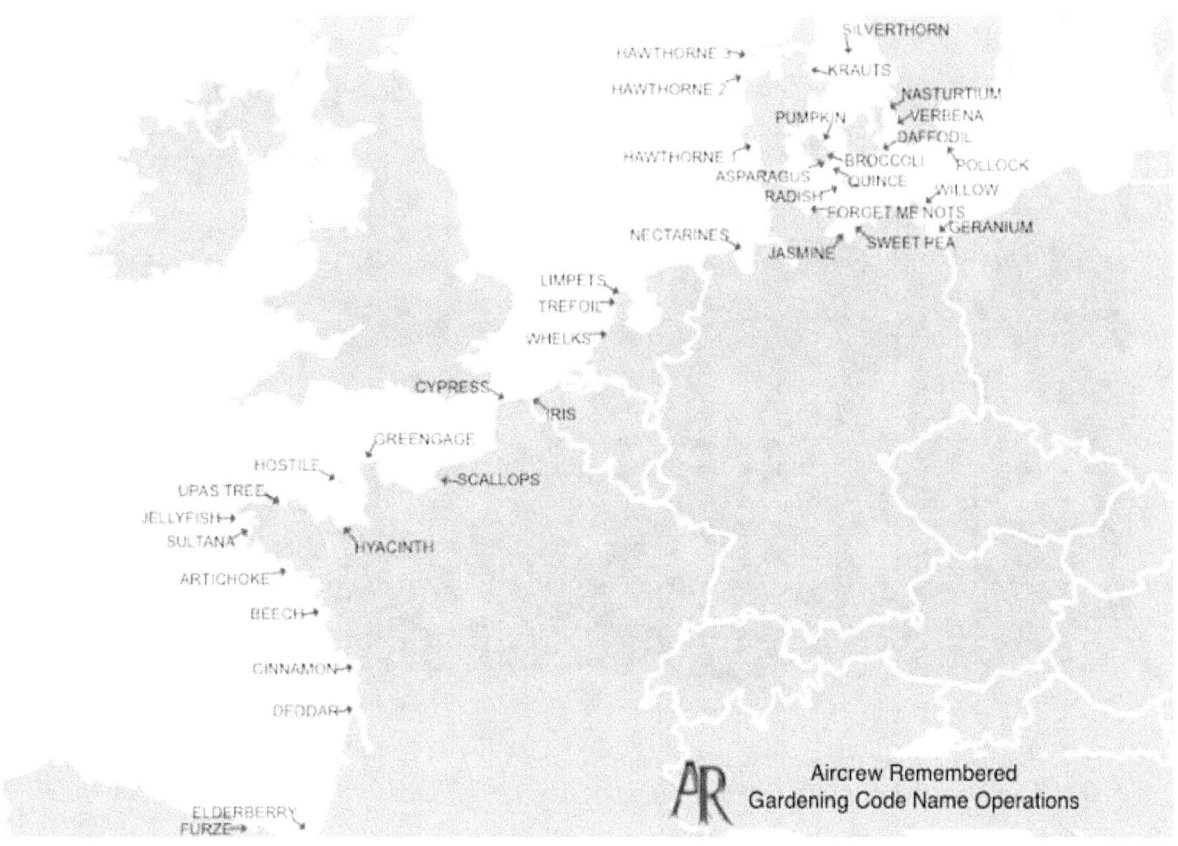
Mining (Gardening) Codenames

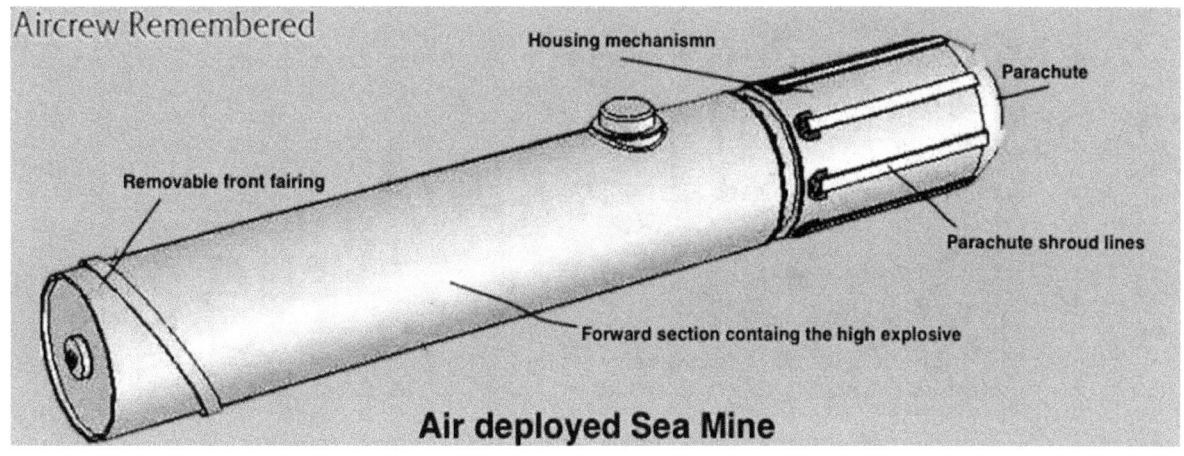

The Collins Crew after completing tour of operations April 1945 – F/Sgt J C Cutler, F/Sgt W Riley, F/O H A Smith, F/L F Collins, F/O R C Dalgetty, F/Sgt W.Millard, F/Sgt K Tamkin. (Harry Holmes)

Lancaster NX562 UL-F March 1945. (Harry Holmes)

F/L Collins and crew. Lancaster SW276   *(Harry Holmes)*

Lancaster SW276 UL-G   *(Harry Holmes)*

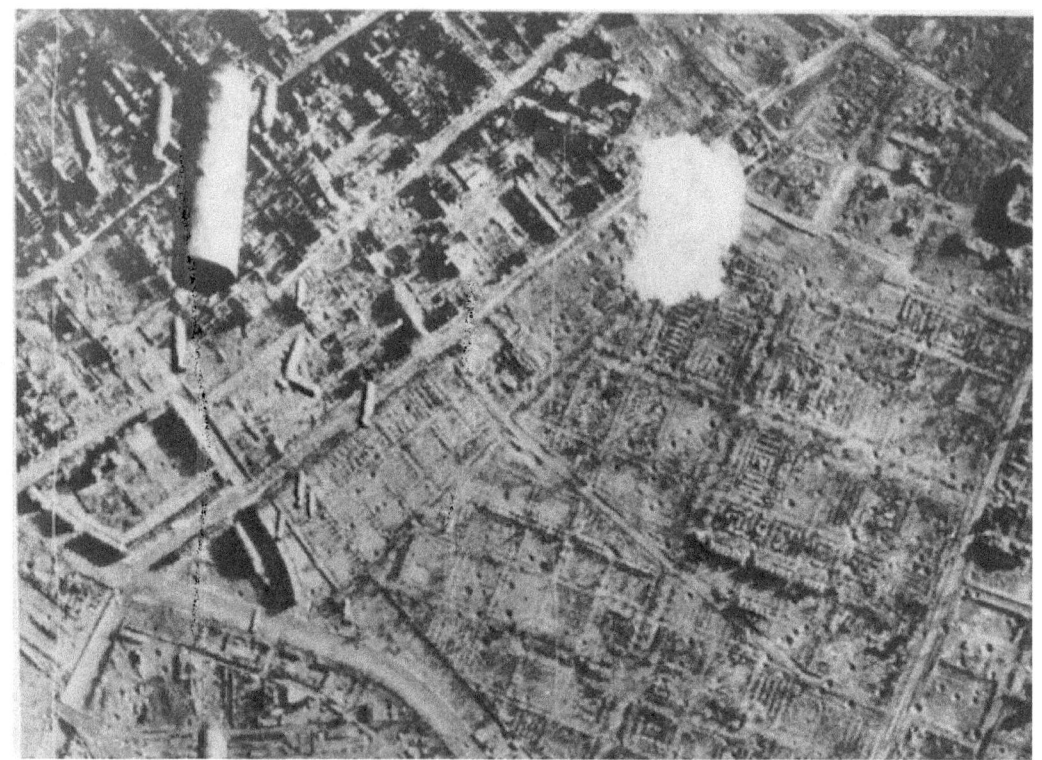

Cologne, Germany 2nd March 1945. Bombs falling from an RAF Lancaster aircraft of Bomber Command during an attack on the already severely damaged city of Cologne, in support of the advancing Allied ground forces. Below: Devastation in Cologne.

Berchtesgaden attack April 1945

Lancaster NN806 UL-M.
Crashed at Fiskerton on take-off 8th May 1945   F/O G L Scott & crew safe. (Harry Holmes)

*Bombing of Lutzkendorf, Germany April 1945.
An Allied bombing raid, seen from one of the participating aircraft.*

Bombing of Nordhausen April 1945

Nordhausen
Aftermath of the British bombing raid of 3/4th April 1945 that destroyed the Boelcke-Kaserne (Boelcke Barracks) located in the south-east of the town of Nordhausen and killed around 1300 inmates. The barracks was a subcamp of the Mittelbau-Dora Nazi concentration camp. Used as an overflow camp for sick and dying inmates from January 1945, numbers rose from a few hundred to over 6000, and the conditions saw up to 100 inmates die every day. Below: Mourning Man memorial to the victims of the bombing.

Loading a 514 Squadron Lancaster for Operation Manna (514 Squadron Association)

The Dutch show their appreciation in tulips.

Operation Exodus - Repatriation of Allied Prisoners of War (Not 576 Squadron photos)

576 Squadron Memorials at Elsham Wolds and Fiskerton.

December 1944

December would follow a similar pattern of operations, with the accent remaining on oil and communications, but with city-busting interspersed, and began with a heavy attack on the town of Hagen, situated on the south-eastern edge of the Ruhr, ten miles south of Dortmund. It had never been the subject of a major raid before, and now, on the evening of the 2nd, faced a force of 504 heavies, predominantly from 4 and 6 Groups, with Path Finder support and seven Lancasters of 101 Squadron to provide RCM cover. The result was a catastrophe for the town, which suffered the destruction of or serious damage to more than sixteen hundred houses and ninety industrial concerns, some of which lost three months production. Among the factories destroyed was one producing accumulator batteries for the new Type XXI U-Boot currently under construction in Hamburg.

The first outing of the month for 576 Squadron was announced on the morning of the 3rd, when a dozen crews were called to briefing to learn that they were to join 145 other crews from 1 Group to act as the main force for an attack on the Urft Dam, situated near Heimbach in the Eifel region of Germany adjoining the Belgian frontier. With American ground forces advancing upon Germany through Belgium, it was thought that the enemy might release large quantities of water to create difficult terrain and bog them down. The 576 Squadron aircraft had fourteen 1,000-pounders winched into their bomb bays, before departing Fiskerton between 07.35 and 08.10 with S/L Masters the senior pilot on duty and recorded in his elevated rank for the first time. They climbed away into heavy cloud that hid Orford Ness from view, and although it broke up over Belgium to leave almost clear skies, a front materialised as the bomber force approached the German frontier at Aachen, and it extended beyond the target area, concealing all ground detail. As it was a precision target, the Master Bomber was left with no option but to abandon the operation at 09.51 and send the aircraft home with their bomb loads intact. There would be further attempts on this target over the ensuing days, the first by 8 Group on the following day, which failed to cause a breach, and even 617 Squadron would be unable to cause more than superficial damage with its Tallboys.

On the evening of the 4th, 535 aircraft of 1, 6 and 8 Groups set off for an operation against Karlsruhe in southern Germany, for which 1 Group contributed 259 Lancasters, fifteen of them provided by 576 Squadron. Thirteen of them received a bomb load of thirteen 1,000-pounders, while four would carry a cookie supplemented with cluster bombs and standard 4lb incendiaries and one a cookie with four 1,000 and nine 500-pounders for company. They departed Fiskerton between 16.30 and 16.45 with F/Ls Arthur, Dotten, Leyton-Brown and Living the senior pilots on duty and set course via Beachy Head for the French coast near Dieppe. The weather conditions throughout the operation were generally favourable, with cloud building and decreasing in turns across the Channel and France, and on arrival over the target, the crews found nine to ten-tenths white stuff with tops at around 14,000 feet. As they approached, a few crews were able to see red and green TIs through gaps, but the majority had to rely on the glow of greens coming through and confirm their accuracy by means of H2S or Gee. It was difficult to assess what was happening because of a scarcity of red TIs, and, although the greens were plentiful, they were scattered, however, the cloud was moving eastwards, and later arrivals were able to identify the built-up area visually. The 576 Squadron crews delivered their attacks on the evidence of TIs from an average of 18,500 feet between 19.29 and 19.43 and reported fires visible from up to a hundred miles into the homeward flight. Mention was made at debriefing of two parachutes descending into cloud in the target area at 19.38½, and a Lancaster bursting into flames and disappearing into cloud at 19.45. It was established ultimately, that severe damage had been inflicted upon the city, particularly in western and southern districts, at a cost of just two aircraft.

This paled into insignificance when compared with 5 Group's simultaneous assault on the virgin town of Heilbronn, situated some fifty miles east-north-east of Karlsruhe and north of Stuttgart. It sat astride the River Neckar and had the misfortune to be served by a north-south railway line, but was otherwise of no genuine strategic importance, and would not have been expecting to be attacked. The aiming-points were the marshalling yards and the town, and by the time that the force retreated westwards into electrical storms, 82% of the city's built-up area was in the process of being destroyed by what probably amounted to a firestorm. The post-war British Bombing Survey estimated 351 acres of destruction and a death toll of at least seven thousand people.

On the following night, a force of 497 aircraft from 1, 4, 6 and 8 Groups was sent against the town of Soest, situated just to the north of the Ruhr and five miles from the now famous Möhne Reservoir and its rebuilt dam. The 1 Group element was provided by ten ABC Lancasters of 101 Squadron for RCM duties. The town contained one of a number of important railway hubs linking the Ruhr with greater Germany that would face attacks until the end of hostilities, and on this night suffered the destruction of a thousand houses mainly in its northern half, where the marshalling yards were situated.

Three major operations were mounted on the night of the 6/7th, against the oil refinery at Leuna (Merseburg) a dozen miles or so west of Leipzig in eastern Germany by 1, 3 and 8 Groups, railway yards at Giessen in west-central Germany by 5 Group, and Osnabrück in the north-west by 4, 6 and 8 Groups. 1 Group contributed 291 Lancasters to the attack on the I G Farbenindustrie A.G Merseburg-Leuna refinery, which lay some 250 miles from the Dutch frontier and five hundred miles from the bomber bases of eastern England, and was one of many oil plants located in an arc from north to south to the west of Leipzig. 576 Squadron made ready eighteen Lancasters in an overall heavy force of 475 of the type, which was unusually large for an oil target and reflected the importance of this particular one in the context of the oil offensive. It was the second largest of Germany's many homebased refineries, occupied a site of one-and-a-quarter square miles and employed around fifty thousand workers in its ammonia, chemicals, fertiliser and synthetic oil production departments. It was also the site at which the Bergius process of synthetic oil refining had been developed. The Fiskerton contingent took to the air between 16.30 and 16.50 with F/Ls Campbell and Leyton-Brown the senior pilots on duty and each bomb bay containing a cookie, eleven supplemented with a mix of 1,000 and 500-pounders and seven with cluster bombs and standard incendiaries.

The Lancasters climbed away from their respective stations into complete cloud cover over England and passed unobserved from the ground over Newhaven on their way to the French coast, from where patchy cloud accompanied them along the route to the German frontier south of Aachen. The cloud built again as the bomber stream undertook the 250-mile final leg across Germany, but the Path Finders had prepared for "Newhaven" marking (ground), with emergency Wanganui (skymarking) if required, and this proved to be the case as ten-tenths stratocumulus was unexpectedly encountered over the target area with tops at 10,000 feet. The early arrivals observed

TIs cascading into it, but they were not visible by the time that the main force crews came in to bomb, and the Path Finders quickly changed to skymarking. Release-point flares were in plentiful supply, their accuracy checked by H2S, and in the absence of instructions from the Master Bomber, they provided the main reference for bombing. The skymarkers continued to provide a firm and concentrated reference throughout the raid, which took place in the face of a strong flak defence that, fortunately, was exploding below the bombers' flight level. The Fiskerton crews carried out their attacks from 17,500 to 20,500 feet either side of 20.45 and returned to report large explosions and the glow of fires for around sixty miles into the return journey. F/L Leyton-Brown and crew lost their port-inner engine shortly after leaving the target and came home on three to attend debriefing, where F/O Harman and crew reported an encounter with what was believed to be a Me410. It was observed approaching on the port beam down and was fired upon by both turrets without itself returning fire and was seen later on the starboard beam with its port engine on fire and descending into cloud to be claimed as probably destroyed. When F/O Mills and crew realised that they were being stalked by a BF109 approaching from astern, both gunners opened fire, and an explosion was followed by a red glow below the clouds. Post-raid reconnaissance confirmed much damage to the oil plant, but it would continue to feature on the target list right through to the final month of the bombing war.

The next briefing at Fiskerton took place on the 12th and provided nineteen crews with the details of that night's operation to Essen by a force of 540 aircraft drawn from 1, 4 and 8 Groups. The 1 Group contribution amounted to 266 Lancasters, those representing 576 Squadron each receiving a bomb load of a cookie and sixteen 500-pounders, before taking off between 16.00 and 16.20 with S/L Templeman-Rooke the senior pilot on duty. They climbed into poor weather conditions with low cloud, which persisted as they passed out over Beachy Head and set course for the French coast on the southerly route to the central Ruhr. While they were heading north over Germany between Cologne and Düsseldorf, the cloud began to clear but built-up again south of the Ruhr to leave the target completely obscured. The Path Finders were a little late in opening the attack, and a few red TIs were seen to enter the cloud tops at up to 16,000 feet and disappear, whereupon red and yellow release-point flares were dropped at 19.27 to be followed by greens three minutes later. Initially, they appeared to be scattered, but soon became plentiful and concentrated, although some crews would complain that they ignited too high, in the region of 18,000 to 20,000 feet. Generally, however, the marking and bombing were accurate, and many large explosions lit up the clouds, followed by a column of black smoke rising up to 20,000 feet. The 576 Squadron crews bombed from an average of 18,500 feet between 19.30 and 19.50, before returning with the general opinion that the attack had been scattered and probably ineffective. In fact, it had been very successful and had caused much damage to residential and industrial buildings, including the Krupp complex, which was now effectively finished as a major producer of war materials.

On the 15th, 1 and 6 Groups combined to assemble a main force of 327 Lancasters to send to the city of Ludwigshafen, located on the western bank of the Rhine opposite Mannheim, where the city's northern half and the nearby town of Oppau were to be targeted, both locations containing an important I G Farben factory, which were engaged in the production of synthetic oil and relying heavily upon slave labour. 1 Group contributed 224 Lancasters, of which thirteen belonged to 576 Squadron, each of which had a cookie winched into its bomb bay, a dozen to be accompanied by four 1,000 and seven 500-pounders, and one, carried by P/O Collins and crew, by fourteen Type-14 cluster incendiaries and two SBCs of standard 4-pounders. They departed Fiskerton between

14.40 and 14.55 with W/C Sellick the senior pilot on duty and flew south to begin the Channel crossing in the Newhaven area. Cloud came and went as the bomber stream traversed enemy territory until fifty miles from the target, when a bank of thick stuff appeared with tops at 20,000 feet, only, with great fortune, to end abruptly just a short distance from the target and leave clear skies and visibility marred only by ground haze. It seems that a tail-wind had propelled some aircraft to the target a little ahead of schedule, and they had to orbit to await the arrival of the Path Finder element, which dispensed the first red TIs punctually at 18.26 and backed them up with greens soon afterwards. Release-point flares were also in evidence, but they were ignored in favour of the clearly-observed TIs, which the 576 Squadron crews bombed from an average of 18,000 feet either side of 18.30. All returned safely to report a concentrated raid with explosions, green and orange smoke and fires that remained visible on the horizon for a hundred miles. Post-raid reconnaissance and local sources confirmed that the Ludwigshafen I G Farben factory had sustained severe damage and fires, and the Oppau plant was put out of action completely, all for the loss of a single Lancaster.

It was on the 16th that German ground forces began a new offensive in the Ardennes, in an attempt to break through the American lines and reach the port of Antwerp in what would become known as the Battle of the Bulge. The German advance surprised overwhelmed the inexperienced American forces, breaking through with ease and making enormous gains under conditions of persistent low cloud that protected it from an assault from above for the next ten days. In the meantime, the city of Ulm, situated on the Danube to the south-east of Stuttgart and west of Augsburg in southern Germany, was the next virgin target to be earmarked for attention. It was similar in nature to the recently-bombed Heilbronn, and because of the catastrophic raid visited upon that city, the local Gauleiter had urged the women and children to evacuate the inner city urgently. Plans were put in place to begin evacuation on Monday the 18th, so that Advent could be observed on the Sunday, but something caused a change of plan and loudspeaker vans toured the city on Sunday the 17th, urging the population to leave at once in what proved to be a fortuitous move in the nick of time. Unlike Heilbronn, Ulm contained industry, including the important Magirus-Deutz and Kässbohrer lorry factories, and it was also home to military barracks and depots.

A main force of 263 Lancasters of 1 Group contained seventeen representing 576 Squadron, and they would benefit from the marking and support of fifty-four Lancasters and thirteen Mosquitos from 8 Group. The Fiskerton Lancasters were each loaded with a cookie and mix of cluster bombs and standard incendiaries and took off between 15.10 and 15.30 with five pilots of flight lieutenant rank the most senior crew captains on duty. F/O Rouse and crew discovered a hydraulics leak during the climb out, which rendered the rear turret unserviceable, and they were soon back on the ground, leaving the others to encounter cloudy, but fairly good conditions as they headed south to rendezvous with the rest of the bomber stream as it began the Channel crossing at Newhaven. Having made landfall south of Dieppe, crews found the weather deteriorating as they traversed France and much of the outward flight was spent in cloud. The skies became clear at the Rhine to leave excellent visibility, which allowed the crews to map-read their way to the target, until some twenty miles short, when a layer of thin stratus slid in with tops at 2,000 feet to completely obscure the ground. The Path Finders opened the attack with red TIs at 19.24, but they quickly became swallowed up in the cloud or were extinguished by the heavy snow on the ground. Release-point (Wanganui) flares were dropped at the same time, and at 19.31, the 35 Squadron Master Bomber,

F/L Cook, ordered these to be bombed and orbited the target from H-3 to H+14, trying to persuade the main force crews to comply and not undershoot on a bunch of errant incendiaries. The 576 Squadron crews attacked from an average of 11,500 feet between 19.30 and 19.45, F/O Hardman's LM294 surviving falling incendiaries that left large holes in the starboard mainplane. The squadron played its part in an accurate and concentrated raid, which resulted in fierce fires that consumed a square kilometre of the city's built-up area. It would be established later that almost 82% of the buildings had sustained damage to some extent, including both lorry factories and twenty-seven other industrial premises. There is no question that the evacuation saved many thousands of lives and restricted the civilian death toll to around six hundred.

Operations were not yet over for the night of the 17/18th, and it was well into the early hours of the 18th when a force of 523 aircraft from 4, 6 and 8 Groups departed their stations for Duisburg, and arrived to find it completely hidden beneath ten-tenths cloud with tops at 6,000 to 8,000 feet. Two aiming-points were marked by Oboe Mosquitos, but the TIs disappeared into the cloud to leave a glow as the only reference point for bombing, and most crews confirmed their positions by H2S and Gee before releasing their loads. Despite doubts about the effectiveness of the bombing, 346 houses were destroyed and more than five hundred seriously damaged, and the likelihood is that industry also suffered to some extent.

The city of Bonn would become prominent after the war as the capital city of Western Germany and had received a number of small-scale visits from the Command during 1944. It was now to be the objective for seventy-seven Lancasters of 1 Group on the 21st, with Path Finder Lancasters and Mosquitos to carry out the marking of the railway yards. It had been intended to send a force of 260 Lancasters but doubts about the state of the weather for their return prompted a reduction in the force to involve just 12 Base squadrons and six from 14 Base's 101 Squadron to provide RCM cover. Heavy cloud over the target created an expectation of failure, and post raid-reconnaissance confirmed that the marshalling yards had not been touched. While this operation was in progress, twenty Lancasters from 12 and 13 Bases were engaged in mining duties in the Bay of Pomerania off Germany's Baltic coast.

The dismantling of Germany's railway infrastructure continued on the 22nd with the launching of an attack by a 1 Group main force of 156 Lancasters from all but 12 Base on the Coblenz-Mosel marshalling yards located some thirty miles south-east of Bonn. Ten of the fifteen 576 Squadron Lancasters received a bomb load of thirteen 1,000-pounders and the remaining five a cookie, six 1,000 and seven 500-pounders, before departing Fiskerton between 15.05 and 15.30 with S/L Masters the senior pilot on duty. They began the Channel crossing between Beachy Head and Hastings, making landfall on the French side to the north-east of Dieppe and arriving at the target to find ten-tenths cloud and somewhat scattered skymarkers providing a less-than-ideal bombing reference. The 576 Squadron crews carried out their bombing runs at an average of 19,000 feet either side of 19.00 and were diverted on return because of poor weather over Lincolnshire, nine of them ending up at Charterhall in Berwickshire. According to local sources in Coblenz, the attack largely missed the mark and deposited the main weight of bombs onto farmland a mile or so to the west. However, the eastern fringes of the bombing found the yards and cut several main lines, while also hitting two important road bridges.

As previously mentioned, Cologne contained a number of important marshalling yards, among them Nippes and Gereon, situated to the north of the city centre west of the Rhine and Gremberg and Kalk on the other side of the river. The first-mentioned, which was known to be active in supporting the transportation of men and materials to the Ardennes battle front, had been attacked unsuccessfully by a force of 136 aircraft from 4, 6 and 8 Groups on the 21st, and now, on Christmas Eve, would face eighty-one 1 Group Lancasters predominantly from 12 and 13 Bases, with sixteen Lancasters and five Mosquitos provided by 8 Group as the marker force. The Path Finder marker crews were right on the money and sent red and green TIs cascading into the railway yards, where they attracted the bombs of the main force Lancasters. Extensive damage was inflicted upon track and installations and an ammunition train blew up.

The festivities passed in traditional style uninterrupted by operational activity, but the peace came to an end on Boxing Day, when crews from all groups were roused from any resulting stupor to attend briefings for operations against enemy troop positions at St Vith in Belgium. The German advance towards Antwerp had ground to a halt after its initial successes, and starved of fuel and ammunition, was now attempting to withdraw back into Germany. 1 Group contributed sixty-four Lancasters from 12, 13 and 14 Bases, and they benefitted from clear skies over Belgium, that enabled them to map-read their way to the target area and visually identify the town. The attack opened on time with red Oboe TIs, which were backed up by red and green TIs right on the aiming-point, and the operation appeared to be successful.

Binbrook was somewhat crowded on the 27th as fifty-one Lancasters were being prepared for an operation by two hundred aircraft from 1, 3, 5 and 8 Groups against the marshalling yards at Rheydt on the western edge of the Ruhr to the south of Mönchengladbach. The station had been playing host to Lancasters from 13 and 14 Bases following their diversion on the previous day, and forty-four had to be bombed-up and fuelled along with seven from 460 Squadron. Included in the operation were the 576 Squadron crews of F/Os Button and Phripp, who were already at Binbrook, although it is not clear how they came to be there, the latter having landed at Manston on return from Coblenz on the 22nd, and the former not having operated since Ludwigshafen on the 15th. One must assume that the continuing adverse weather conditions had prevented their return to Fiskerton. They learned at briefing that the force was to adopt what 1 Group referred to as the "Group Column" formation, which consisted of vics of three in line astern. They took off at 12.05 and 12.10 respectively, each carrying eight 1,000 and eight 500-pounders, and after climbing out joined the formation, which held together satisfactorily after rendezvousing with the other groups until the final leg from Liege, when the 3 Group gaggle crossed over 1 Group and inevitably created confusion. Nevertheless, the main weight of bombs was observed to fall in the southern end of the marshalling yards, although some overshot and landed in the town to the east. The target area was covered by a mass of fires emitting brown and grey smoke, which convinced returning crews that they had fulfilled their brief, although F/O Phripp and crew landed at Fiskerton with their bomb load intact after a technical fault had prevented its release.

1 Group divided its forces on the 28th to send 103 Lancasters from 12 and 13 Bases to Mönchengladbach in company with forty-six Halifaxes of 4 Group and twenty-six Lancasters and eleven Mosquitos of 8 Group, while a further 133 from 14 and 15 Bases targeted the marshalling yards again at Bonn. At Fiskerton the armourers got to work loading fifteen Lancasters with a cookie, six 1,000 and eight 500-pounders and two with eight 1,000 and eight 500-pounders, before

sending them on their way between 15.15 and 15.45 with S/L Templeman-Rooke the senior pilot on duty and undertaking the twenty-seventh and final sortie of his second tour. Clear skies over England gave way to six-tenths stratocumulus over the Channel, decreasing slightly over France as far as 6° East, where it built again to leave nine-tenths over the western Ruhr and ten-tenths over Bonn with tops at 8,000 feet and bright moonlight and excellent visibility above. The Path Finders were three minutes late in dispensing large numbers of skymarkers and red and green TIs, which provided a firm reference for the main force crews, who confirmed their positions by H2S before delivering their payloads from 15,000 to 16,000 feet between 18.45 and 18.55. Several large explosions were witnessed at 18.45 and 18.49, and a flak shell, described in the 1 Group ORB as a "scarecrow", allegedly caused damage to a nearby Lancaster. This may have been 576 Squadron's NN750, which was skilfully and gently nursed back across the Channel minus its flight engineer and with only trimming tabs to provide a modicum of stability. F/O Fletcher attempted a landing at Manston, which failed, and forced him to open the throttles for a "go-around", during which the Lancaster lost flying speed, stalled and crashed, killing all on board. Flight engineer, Sgt Lake, had baled out over Germany and had been taken into captivity. Post-raid reconnaissance and local sources confirmed that, in fact, a modest 128 houses and nineteen public buildings had been destroyed along with forty-five houses and various other buildings in nearby Rheydt, while forty miles to the south, extensive damage had been inflicted across the city of Bonn but not on the railway yards.

Sixteen 576 Squadron crews attended briefing on the 29th to learn that they would be heading to the Ruhr later that evening to target the Hydrierwerke synthetic oil refinery at Scholven-Buer in the north-western quarter of Gelsenkirchen. They were part of a 1 Group force of 239 Lancasters bolstered by fifty-seven provided by 6 Group, with twenty-eight from 8 Group and twenty-two Mosquitos to take care of the marking. The Fiskerton Lancasters each received a bomb load of a cookie and sixteen 500-pounders and took off between 15.10 and 15.30 with S/L Masters the senior pilot on duty. They enjoyed favourable weather conditions on the way out over the Channel to a point north-east of Dieppe and were greeted at the target by bright moonlight over a thin veil of ten-tenths cloud topping out at 5,000 feet. Skymarkers had to be employed, and the first Oboe red went down a fraction early at 18.53, followed precisely at Zero-Hour by a good concentration of others to leave their red glow clearly visible. The 576 Squadron crews delivered their payloads from an average of 18,500 feet either side of 19.00, before returning safely to report numerous large explosions, smoke rising to 15,000 feet and fires visible for a hundred miles into the return flight. A local report detailed three hundred high-explosive bombs hitting the area of the plant, causing fires and inflicting severe damage upon the installations. A further 3,100 bombs fell in other parts of Scholven, causing much residential and industrial destruction, and surface buildings at two coal mines were also hit and severely damaged.

The final operation of the month for 1 Group was posted on the 31st and involved 133 of its Lancasters in an attack on the railway yards at Osterfeld, a town deep inside Germany some twenty miles south-west of Leipzig, for which the marking was to be provided by sixteen Lancasters and seventeen Mosquitos of 8 Group. Ten of the eleven 576 Squadron Lancasters each received a bomb load of a cookie supplemented with six 1,000 and six 500-pounders, while one had a cookie and type-14 and 15 incendiary cluster bombs plus two SBCs containing a total of 120 x 4lb incendiaries. They departed Fiskerton between 14.45 and 15.05 with F/Ls Acheson, Boullier and Living the senior pilots on duty and adopted the well-trodden route via Newhaven to the French coast north-east of Dieppe. Initially, they enjoyed favourable weather conditions, until cloud began to build over France and Belgium and a headwind of 120 mph over the latter delayed the arrival of the force at the target. Faced with seven to ten-tenths cloud with tops at 10,000 feet, the Path Finders struggled to provide adequate concentrated marking after arriving a few minutes behind schedule and the first markers were observed at 18.45. The red TIs appeared to be fairly concentrated and the greens scattered, and it was at the glow of the former that the 576 Squadron crews aimed their bombs from an average of 18,500 feet between 18.47 and 19.02. Fires and several large explosions were observed, and the return flight proved to be uneventful and the landing in time to see in the New Year.

S/L Templeman-Rooke had now completed twenty-seven sorties in his second tour and was rewarded with a Bar to his DFC. It had been a hectic and demanding year, which had seen the Command rise phoenix-like from the traumas of the winter campaign and pave the way for the land forces to sweep across the occupied countries to the frontiers of Germany itself, which lay in ruins, its transport system in chaos and its manufacturing base no longer able to support the war effort. The New Year beckoned with the scent of victory in the air, but much remained to be done, and any thoughts that the enemy defences were spent were misplaced. Even though dwindling resources in manpower and fuel meant that they were unable to protect every corner of the Reich, they would continue to provide stubborn resistance for a further three months and claim more Bomber Command lives.

During the course of the month, the squadron took part in eleven operations and dispatched 155 sorties for the loss of a single Lancaster and its crew.

January 1945

The final year of the war began with a flourish, as the Luftwaffe launched its ill-conceived and, ultimately, ill-fated Operation Bodenplatte (Baseplate) at first light on New Year's Day. The intention to destroy the Allied air forces on the ground at the recently liberated airfields in France, Holland and Belgium was only modestly realised, and it cost the German day fighter force around 250 aircraft. Many of the pilots were killed, wounded or fell into Allied hands, and it was a setback from which the Tagjagd would never fully recover, while the Allies could make good their losses within hours from their enormous stockpiles.

The old enemy of Nuremberg was posted on the 2nd as the first major urban target of 1945 and would face a main force of 445 Lancasters drawn from 1, 3 and 6 Groups with a further sixty-nine Lancasters representing 8 Group to provide the marking and bombing support. A simultaneous operation involved 351 Halifaxes of 4 and 6 Groups in attacks on two I G Farben chemical plants, one in Ludwigshafen and the other close by in Oppau. Both operations would also benefit from Oboe Mosquitos, seven for Nuremberg and twenty-two for Ludwigshafen, their participation made possible by the mobile Oboe stations now established in liberated territory. 576 Squadron made ready seventeen Lancasters in a record 1 Group effort of 296, and loaded each with a cookie, nine supplemented with fourteen 500-pounders, seven with cluster bombs and standard incendiaries and a singleton with four 1,000 and five 500-pounders. They departed Fiskerton between 14.50 and 15.10 with F/L Arthur the senior pilot on duty and headed via Beachy Head for the French coast north-east of Dieppe, adopting a course, thereafter, parallel to the Franco/Belgian frontier, before turning east to enter Germany north of Saarbrücken. The two forces would then follow a similar route until diverging shortly before reaching Ludwigshafen, at which point the Nuremberg force would still have 140 miles and forty-five minutes flying time to negotiate before arriving at its destination.

They began the outward flight over six-tenths cloud, which thickened over the Channel and remained at ten-tenths until breaking up from 7° East, by which time, shortly after turning to the east at Reims, NF976 was hit by flak, which damaged flying surfaces and the hydraulics system and left F/O Sowerbutts with no option but to turn back and jettison the bombs into the Channel. Nuremberg lay under clear skies and effectively naked to the bomb sights high above, the built-up area contrasting sharply with the snow-covered countryside, as the Path Finder illuminating flares highlighted the River Pegnitz, railway tracks and buildings. Some main force aircraft arrived a little early courtesy of a tail wind, and orbited as they awaited the Path Finders, who opened the attack a few minutes early with the first salvoes of mixed red and green TIs. They fell across the marshalling yards in the city centre in good concentration and attracted the main force bombs under the guidance of the Master Bomber. The 576 Squadron crews carried out their attacks on red and green TIs from 16,000 to 18,000 feet between 19.25 and 19.55, those at the tail end aiming at the upwind edge of the smoke in accordance with the master Bomber's instructions after the ground became enveloped. A glow from the burning city remained on the horizon for 150 miles and returning crews were confident of a successful outcome. Night-fighter activity was reported at debriefings with a particular mention of jet-propelled aircraft, despite which the Command registered the failure to return of a modest six aircraft. One other belonging to 1 Group was abandoned over liberated France with all but one crew member safe, and two 15 Base Lancasters from Hemswell and Scampton collided on return north of the Fiskerton circuit leaving all fourteen occupants dead. Post-raid reconnaissance and local sources confirmed that the raid had destroyed more than 4,600 houses and apartment blocks along with a further two thousand preserved medieval houses, while industrial districts and railway areas had also sustained heavy damage.

Meanwhile, the success of the Ludwigshafen operation was confirmed by local reports that five hundred high-explosive bombs and many thousands of incendiaries had fallen within the confines of the two I G Farben production plants. This had put an end to all production of synthetic oil, and adjacent industrial buildings, residential property and railway installations had also been destroyed.

Briefings were held for ninety-eight crews on 14 and 15 Base stations during the evening of the 4th in preparation for an operation in the early hours of the 5th by elements of 1, 5 and 8 Groups against the coastal town of Royan, located on the eastern bank of the Gironde estuary some sixty miles north of Bordeaux. The established pattern for joint operations with 5 Group was a two-wave attack, in this case separated by an hour, in which 5 Group opened proceedings employing its highly accurate low-level marking system followed by an assault by the heavy brigade, to leave a burning beacon for the second wave force. The operation was mounted in response to requests from Free French forces, who were laying siege to the town on their way to attempt to capture the city and port of Bordeaux. 576 Squadron contributed seventeen Lancasters, each loaded with a cookie and sixteen 500-pounders, before departing Fiskerton between 01.35 and 02.43 with F/Ls Acheson, Boullier, Campbell, Dotten and Living the senior pilots on duty. They headed south, passing over Cheltenham on their way to begin the Channel crossing at Christchurch, and found the cloud over the sea and north-western France diminishing until there was none between the approaching bomber force and the well-illuminated Biscay coastline. The Master Bomber called "basement" at 11,000 feet and instructed crews to bomb two hundred yards to starboard of the red TIs and overshoot by one second. The aiming point was maintained throughout with red and green TIs and the 576 Squadron crews delivered their attacks unopposed from an average of 9,500 feet in a fifteen-minute slot from around 05.28, observing a large explosion at 05.32. The town was effectively erased from the map and the tragedy was that the residents had been offered the opportunity by the German garrison commander to evacuate. Two thousand people opted to remain, quite reasonably in the belief that nothing untoward would result, and up to eight hundred of these are believed to have lost their lives. In an ironic twist of war, the town was not taken, and the garrison remained in place until mid-April.

Briefings took place on the 5th for the first major assault on the city of Hannover since the series in the autumn of 1943 and was to be conducted by 650 Lancasters and Halifaxes and fourteen Mosquitos drawn from 1, 4, 6 and 8 Groups. The plan called for the 4 and 6 Group Halifaxes to go in first to be followed two-and-a-half hours later by the Lancasters, the 8 Group Lancaster element split fifty-nine and thirty-one between the first and second phases with seven Mosquitos assigned to each. 1 Group detailed 163 Lancasters, with Hemswell representing 15 Base, while the Fiskerton and Scampton squadrons were rested. The route over the North Sea and Holland and as far as 7° East was covered by a layer of up to ten-tenths cloud between 5,000 and 12,000 feet, but from south of Bremen to the target, clear skies prevailed, and the burning city acted as a beacon to draw the second phase Lancaster element on for the last one hundred miles. The Halifax attack had taken place over ten-tenths low cloud with tops at between 2,000 and 5,000 feet, but good H2S returns enabled the Path Finder element to establish its position over the aiming-point in the northern half of the city, and the bombing had been accurate and concentrated. Numerous fires were spread across the city, the glare and smoke from which created challenging conditions, and most TIs were soon lost to view. In truth, marking was somewhat superfluous, but the 1 Group participants found sufficient red and green TIs to satisfy their needs and disgorged the contents of their bomb bays from 19,000 to 21,000 feet between 21.49 and 21.57. The second phase attack added to the destruction, and once the fires had been extinguished and the dust had settled, the local authorities were able to assess that almost five hundred apartment blocks had been destroyed with their 3,600 individual dwelling units.

Orders were sent out to 1, 3, 4, 6 and 8 Group stations on the 6th to prepare for operations against two marshalling yards, one in the town of Hanau-am-Main, situated a short distance to the east of Frankfurt and the other in Neuss in the southern Ruhr. A force of 482 aircraft was assigned to the former and included a contribution from 1 Group of fifty-two Lancasters from 12 and 14 Bases, which found the target under ten-tenths cloud and bombed on the glow of TIs until skymarkers were employed. Returning crews reported the glow from the target to be visible from seventy-five miles away, but it had not been possible to assess the outcome, and it was left to local sources to confirm damage in the area of the railway yards and also in other parts of the town resulting in the destruction of 40% of the built-up area. Meanwhile, the raid on Neuss, which had included thirty-three 1 Group Lancasters also from 12 and 14 Bases, had destroyed or seriously damaged almost eighteen hundred buildings.

A major operation against Munich was planned for the 7th, for which a two-wave force of 645 aircraft was drawn from all five of the Lancaster-equipped groups, 5 Group, which was unused to sharing this target, leading the way with 213 Lancasters and three Mosquitos, leaving the second wave to follow two hours later. 576 Squadron made ready fifteen Lancasters with bomb loads that included a cookie and mix of cluster bombs and standard incendiaries and dispatched them from Fiskerton between 18.00 and 19.00 with S/L Masters the senior pilot on duty and undertaking the final sortie of his tour, as was F/O Moore. They set course via Beachy Head for the French coast to rendezvous with the rest of the bomber stream, while ahead the 5 Group element was about to cross the Franco-German frontier near Strasbourg with an hour's flight still ahead of it. On arrival at Munich, the 5 Group spearhead encountered broken medium-level cloud at 14,000 feet, with haze or thin cloud below, by which time, the Master Bomber had made a visual identification of the aiming-point and sent the first two primary blind markers in to deliver their TIs at the same time thirty seconds ahead of the planned opening of the attack. The flare force went in immediately afterwards, and illuminated the city very effectively, allowing ground detail to be identified. Red TIs went down west and east of the River Isar, bracketing the aiming-point, and the Master Bomber ordered the backers up to drop their TIs between the reds, after which, the next batch of flares formed a circle around the aiming point. The main force was then called in, and as they withdrew with empty bomb bays minutes later, they left behind a burning city that would act as a beacon visible to the second phase crews from 130 miles away.

Soon after crossing the French coast, the second phase force had met an ice-bearing front extending up to 20,000 feet, and although this diminished to a layer of thin cloud at 10,000 feet, the ground remained hidden. The target itself was concealed beneath ten-tenths cloud with tops at 12,000 feet as the attack began well on time with green TIs and red flares with green stars, the former quickly disappearing into the cloud tops and leaving the skymarkers to provide a concentrated reference for the bombing element. The Fiskerton crews delivered their bombs from an average of 17,500 feet either side of 22.30, and some observed five large explosions between 22.27 and 22.41, the last-mentioned resulting in a mushroom of smoke breaking through the cloud tops. The loss of fifteen Lancasters included nine from the ranks of 1 Group, one partially abandoned over France after a mid-air collision, while 576 Squadron posted missing the predominantly RCAF crew of F/O Saslove RCAF in PA173. The pilot and both gunners lost their lives, and the four survivors fell into enemy hands to spend a relatively short time in captivity. This proved to be the final large-scale attack of the war on Munich, but joint operations led by 5 Group would become an established format for the remainder of the war.

The following week was relatively busy for the independent 3 Group, while other groups were employed sparingly and 1 Group not at all, largely as a result of the weather, a heavy fall of snow arriving on the 9th, which needed to be cleared over the ensuing days. On the 14th, 1, 5, 6 and 8 Group stations were alerted to a major two-phase operation against the previously targeted I G Farbenindustrie synthetic oil refinery at Leuna near Merseburg. They were part of an overall force of 573 Lancasters and fourteen Mosquitos, of which the 5 Group contingent of 210 Lancasters and nine Mosquitos would form the first phase and be followed up three hours later by a 306-strong main force consisting of 245 Lancasters of 1 Group and sixty-one from 6 Group. The 5 Group element began to depart their stations at around 16.00 for the three-and-a-half-hour outward flight, which would take them via the southerly route across France and into eastern Germany. They reached the target area to find clear skies but poor vertical visibility due to a layer of haze, which, in the event, was no hindrance to the primary blind markers, whose job was to establish their position over the aiming-point by means of H2S. They delivered their TIs from 18,000 feet, after which, the first element of the flare force went in and the Master Bomber called for ground marking only, which was carried out by the low-level Mosquito element. By 20.50, he was satisfied and sent the marker aircraft home.

As the 5 Group main force crews went in to attack, 550 miles to the west-north-west, those of the second phase were in the process of taking off, eighteen at Fiskerton departing between 19.05 and 19.37 with F/Ls Acheson, Campbell and Living the senior pilots on duty and each Lancaster carrying a cookie and a dozen 500-pounders. They set course via Beachy Head for the French coast and the standard route into Germany in good weather conditions over thin cloud, which would prevail throughout the almost nine-hour round trip. The target was reached early by some crews and found to be covered by ten-tenths thin cloud or smoke, with the glow from the 5 Group raid clearly visible. The illuminating flares went down at 23.54, followed by red and green TIs, and although they could be seen dimly, the ground itself was completely obscured and the Master Bomber experienced difficulty in identifying the aiming point, eventually instructing the main force to bomb on the red and yellow release-point flares. The Fiskerton crews complied with his instructions from an average of 21,000 feet between either side of midnight, and large explosions were reported at 23.59 and 00.18, one of which sent dense clouds of smoke rising through the cloud tops. At debriefing, the crews of F/Os Dalziel and Pegg each claimed the destruction of a jet fighter, which other crews were able to confirm. Many returning crews thought the operation to have been scattered and probably ineffective, when, in fact, it had been among the most devastating attacks on the synthetic oil industry of the war.

Feverish activity across the Command on the 16th prepared more than twelve hundred aircraft for action, the majority to participate in four major operations that night, three to target oil refineries and the largest to deliver an area attack on the eastern city of Magdeburg, which also contained the Braunkohle A.G Bergius process hydrogenation plant, located in the Rothensee district to the north of the city centre. The independent 3 and 5 Groups were handed the refineries at Wanne-Eickel in the Ruhr and Brüx in Czechoslovakia respectively, leaving 320 Halifaxes of 4 and 6 Groups to take care of Magdeburg and 283 Lancasters of 1 and 6 Groups to ply their trade at Zeitz-Tröglitz, the location of another Braunkohle-Benzin A.G plant, situated some twenty miles south-west of Leipzig. 1 Group detailed 232 Lancasters for Zeitz and 8 Group forty-five, and the eighteen-strong 576 Squadron contingent departed Fiskerton between 17.30 and 17.45 with F/Ls Acheson, Collins and Dotten the senior pilots on duty and each Lancaster carrying a cookie and twelve American-built 500-pounders. Ten-tenths cloud over England and the Channel began to disperse at the French coast and the skies were clear from 6° East for the rest of the outward flight, although extremely dark in the absence of a moon. A strong tail wind resulted in some crews arriving up to six minutes ahead of schedule and not all were prepared to wait for the marking to begin, preferring instead to bomb by H2S before heading home. The first salvoes of mixed red and green TIs fell on the northern edge of the plant and were backed up plentifully and continuously throughout the attack, which was tightly controlled by the Master Bomber, who called in the main force at 22.09. The Fiskerton crews delivered their loads from an average of 17,500 feet either side of 22.15 and at debriefing reported a series of large explosions between 22.13 and 22.23, the largest at 22.19 sending a mushroom of black smoke to 10,000 feet and beyond. They also reported the oil plant and parts of the town to be ablaze. F/O Phripps was on the final sortie of his tour and his gunners claimed the destruction of two jet fighters, one identified as a rocket-fuelled Me163 Komet. Absent from debriefing was the predominantly RAAF crew of F/O Pegg RAAF, who had sent a message at 01.20 to the effect that they were about to abandon PD309 over Belgium. They were reported later to be safe, with one broken ankle between them, and also claimed the possible destruction of a jet fighter.

Following a frustrating five-day period of inactivity for the heavy brigade, the Ruhr city of Duisburg was posted on the 22nd as the destination for a 1, 3 and 8 Group force of 286 Lancasters and sixteen Mosquitos. The 1 Group ORB is not specific about the precise target for its 130 Lancasters, but the 576 Squadron ORB cites the Hamborn steelworks (Thyssen), while other ORBs identify a benzol plant in the Bruckhausen district, both locations situated to the north of the city centre. 576 Squadron's seventeen participants departed Fiskerton between 16.40 and 17.00 with F/Ls Acheson, Leyton-Brown and Living the senior pilots on duty and each crew sitting on a cookie and sixteen 500-pounders. Onlookers were nervous about the prospects for an incident-free take-off as the runways were covered by a treacherous coating of snow, despite having been cleared during the course of the day, and there was great relief when the last Lancaster lifted off into the gathering gloom. They headed south over low cloud between northern Lincolnshire and the French coast, where it gradually diminished to leave the target area clear under moonlight and in excellent visibility. Crews were able to confirm visually the accuracy of the Path Finder markers, and apart from one stray red TI in the Ruhrort docks complex, they all fell around the aiming points and attracted the bomb loads. The 576 Squadron crews delivered their attacks onto red and green TIs from an average of 18,500 feet between 20.00 and 20.15 and returned home full of praise for the work of the Path Finders. They missed a particularly large explosion at 20.37, probably emanating from the benzol plant, which was observed by the last crews to leave the target area, and bombing photos supported the claims of a highly destructive raid. At debriefing, F/O Ridge and crew reported that they had undertaken most of the outward flight on three engines and had bombed a little short of the target as they struggled to maintain height. F/L Living and crew returned in a damaged ME735, claiming to have been struck by the fallout from a mythical "scarecrow", which in reality was one of two 153 Squadron Lancasters to be lost over the target. Post-raid reconnaissance revealed also that the Thyssen steelworks had sustained severe damage after being hit by five hundred bombs, and there was much collateral damage in adjacent residential districts.

Orders were received at all 1 Group bases on the 28th to prepare for an operation that night to Stuttgart by 602 aircraft divided into two forces separated by three hours, each with its own specific target. The first phase, by 226 aircraft, was to be directed at the marshalling yards in the town of Kornwestheim, situated just beyond the northern boundary of Stuttgart, while the second phase would target the Hirth aero-engine factory at Zuffenhausen, fewer than two miles to the south. 1 Group put up 150 Lancasters for the latter, the fifteen representing 576 Squadron each receiving a bomb load of a cookie and a dozen 500-pounders, before departing Fiskerton between 19.38 and 20.00 with seven pilots of flight lieutenant rank leading the way. They flew out over the Sussex coast over five-tenths cloud as far as the French coast north-east of Dieppe, from where they encountered large gaps until reaching the German frontier north of Strasbourg. Here, the cloud built until it was at ten-tenths over the target with tops at 10,000 feet, a situation requiring a skymarking plan.

The Path Finders were three minutes late, and some main force crews arrived early and carried out their attacks before any release point flares were evident. The first red and yellow flares appeared at 23.30 and were initially sparse and scattered, but the density of marking increased as the raid progressed, and the 576 Squadron crews had adequate numbers to aim at as they delivered their attacks from an average of 19,000 feet between 23.30 and 23.40. Large explosions were observed at 23.36 and 23.38 and the glow of fires beneath the clouds suggested some success, although returning crews believed the raid to have been scattered. Crews returning to Fiskerton reported much night-fighter activity, but no combats, and after landing safely, F/O Mills and crew were declared tour-expired. Local sources confirmed the extent of the damage at both targets, reporting that many parts of the city had been hit, while a decoy fire site had also attracted some bomb loads as the Germans fired dummy TIs into the air. The railway installations at Kornwestheim sustained damage and a number of important war industry factories, including the Robert Bosch works, were also reported to have been hit. This would prove to be the last of fifty-three major raids on this important industrial city, which had now been largely destroyed.

During the course of the month the squadron took part in seven operations and dispatched 117 sorties for the loss of two Lancasters and one crew.

February 1945

The weather at the start of February provided difficult conditions for marking and bombing, and several operations would struggle to achieve their aims in the face of thick, low cloud and strong winds. Three major operations were laid on for the night of the 1/2nd, the largest by 382 Lancasters and fourteen Mosquitos of 1, 6 and 8 Groups against Ludwigshafen, while thirty-five miles to the north, 340 aircraft from 4, 6 and 8 Groups attended to the city of Mainz. Further north still, 5 Group's target was the marshalling yards in the town of Siegen, situated some fifty miles east of Cologne. 1 Group would be represented at Ludwigshafen by 277 Lancasters, the fourteen belonging to 576 Squadron receiving a bomb load of a cookie supplemented with a mix of cluster bombs and standard incendiaries, before departing Fiskerton between 15.55 and 16.10 with W/C Sellick the senior pilot on duty. The skies were largely clear from the Sussex coast until around 6° East, where cloud began to build and was at nine-tenths with tops at 6,000 feet by the time that the spearhead of the bomber stream arrived in the target area at the end of a three-hour flight. The Path Finders opened the attack punctually at 19.11 with cascading red TIs backed up by greens and followed by release point flares, and these could be seen by the approaching main force crews until the start of their bombing runs, when the ground became concealed by cloud. They then had to rely on the flares, which resulted in scattered bombing and a degree of undershooting. Small gaps in the cloud revealed incendiary fires on both sides of the Rhine, and several large explosions were observed at 19.20, 19.25, 19.36 and 19.42, the last-mentioned by crews fifty miles into their homeward flight. The Fiskerton crews carried out their bombing runs from an average of 16,500 feet either side of 19.30 employing red and green skymarker flares as their reference, and all returned home safely, some to report observing an aircraft on fire at 18.57, which crashed, and another at 19.24 from which two parachutes were seen to enter cloud. Local sources confirmed that bombs had fallen right across the city and that nine hundred houses had been destroyed or seriously damaged along with the marshalling yards, and a Rhine bridge had been forced to close for repairs.

When briefings took place on the 2nd, they came with the bad news that a tour of operations for main force crews was to be increased again to thirty-six sorties. On 5 Group stations in drizzly

Lincolnshire, 250 crews were told further, that the night's operation was to be against Karlsruhe in southern Germany, and that this was one of three major undertakings involving a total of 1,150 aircraft. Elsewhere, 495 crews from 1, 3, 6 and 8 Groups were informed that Wiesbaden would be their destination and that it would the first time that this city, separated from nearby Mainz to the south by the River Rhine, had been targeted by Bomber Command. The third operation on this night would bring a return to the Ruhr for 277 Halifaxes of 4 and 6 Groups with twenty-seven 8 Group Lancasters and nineteen Mosquitos to provide the marking for an attack on the Krupp Treibstoffwerke synthetic oil plant in the Wanne-Eickel district of Herne. 1 Group put up 233 Lancasters for Wiesbaden, thirteen of them made ready at Fiskerton, where each received the same bomb load as for the previous operation, before taking off between 20.40 and 21.35 with S/L Templeman-Rooke the senior pilot on duty and mentoring the freshman crew of P/O Croft. They adopted a similar course to that of the previous night and from 3° East encountered a build-up of cloud to ten-tenths in layers up to 20,000 feet, which would persist all the way to the target. PD312 had progressed some fifty miles inland from the French coast when afflicted by an uncontrollable engine fire over the Beauvais area, which persuaded F/L Boullier and crew to abandon it to its fate at 22.50 and arrive safely on the ground in Allied-held territory. At around the same time, F/O Dalziel and crew, who had been the last to take off and too late to reach the target in the allotted window, were recalled. Winds were lighter than forecast, resulting in the late arrival of the force, and the cloud completely nullified the attempts to mark, leaving crews with no option but to bomb on Gee and H2S. The 576 Squadron crews carried out their attacks from an average of 20,000 feet between 23.35 and 00.02, and none had a clue as to the outcome of the operation. NG119 failed to return with the crew of F/O Sowerbutts, who all lost their lives when the Lancaster came down at Kautenbach in Luxembourg.

Two Ruhr oil production sites were the focus of attention on the evening of the 3rd, one of them the Prosper coking plant at Welheim, an eastern district of Bottrop, situated about five miles to the north-east of Duisburg and Oberhausen, while the other was the Hansa benzol plant at Dortmund. The former was assigned to a 1 and 8 Group heavy force of 192 Lancasters, of which 1 Group contributed 164, and the latter was entrusted to 3 Group and its highly effective G-H bombing system. The eleven 576 Squadron Lancasters each received a bomb load of a cookie and sixteen 500-pounders, two of the latter with long-delay fuses, and departed Fiskerton between 16.07 and 16.31 with a quintet of flight lieutenant pilots leading the way. They adopted the familiar route to southern Germany and flew out under largely clear skies until a few miles from the target, where a little low cloud began to form at 3,000 feet, but insufficient to interfere with the progress of the raid. The first red TIs appeared punctually at 19.26 and were observed to be both accurate and concentrated, and they were followed by greens which also fell right on the aiming point. Many crews were able to confirm visually the effectiveness of the marking and proceeded to bomb in a very tight pattern, those from Fiskerton from an average of 17,000 feet between 19.33 and 19.40. Fires and explosions were evident along with much black smoke and it was clear to most that a successful operation had taken place, albeit in the face of a spirited and accurate flak defence supported by some two hundred searchlights in cones of between ten and twenty. A number of crews reported observing two aircraft crash, at 19.37 and 19.53, and post-raid reconnaissance confirmed eventually that extensive damage had been inflicted upon the plant.

Three main operations were posted again on the 4th, against the Gutehoffnungshütte Oberhausen A.G benzol plant at Osterfeld near Leipzig, the Gelsenkirchener Bergwerke A.G (Nordstern) coking plant in the Ruhr and an area attack on the city of Bonn, all of which 1 Group sat out. However, the group detailed and briefed fifteen crews for mining operations in the Rosemary and Eglantine gardens, respectively in the Heligoland Bight and the Elbe estuary, five each at Binbrook, Elsham Wolds and Scampton, and all returned safely having carried out their assigned tasks.

The towns of Cleves and Goch are separated by around eight miles and lie east of the Reichswald and to the south of the Rhine and formed part of the enemy's defensive line towards which the British XXX Corps was preparing to advance. Briefings took place on the 7th at which it was learned that a 1 Group force of 250 Lancasters was to join up with forty-five Lancasters and ten Mosquitos from 8 Group to attack the former, while 464 aircraft of 4, 6 and 8 Groups attended to the latter. The bomb bays of a dozen 576 Squadron Lancasters swallowed up a cookie and sixteen 500-pounders each, which were lifted into the air from Fiskerton between 18.55 and 19.15 with S/L Templeman-Rooke the senior pilot on duty. The weather was good as they climbed out over the Lincolnshire Wolds and headed south to the exit point at Hastings on course for the Boulogne coastal area. The route out was virtually cloud-free, but a dozen miles from the target it began to build and was at seven to ten-tenths in a band from 5,000 to 7,000 feet when the raid began. This prompted the Master Bomber to bring the main-force crews down to 5,000 feet to provide them with a view of the red and green TIs on the brilliantly-illuminated aiming-point. He was clear and concise and maintained excellent control of proceedings, and the 576 Squadron crews delivered their attacks in accordance with his instructions from 5,000 feet between 22.01 and 22.16. S/L Templeman-Rooke had been tasked with compiling a report of the raid, and after bombing, descended to 2,000 feet and was able to confirm "Altogether, a good show", during which there had been no interference from the enemy defences. Returning crews reported many fires and multi-coloured explosions with smoke rising through 4,000 feet as they turned away, and post-raid reconnaissance revealed almost total destruction of the town, which had been largely evacuated by the civilian population.

Fourteen crews were called to briefing at Fiskerton on the afternoon of the 8th to learn that they were to take part in the third and what would prove to be the final raid in a series against the I G Farben-owned Wintershall synthetic oil refinery at Politz, which had begun in December. Situated to the north of Stettin in what is now Poland, it represented a long round-trip of some 1,400 miles and was to be another two-phase attack led by a 5 Group force of 227 Lancasters and seven Mosquitos and completed two hours later by 184 Lancasters from 1 Group and fifty-seven representing 8 Group. All of the 576 Squadron aircraft were carrying a cookie and ten 500-pounders as they departed Fiskerton between 19.05 and 19.30 with W/C Sellick the senior pilot on duty and undertaking his ninth and final sortie as the squadron commander. They began the North Sea crossing at Mablethorpe and were accompanied by low cloud as far as 7° East, before climbing to cross the German coast under clear skies, which then persisted all the way to the target. An engine fire had forced F/L Living and crew to turn back when over Jutland and they jettisoned their payload off the western coast into the Waddensee. The others were drawn on by six fires resulting from the earlier 5 Group raid, and the attack opened on time with flares illuminating the plant, before marking began with red and green TIs from the Deputy Master Bomber at 23.10. These were well-placed on the aiming-point and were soon backed up by others to form an excellent concentration within the boundaries of the site. The marking was maintained throughout the attack, and the main force element exploited the opportunity to deliver a decisive blow against this important contributor to Germany's war effort, the 576 Squadron crews delivering their attacks from an average of 13,500 feet between 23.15 and 23.25. The entire area was soon covered by smoke, through which numerous explosions were observed, one of particular violence that lasted seconds and added another column of smoke to the pall that had reached 10,000 feet by the time that the last of the bombers had turned for home. The glow remained visible on the horizon for a hundred miles, and post-raid reconnaissance confirmed that the plant's ability to produce oil had been ended for good.

Two major operations were planned for the night of the 13/14th, the first by a main force of 326 Halifaxes from 4 and 6 Groups with thirty-four Lancasters and eight Mosquitos of 8 Group to provide the marking at the Braunkohle-Benzin oil plant at Böhlen, situated some seven miles to the south of Leipzig. On the Lancaster stations, meanwhile, briefings took place for the first round of Operation Thunderclap, the Churchill-inspired offensive against Germany's eastern cities, which was devised partly to act in support of the advancing Russians, and also as a demonstration to Stalin of RAF air power, should he turn against the Allies after the war. The historic and culturally significant city of Dresden was selected to open the offensive in another two-phase affair, with a 5 Group force of 246 Lancasters and nine Mosquitos leading the way, to be followed three hours later by 529 Lancasters of 1, 3, 6 and 8 Groups. It had proved to be a successful policy thus far, with the 5 Group low-level marking system and main force attacks providing a beacon for the second force, and should it be required on this night, 8 Group would provide any necessary marking for phase two from high level. The crews involved had absolutely no concept of the ramifications of the operation, both in terms of its outcome on the ground and its hysterical aftermath. Dresden was Germany's seventh largest city and its largest remaining intact built-up area, which, according to American sources, contained more than a hundred factories and fifty thousand workers contributing to the war effort. It was also an important railway hub, to the extent that the marshalling yards had been attacked twice in late 1944 by the USAAF.

The heavy force was two hours out when W/C Maurice Smith of 54 Base, the Master Bomber for the 5 Group attack, lifted off the Woodhall Spa runway at a few minutes before 20.00 hours in Mosquito KB401 AZ-E, a 627 Squadron aircraft, and he was followed away by eight others from 627 Squadron. The heavy brigade and the Mosquitos arrived in the target area at the same time to encounter three layers of cloud between 3,000 and 5,000 feet, 6,000 to 8,000 feet and 15,000 to 16,000 feet, but otherwise good visibility. The first primary blind marker crew delivered green TIs from 15,000 feet at 22.03 and was followed in by the flare force, which lit the way for the low-level Mosquitos. The main force Lancasters were carrying eight hundred tons of bombs, mostly in the form either of a cookie and twelve 500-pounders or one 2,000-pounder and fourteen cluster bombs, which were delivered onto the glow of red TIs in accordance with the Master Bomber's instructions. As far as the crews were concerned, this was no different from any other attack, and the fires visible for more than a hundred miles into the return journey were nothing out of the ordinary.

At Fiskerton, seven of fourteen participating 576 Squadron Lancasters were loaded with a 2,000-pounder supplemented with either cluster bombs or standard incendiaries, while the remaining seven had a cookie and mix of cluster bombs and incendiaries in the bomb bay as part of a 1 Group contribution to the operation of 260 aircraft. The 576 Squadron contingent took off between 21.15 and 21.35 with S/L Templeman-Rooke the senior pilot on duty, accompanied by the station commander, G/C Arbuthnot, while W/C Morton was flying as second pilot to F/O Hardman to gain experience before assuming command of 100 Squadron in March. The operation began badly for 1 Group when a 300 Squadron Lancaster collided with another from 550 Squadron, and both aircraft fell to earth near Fiskerton, in response to which the Fiskerton fire crews and crash tenders raced to the scene to render whatever assistance they could, sadly to no avail as far as saving lives was concerned. The others began the Channel crossing at Hastings en-route to making landfall on the French side near Abbeville, by which time, F/L Campbell and crew had landed at Carnaby complaining of an unserviceable air speed indicator. The bomber stream pressed on under clear skies until arriving at 3° East, when large amounts of broken cloud reached 18,000 feet, only to disperse from 12° East to leave clear skies over the target and a large bank of cloud threatening a short distance away to the east. By the time that this second force of 1, 3, 6 and 8 Group Lancasters arrived over Dresden three hours after 5 Group, the fires created by the earlier attack provided the expected reference point. The 576 Squadron crews delivered their attacks on green and then red TIs from an average of 18,500 feet between 01.30 and 01.50, their bombs among a further eighteen hundred tons raining down onto the historic and beautiful old city, setting off the same chain of events that had devastated parts of Hamburg in July 1943 and a number of other cities since. F/O Carter had shut down an ailing engine before reaching the target, but pressed on to bomb from 12,000 feet, and after losing a second engine on the way home, landed safely at Juvincourt. A homebound SW276 lost its starboard-inner engine to predicted flak at Nuremberg, and having reached Strasbourg, S/L Templeman-Rooke abandoned the briefed route and headed directly for home.

Dresden's population had been swelled by masses of refugees fleeing from the eastern front, and many were engulfed in the ensuing firestorm, which was still burning on the following morning, when three hundred American bombers carried out a separate attack under the umbrella of a fighter escort and completed the destruction. There were claims in Germany that RAF aircraft had strafed the streets and open spaces to increase the level of terror, and such accusations abound in the city to this day. In fact, American fighters were responsible and were trying to add to the general confusion and chaos. Initial propaganda-inspired reports from the Office of the Propaganda Minister, Joseph Göbbels, falsely claimed a death toll of 250,000 people, but an accurate figure of twenty-five thousand has been settled upon since. The operation cost Bomber Command only eight Lancasters, including 576 Squadron's PD232, which crashed in southern Germany with no survivors from the crew of F/O Young.

The destruction of Dresden has been used by some in this country also as a weapon with which to denigrate Bomber Command and Harris, and label them as war criminals. Curiously, no accusations have been levelled at the Americans. It should also be understood that Harris had no interest in attacking Dresden and had to be nagged by Chief-of-the-Air-Staff Portal to fulfil Churchill's wishes. The aircrew simply did the job asked of them, and the Dresden raid was no different from any other attack on a city. The death toll at Hamburg was much higher, and yet, there has been no similar outcry. The legacy of this operation served to deny Harris and the men under his Command their due recognition for the massive part they played in the ultimate victory, and only in recent times has a monument been erected in Green Park in London and a campaign clasp awarded, sadly, far too little and far too late for the majority. Churchill, with his eyes set on a peacetime election, betrayed Harris and the Command in a typical politically motivated U-turn, in which he accused Harris of bombing solely for the purpose of inflicting terror. In the post-war honours, Harris was the only commander in the field to be omitted.

Briefings for round two of Operation Thunderclap took place across the Command on the 14th, when crews learned that the highly industrialised city of Chemnitz would be the target for 717 aircraft drawn from 1, 3, 4, 6 and 8 Groups, which would be divided into two waves separated by three-and-a-half hours. The city contained many factories manufacturing military hardware, including the Siegmar tank-engine works and an oil refinery and was home to the headquarters of the Auto Union automotive company. The Flossenbürg female forced workers camp had a subcamp in the city to provide slave labour for the Astrawerke A.G factory that produced calculator machines. 5 Group would also be in the area on this night with 224 Lancasters and eight Mosquitos to target an oil refinery in the small town of Rositz, situated twenty-five miles due south of Leipzig and thirty miles north-west of Chemnitz. 1 Group put together a force of 202 Lancasters for the second phase of the main event, fourteen of them made ready by 576 Squadron, of which six were loaded with a 2,000-pounder supplemented by eleven cluster bombs, one with a 2,000-pounder and standard incendiaries and the rest with a cookie and 1,170 x 4lb incendiaries. In addition to supporting the main event, 1 Group detailed twenty Lancasters for mining duties in the Sweet Pea Garden in the Kadet Channel between Denmark's Lolland Island and Warnemünde on Germany's Mecklenburg Bay coast.

The 576 Squadron element departed Fiskerton between 20.00 and 20.30 with F/Ls Acheson, Campbell, Collins, Halnan, Living and Thieme the senior pilots on duty, and enjoyed favourable conditions during the outward flight via Hastings and Abbeville, until reaching 11° East, where cloud built to ten-tenths with tops at between 10,000 and 18,000 feet, and extended to the target and beyond. The Master Bomber issued a time check at 00.15, and he was then heard to call for markers at 00.25, to which the Path Finder blind markers responded with green TIs delivered on H2S. These disappeared quickly into the cloud, forcing the Master Bomber to call for skymarking, in response to which four Path Finder aircraft released green/red flares without achieving concentration. The Master Bomber ordered the main force crews to aim for the skymarkers until 00.30, at which point, with so few remaining visible, he instructed them to bomb on navigational aids. Any marking that took place was sparse and inadequate and the subsequent bombing became scattered over a wide area. The Fiskerton crews carried out their attacks on H2S from an average of 18,000 feet between 00.30 and 00.50 and had no clue as to what was happening beneath the clouds. Most crews returned home dissatisfied with the conduct of the raid but reported that fires appeared to be taking hold across the target area, the glow from which lingered on the horizon for at least an hour into the homeward flight. Meanwhile, the gardeners had enjoyed excellent conditions and had planted thirty mines between them on H2S from 12,000 feet between 21.06 and 21.17. Post-raid reconnaissance at Chemnitz confirmed that many parts of the city had been hit, but that much of the effort had been wasted in open country.

Preparations for the next operation were put in hand on the 20th, when a major assault was planned on the southern half of Dortmund, for which a force of 514 Lancasters was assembled from 1, 3, 6 and 8 Groups. 1 Group detailed 271 Lancasters, seventeen of them belonging to 576 Squadron, nine of which had a cookie as the main armament, while eight received a 2,000-pounder, and the remaining space in the bomb bays was filled with cluster bombs and standard incendiaries. They departed Fiskerton between 21.30 and 21.55 with the newly promoted and B Flight commander-elect, S/L Dutton, the senior pilot on duty, and as they climbed away into clear skies, further north a force of 156 Halifaxes of 4 Group was climbing out over Yorkshire before heading south the join up with a Path Finder element for an attack on the Rhenania-Ossag oil refinery in the Reisholz district of Düsseldorf. As the two bomber streams made their way to their respective targets via the Sussex coast, the sky filled rapidly with cloud from 5° East and was at eight to ten-tenths over the north-eastern Ruhr, but very low and thin enough for the red Oboe TIs to be clearly visible. At 00.58, the Path Finder visual centerer crews released green TIs, and from then onwards the ground marking was well concentrated and maintained and was supplemented by green skymarkers, which, unfortunately, tended to fall short and, as a result, created a marking creep-back for fourteen miles along the line of approach. The bombing in the early stages was accurate, but as the cloud thickened and the glow through the clouds diminished, it became scattered and much of it fell short. The 576 Squadron crews carried out their attacks from an average of 18,000 feet between 01.03 and 01.20, and all but one returned home safely to report developing fires but no detail. It was an expensive night for the Command for the period and cost fourteen Lancasters, ten of them belonging to 1 Group, among which was 576 Squadron's NF975, which disappeared without trace with the crew of F/O Bastick. The authorities in Dortmund were beyond the ability to produce an account of the raid, and the next major attack in three weeks' time would obliterate all traces of this night and leave the city totally paralysed.

Responsibility for the final heavy raid of the war on the much-bombed city of Duisburg was handed to 362 Lancasters of 1, 6 and 8 Groups on the night of the 21/22nd, for which 1 Group assembled a force of 245 Lancasters, sixteen of them made ready by 576 Squadron. Each received a bomb load of a cookie supplemented with eleven deep SBCs, each containing 150 x 4lb incendiaries and two other SBCs of 60 x 4lbs, before departing Elsham Wolds between 19.30 and 20.13 with no fewer than nine pilots of flight lieutenant rank taking the lead. After climbing away, they headed south to the Sussex coast in conditions of little or no cloud, which persisted until shortly before the target was reached, when a band of stratus a thousand feet thick slid over the city at 15,000 feet to cover it completely. The winds outbound were different from those forecast at briefing, and this delayed the arrival of the main force by a few minutes. As they approached, the crews could see the first red TIs cascading at 22.56, but by the time they arrived to bomb, these had disappeared below the cloud and no more were evident until 23.08. Some considerable difficulty was experienced in identifying the target, and incendiaries were seen to be dropped all the way from Krefeld to Duisburg. By 23.10, the cloud was beginning to break up and a better concentration was achieved, and had a Master Bomber been present, he might have been able to compensate for the scarcity of the marking. The Fiskerton crews delivered their attacks from an average of 17,500 feet between 23.03 and 23.22, and on return reported large explosions. It had been an eventful night for 576 Squadron crews, many of whom reported single-engine jet/rocket propelled fighters, F/O Croft's mid-upper gunner engaging one from 500 yards range as it attacked from head-on, observing it to explode and fall in pieces. At 00.10, a signal was received from F/L Halnan and crew to the effect that flak had set off a fire in the bomb bay and that they were abandoning NG464 to its fate between Reims and Juvincourt, a later message confirming that they were safe. Less fortunate was the crew of F/L Living RCAF in ME735, which crashed with great force and exploded south of Kevelaer on Germany's frontier with Holland, killing all on board. RA516 crashed further south near Roermond in liberated Holland, killing three members of the crew, while F/L Thieme and three others survived. Post-raid reconnaissance eventually confirmed the operation to have been successful.

A Halifax main force of 297 aircraft from 4 and 6 Groups was made ready on the morning of the 23rd to send against Essen in the afternoon, and despite complete cloud cover and the use of skymarking, most of the bombing fell squarely into the Krupp districts. The day's operations were not yet over, however, and a force of 366 Lancasters, plus one from the Film Unit and thirteen Mosquitos, was drawn from 1, 6 and 8 Groups to send against the city of Pforzheim, situated in southern Germany between Karlsruhe to the north-west and Stuttgart to the south-east. This would be the first area raid on the city, which was known as a centre for jewellery and watch manufacture but was believed by the Allies to be involved also in the production of precision instruments in support of Germany's war effort. 1 Group detailed 258 Lancasters, fifteen of them representing 576 Squadron, each of which received a bomb load of a cookie and twelve SBCs of 4lb incendiaries, before departing Fiskerton between 15.45 and 16.00 with S/L Dutton the senior pilot on duty. They climbed out through ten-tenths low cloud, which persisted until the bombers had crossed the French coast near Abbeville, where it began to break up, leaving the skies clear under a bright moon as the target drew near. The thin veil of ground haze proved to be no impediment, and the first red Oboe TIs went down at 19.52, to be followed quickly by illuminator flares and salvoes of concentrated reds and greens. The Fiskerton crews delivered their attacks from an unusually low 7,000 to 9,000 feet between 20.00 and 20.10, and fires rapidly took hold until the whole town north of the river looked like a sea of flames. By 20.06, the fires were too dazzling for the TIs to be visible, after which, the Master Bomber ordered the smoke to be bombed.

The raid lasted twenty-two minutes, during which 1,825 tons of bombs fell into the built-up area, reducing 83% of it to ruins and setting off a firestorm in which 17,600 people lost their lives. This was the highest death toll to result from a single attack on a German city after Hamburg (40,000) and Dresden (25,000). It was during this operation that the final Victoria Cross was earned by a member of RAF Bomber Command. It went posthumously to the Master Bomber from 582 Squadron, Captain Ed Swales of the South African Air Force, who continued to control the attack in a Lancaster severely damaged by a night-fighter, before sacrificing his life to allow his crew the opportunity to save themselves. At debriefing, F/L Leyton-Brown and crew claimed a Ju88 destroyed after it was seen to crash, and F/O O'Neill and crew claimed another as damaged.

S/L Templeman-Rooke was posted from the squadron on the 25th to take command of 170 Squadron at Hemswell and having proved to be a popular and inspirational A Flight commander, would be missed by the squadron and station communities. W/C Sellick DFC & Bar concluded his third tour at the end of the month, during the course of which, the squadron had taken part in ten operations and dispatched 140 sorties for the loss of seven Lancasters, four complete crews and three additional airmen.

March 1945

Just when the crews must have been thinking that bomber operations were becoming safer, March came along to prove them wrong. The new month would see the Command continue to bludgeon its way across Germany, concentrating on oil, rail and road targets, along with the few towns still boasting a built-up area, and began for 576 Squadron with the arrival of a new commanding officer. Neither the squadron nor 1 Group ORBs make mention of W/C Commander F R McAllister's previous appointments, and the author can find no record of his service. As his first sortie with the squadron, towards the end of the month, would be as a second pilot, the likelihood is that he arrived with no previous operational experience, possibly having spent the war as an instructor. It was not unusual at this stage of the war for operationally inexperienced officers to be given a command, despite the annoyance it must have caused to flight commanders who had been putting their lives on the line only to be overlooked when a vacancy arose. The city of Mannheim was selected to host the first operation of the penultimate month of the bombing war, which would take place in daylight on the 1st and prove to be the final one of the many visited upon this particular target. It was a 1, 6 and 8 Group force of 372 Lancasters and ninety Halifaxes that prepared for take-off that morning, among them 248 Lancasters representing 1 Group. At Fiskerton, 576 Squadron loaded thirteen Lancasters with a cookie and thirteen SBCs of 4lb incendiaries and sent them on their way between 11.40 and 12.00 with the station commander, G/C Arbuthnot, the senior pilot on duty.

After climbing out, they made for the Sussex coast, joining up with the rest of the 1 Group force and forming into vics in line astern led by the Hemswell units, which were employing yellow verey lights, yellow trailing lights and light green fins to aid identification. They began the Channel crossing over five-tenths cloud and maintained good formation as the cloud built to ten-tenths from the French coast, the tailwind lighter than forecast, despite which, no attempt was made to make up time. They arrived at the target some six minutes later than planned, and at 14.47, the Master Bomber was heard to ask his Deputy if he could see the main force, to which he received a negative response and ordered the marker force to orbit above the 12,000-foot cloud tops until 15.03, when he called for release-point flares. Blue smoke-puff skymarkers went down accurately and in concentration, and the main force crews were instructed to aim for the centre of these, the Fiskerton crews complying and delivering their loads from an average of 18,000 feet between 15.07 and 15.15. On return, they were unable to provide an assessment of the results and there was no post-raid reconnaissance or local report to provide clarity, but it is known that many bombs fell on neighbouring Ludwigshafen and its surrounds, where much damage occurred.

With Cologne now almost on the front line, it, too, was earmarked for its final attack of the war on the morning of the 2nd, for a which a two-phase operation was planned, the first by 703 aircraft from 1, 4, 6 and 8 Groups, and the second, a G-H attack by 155 Lancasters of 3 Group. 1 Group contributed 244 Lancasters, fourteen of them belonging to 576 Squadron, each loaded with a cookie, a dozen 500 and four 250-pounders, before departing Fiskerton between 07.00 and 07.15 with F/Ls Acheson, Campbell, Crowther, Dotten and Sleight the senior pilots on duty. After climbing out, they pointed their snouts towards Beachy Head to take their place in the elongated bomber stream, before beginning the Channel crossing and reaching the target to find near perfect bombing conditions with a little cloud topping out at around 6,000 feet. A Master Bomber was on hand to tell crews where to bomb, although the city's landmarks, the cathedral and nearby main railway station and the Hohenzollern railway bridge stood out in the sunshine, almost inviting the bombs to fall. The 576 Squadron crews released their bombs onto red and green TIs from an average of 17,000 feet between 10.00 and 10.06, and many, for a change, were able to see the fall of their bombs. It wasn't long before a mushroom of black smoke began to conceal the ground, and later crews were instructed to bomb the up-wind edge of that. The main concentration of bombing was on the western side of the Rhine, and the western end of the Hohenzollern railway bridge appeared to have been demolished and had collapsed into the Rhine. The second wave by 3 Group was ruined by the failure of a G-H station in England and had to be halted after only fifteen aircraft had bombed. It mattered little, as the damage was done, and the once proud city fell to American forces four days later.

The night of the 3/4th brought mining sorties in one of the Silverthorn gardens of the Kattegat for fifteen 1 Group crews from 12, 14 and 15 Bases, and it was also the night chosen by the Luftwaffe to launch Operation Gisella, which involved some two hundred intruders stalking returning bombers as they prepared to land. They succeeded in bringing down twenty bombers, including one Lancaster from 460 Squadron RAAF returning to Binbrook from the Kattegat and two from 12 Squadron which were on training exercises.

Preparations for Operation Thunderclap to return to Chemnitz were put in hand on the 5th, and a force of 760 aircraft assembled from all but 5 Group, which itself would be active some thirty-five miles to the north, attacking the oil refinery at Böhlen. 1 Group dispatched 239 Lancasters, eight of the fifteen representing 576 Squadron loaded with a cookie and eleven SBCs of 4lb incendiaries and seven with a 2,000-pounder plus a dozen SBCs, before departing Fiskerton between 16.40 and 17.20 with F/L Leyton-Brown the most senior of the flight lieutenant pilots taking part. Those taking off from the more northerly stations, particularly those of 6 Group, climbed into ten-tenths cloud with severe icing conditions, which caused nine of them to crash. Aside from a slight reduction over the Channel and northern France, the complete cloud cover remained in place all the way to the target area, and there were reports of predicted flak around Leipzig and Halle, which had probably been stirred-up by the above-mentioned 5 Group operation. F/L Dotten and crew lost an engine when some sixty miles east of Kassel but pressed on to the target, struggling to maintain height at 13,500 feet over the ten-tenths cloud five hundred feet below them that concealed the city. They and the rest of the main force element had to listened out for the Master Bomber's instructions as they lined up for the bombing-run, and on observing cascading red and green skymarkers, complied with instructions at 21.50 to bomb them with a twelve-second overshoot from 15,000 feet. When the skymarkers went out at 21.55, a new instruction was issued, to bomb the glow in the clouds, before further skymarkers appeared and the original order was reinstated.

The 576 Squadron crews carried out their attacks from an average of 16,000 feet between 21.46 and 22.04 in the face of negligible opposition from the ground, but were unable to assess the outcome, reporting only a bright glow beneath the clouds that seemed to cover an area a mile wide. As they turned south towards the Czechoslovakian frontier for the homeward flight across southern Germany, they left behind them F/O Rouse RCAF and his mixed RAF/RCAF crew, who all lost their lives when PD403 crashed in the target area. Some were pestered on the way home by enemy night-fighters, which were probably responsible for the failure to return of fourteen Lancasters and eight Halifaxes. It was established eventually that the operation had been a major success, which had destroyed by fire much of the central and southern districts of the city and also resulted in damage to some important war-industry factories, including the Siegmar tank-engine works, which suffered destruction.

The main operation on the 7th was to be undertaken by 526 aircraft of 1, 3, 6 and 8 Group against the virgin target of Dessau, a city in eastern Germany between Berlin to the north and Leipzig to the south. While this was in progress, 256 Halifaxes and twenty-five Lancasters of 4, 6 and 8 Groups were to target the Deutsche Erdöl oil refinery at Hemmingstedt on the western side of Schleswig-Holstein, while 5 Group went for a similar target at Harburg on the south side of the

River Elbe opposite Hamburg. 1 Group contributed 243 Lancasters to the Dessau raid, seventeen of them belonging to 576 Squadron, ten of which carried a cookie as their main armament, while the rest received a 2,000-pounder, and all loads were supplemented with SBCs of incendiaries. They departed Fiskerton between 16.55 and 17.15 with F/L Leyton-Brown the most senior among six participating pilots of similar rank, and climbed out through complete cloud-cover, which persisted as the stream adopted a circuitous route via the Sussex coast to make landfall on the French side of the Channel north-east of Dieppe. The briefed route traversed Belgium and skirted the southern Ruhr, where the cloud thinned to up to five-tenths, before building again to eight to ten-tenths with tops at 10,000 feet as the bombers headed on a north-easterly track to the target. Night-fighters had infiltrated the bomber stream from the Rhine, and flak intensified in the Braunschweig and Magdeburg defence zones.

As the main force crews approached the city, which, since 1925, had been home to the famous Bauhaus architectural school, they observed illuminating flares going down at 21.56, followed by red and green TIs, which proved not to be visible through the cloud. Release point flares soon joined the mix, and they were concentrated at first, but became scattered later, as the Master Bomber's instructions suffered from interference after someone in a main force aircraft left a transmitter on. Fortunately, a large break in the clouds at 22.04 provided a clear view of the ground and the many TIs still burning, and the main force crews were able to take advantage. The 576 Squadron crews carried out their attacks from an average of 14,000 feet between 22.00 and 22.10 and observed widespread fires revealing a distinct pattern of streets, and among many explosions were three particularly large ones at 22.03. 22.13 and 22.15, and another producing a large bluish flash at 22.08. At 22.18, a section of the town burning with white flames suddenly erupted in a terrific red burst and continued to burn red. There was a mention at some debriefings of "scarecrows" over the Ruhr on the way home, which were, of course, the final moments of some of the eighteen Lancasters that failed to return. Among the twelve 1 Group absentee Lancasters were two belonging to 576 Squadron, including PD363 "Mighty Atom", which contained the "wind-finder" crew of F/O Paley, who were last heard from at 21.35 as they passed on wind details to group. The Lancaster crashed somewhere in France on the way to the target and there were no survivors. RF120 came down some thirty-five miles east of Düsseldorf, also while outbound, and only F/O Dalziel and his bomb-aimer survived to fall into enemy hands. The operation caused extensive damage in the town centre and residential, industrial and railway districts, all of which would have to be completely rebuilt after the war, sadly, in the Eastern Bloc style of featureless concrete architecture.

The pace of operations refused to slacken, and what, perhaps, should have been a wind-down towards the German capitulation, became one of the most intense operational periods in the entire war. With six major operations already behind it during the first week of the month, the second week began for 8 Group with orders on the 8th to provide sixty-two Lancasters and ten Mosquitos to mark for 241 Halifaxes of 4 and 6 Groups for an attack on the Blohm & Voss U-Boot yards in Hamburg, where the new Type XXI vessels were under construction. While this operation was in progress, 235 Lancasters of 1 Group would be joining twenty-seven others and fourteen Mosquitos of 8 Group to raid Kassel, some 150 miles to the south. 576 Squadron made ready fifteen Lancasters for what would be the last major raid upon it of the war and the first return to this destination since the devastating raid in late October 1943. Each was loaded with a cookie supplemented with eleven SBCs of 4lb incendiaries and departed Fiskerton between 17.00 and

17.25 with F/Ls Leyton-Brown and Sleight the senior pilots on duty. They climbed out through nine to ten-tenths thin cloud topping out at around 5,000 feet, and this accompanied the bomber stream all the way from the Sussex coast, over France and Belgium, until decreasing slightly as the route swung to the north of the Ruhr. Cloud built again as the force headed south-east for the target, which was found to be covered by eight to ten-tenths topping out at 6,000 feet. The attack opened on time with both sky and ground markers, the latter clearly visible through the cloud, and although the red TIs were a little sparse, greens were plentiful. The skymarking was less accurate, but as most crews focused on the TIs, it mattered little, and when a gap opened up over the city, crews were able to assess for themselves the quality of the marking. Those representing 576 Squadron attacked from an average of 20,000 feet between 21.30 and 21.45 and observed fires building steadily in the western half of the city, the glow from which hung in the sky to remain visible for a hundred miles and more. F/O McClelland and crew were on their thirty-sixth sortie and were forced to land at Juvincourt after both inner engines began to fail. No local report emerged from Kassel to provide details of the damage, which would have been severe.

An all-time record was set on the 11th, when 1,079 aircraft, the largest Bomber Command force ever to be sent to a single target, was assembled to attack Essen for the last time. 1 Group contributed 240 Lancasters, fifteen of them belonging to 576 Squadron, which each received a bomb load of a cookie and sixteen 500-pounders, before taking off from Fiskerton between 11.35 and 12.00 with S/L Dutton the senior pilot on duty. They climbed out through ten-tenths cloud, above which conditions were excellent, but the ground would remain concealed from view throughout the operation. All arrived in the central Ruhr to find the cloud tops at 6,000 feet, which required the Path Finder element to employ skymarkers in the form of blue, and later red smoke puffs, and the first of these went down at 14.59, to be backed up throughout the course of the raid. The 576 Squadron crews delivered their bombs from an average of 17,500 feet between 15.00 and 15.10 as part of a total of more than 4,600 tons to complete the destruction of the already ravaged city and former industrial powerhouse. Smoke and dust emerged through the cloud tops in a tight spiral that had reached 10,000 feet as the last of the bombers retreated, and the city would still be in a state of paralysis when the American ground forces captured it unopposed on the 10th of April.

Twenty-four hours after the Essen raid, the short-lived record was surpassed by the departure from their stations in the early afternoon of 1,108 aircraft, which had Dortmund as their destination. This time 1 Group provided 244 Lancasters, sixteen made ready at Fiskerton, each loaded with a cookie and sixteen 500-pounders, before taking off between 13.00 and 13.25 with F/Ls Acheson, Crowther, Dotten and Leyton-Brown the senior pilots on duty. Having adopted the southerly route, they all reached the eastern Ruhr to find it still under a blanket of ten-tenths cloud with tops again at 6,000 feet, conditions for which the Path Finders had prepared a skymarking plan based on green and blue smoke puffs. The first Oboe-aimed greens appeared at 16.26 to be followed a minute later by blues from the blind primary markers, and the Master Bomber directed the main force crews to aim for the latter. It was not long before brown smoke was observed to be climbing through the clouds to 8,000 feet from the northern end of the city, and crews also reported a ring of smoke encircling the entire area so dense that it remained visible for 120 miles into the return flight. The 576 Squadron crews carried out their attacks from an average of 17,500 feet between 16.30 and 16.40 and contributed to the delivery of a new record of 4,800 tons of bombs. Photo-reconnaissance revealed that the central and southern districts of the city had received the greatest weight of bombs and had been left in chaos with all industry silenced permanently and railway tracks torn up.

Elements of 1 and 8 Groups joined forces on the evening of the 13th, to attack two benzol producers in the Ruhr, the Erin plant at Herne, located between Bochum and Gelsenkirchen, and the Dahlbusch A.G plant, south of the Gelsenkirchen city centre. 1 Group detailed seventy-eight Lancasters from 12 and 13 Bases for the former and eighty-one from 14 and 15 Bases for the latter, while 576 Squadron was given the night off. The partial cloud cover over England gave way to clear skies during the Channel crossing from Hastings to Le Touquet and as far as the Rhine, where cloud built to nine-tenths with tops at 10,000 to 12,000 feet with considerable haze below. The first red and green TIs went down three-and-a-half minutes late at 20.29½ and were visible only by their feint glow beneath the cloud, as a result of which, most crews bombed on H2S or Gee. A large white explosion was witnessed at 20.31, but an assessment of the raid was impossible, and the impression was that much of the bombing had under and overshot the aiming point. This was confirmed by post-raid reconnaissance, which also revealed the Gelsenkirchen raid to have been successful.

Benzol plants at Bottrop and Castrop-Rauxel in the Ruhr occupied elements of 4, 6 and 8 Groups during the afternoon of the 15th, while 1 and 8 Group stations were conducting briefings for the evening operation against the Deurag-Nerag oil refinery at Misburg, on the north-eastern rim of Hannover. 1 Group detailed a main force of 212 Lancasters supported by forty-six Path Finder Lancasters and nine Mosquitos, the 576 Squadron element of fifteen departing Fiskerton between 17.15 and 17.35 with F/Ls Acheson, Collins, Crowther, Dotten and Leyton-Brown the senior pilots on duty and each crew sitting on a cookie and ten SBCs of 4lb incendiaries. The Channel crossing began at Beachy Head and terminated at Le Treport in what was a most circuitous route for a target in northern Germany, that crossed France, Belgium and Holland, before entering Germany to the north of Duisburg and swinging towards Hannover from the south. The passage across enemy territory both out and in benefitted from cloudless skies, and this enabled crews to identify the target visually by the light of illuminator flares. The raid began punctually with red TIs, backed up by mixed reds and greens in great concentration right on the aiming-point, and the Master Bomber called in the main force at 21.12. Almost immediately the target was engulfed in flames, and smoke was observed to rise through 10,000 feet following an explosion at 21.13. The Fiskerton crews delivered their bomb loads from an average of 18,000 feet between 21.14 and 21.30 and returned home to report a highly successful operation, characterised by many explosions and fires that created a glow visible from a hundred miles into the return journey. There was particular praise from the main force crews for the performance of the Master Bomber and the Path Finder element generally.

This was the thirty-eighth and final operation for Australian, F/L Howard Leyton-Brown, and his crew, for which he was awarded a DFC. He had been pursuing a career in music in Europe before the war, and on joining the RAF was sent to Canada to train as a pilot, meeting his future wife there, and bringing her back with him to England. Having survived an eventful tour, he was posted to Canada as an instructor but would return to England postwar to continue his music career, serving for a time as the leader of the London Philharmonic Orchestra, until emigrating to Canada in 1952.

Nuremberg was posted as 1 Group's target on the 16th, for which a main force of 231 Lancasters was assembled, supported by forty-six Lancasters and sixteen Mosquitos of 8 Group. A simultaneous operation by 225 Lancasters and eleven Mosquitos of 5 Group was to take place at Würzburg some fifty miles to the north-west, and the presence of more than five hundred aircraft was likely to draw a Luftwaffe night-fighter response despite the shortage of experienced pilots and aviation fuel. 576 Squadron launched fifteen Lancasters from Fiskerton between 17.15 and 17.35 with F/Ls Acheson, Collins, Crowther, De-Mille, Dotten and Halnan the senior pilots on duty and each crew sitting on a cookie and eleven SBCs of incendiaries. F/L Halnan and crew aborted their sortie during the climb-out when the rear turret became unserviceable, and they headed directly for the jettison area, leaving the others to exit the English coast in the region of Beachy Head and make landfall on the other side near Abbeville. Partial cloud cover increased to ten-tenths at the French coast with tops at 14,000 feet, but this broke up slowly to leave four to six-tenths in the target area with tops at 7,000 to 9,000 feet. A stronger than forecast wind drove the spearhead of the main force to the target ahead of schedule, and half a dozen of these bombed five minutes before H-Hour and before the appearance of any markers. F/L De-Mille and crew were attacked by a Ju88 at 18,000 feet, when short of the target, and sustained extensive damage to the port wing, falling to 4,000 feet before control was regained. Undaunted, they clawed back five thousand feet of altitude and bombed a last-resort target, a small town estimated to be some thirty miles south of Nuremberg. The Path Finder illuminator crews officially opened the attack on time at 21.24, and a large gap opened up in the cloud to reveal the red and green TIs on the ground. The master Bomber provided clear instructions with which the 576 Squadron crews complied as they bombed from an average of 17,000 feet between 21.30 and 21.40, and as smoke began to obscure the ground at around 21.35, the Master Bomber instructed crews to aim for bomb bursts. By this time smoke had risen through 7,000 feet and developing fires were outlining streets before merging into a single conflagration that produced a glow on the horizon for 150 miles.

The flak was relatively ineffective, but night-fighter activity was intense from the Stuttgart area to the target and back as far as the bomb line, and a shocking twenty-four 1 Group Lancasters failed to return, 10.4% of those dispatched. Many 1 Group squadrons posted missing multiple aircraft, 12 Squadron alone having four unaccounted for, while three 103 Squadron dispersal pans stood empty at Elsham Wolds and a similar number at Fiskerton. All three 576 Squadron casualties came down somewhere in southern Germany, PA265 with the crew of F/Sgt Ryan RAAF, from which the rear gunner alone survived in enemy hands. PB785 contained the predominantly RCAF crew of F/L Dotten RCAF, from which none survived, the only RAF member, flight engineer, Sgt Eve, thirty-six years of age and well above the normal for aircrew. There were, at least, three survivors from ME317, pilot, F/Sgt Sattler RAAF, and his navigator and bomb-aimer, who were all taken into captivity. Heavy damage was caused in the southern half of the city and the already devastated Altstadt, and more than five hundred people lost their lives, many in one of the south-western districts ravaged by fire.

Operations continued to come thick and fast, and the next target was also in southern Germany. Hanau's railway system had been attacked in January, and now it was time for an area attack, which was to be carried out by a 1 Group main force of 230 Lancasters, supported as always by a strong Path Finder element. 576 Squadron made ready thirteen aircraft, which departed Fiskerton unusually late for the period, between 00.30 and 01.10 on the 19th, with S/Ls Bradbury and Dutton the senior pilots on duty, the former having arrived on posting as successor to S/L Templeman-

Rooke as A Flight commander. Harold Bradbury had been a Hurricane pilot during the siege of Malta in 1941 and was injured when force-landing at Luqa in January of that year, but his operational career, thereafter, is unclear. Each bomb bay contained a cookie and twelve SBCs of 4lb incendiaries as the Lancasters climbed out through layer cloud and set course for the south coast and the Channel, pressing on with cloud alternately building and dispersing all the way out until 8° East, where the skies cleared but the ground became obscured by thick haze. The first illuminating flares were seen at H-15, and these were followed immediately by both skymarkers and red and green TIs, which fell in excellent concentration and stood out clearly through the haze until obliterated by the ensuing bombing. The 576 Squadron crews carried out their attacks from 10,000 to 12,000 feet between 04.30 and 04.37, at which point the Master Bomber issued instructions to bomb the upwind edge of the smoke. Crews headed for home confident that they had contributed to a highly effective raid, which would be confirmed by post-raid reconnaissance and local sources that revealed the destruction of 2,240 houses, the devastation of the Altstadt and damage to most of the public buildings.

1 Group alerted 13 and 15 Bases on the 21st to prepare for an operation against the Deutsche Vacuum oil refinery in Bremen, for which 104 Lancasters were made ready to act as the main force, with twenty-nine Lancasters and six Mosquitos of 8 Group to provide the marking. 576 Squadron loaded each of a dozen Lancasters with a cookie and sixteen 500-pounders and sent them on their way from Fiskerton between 07.45 and 07.55 with S/L Bradbury the senior pilot on duty. They set course via Wainfleet for Egmond on the Dutch coast, and all arrived in the target area under clear skies and with the Path Finder marking punctual and concentrated on the aiming point. They carried out their attacks from 14,000 to 15,000 feet between 10.00 and 10.03 in accordance with the instructions of the Master Bomber and in the face of an intense and accurate flak barrage, which caused mostly minor damage to five 576 Squadron Lancasters. JB410 was hit in the port-inner engine, which F/O Simpson was unable to feather, and they landed on the former Luftwaffe aerodrome at Eindhoven, returning to base on the following day. Later, that night, 117 Lancasters of 12 and 14 Bases conducted an operation with elements of 8 Group against the benzol plant in the Bruchstrasse district of Bochum in the heart of the Ruhr.

Elements of 1, 6 and 8 Groups were selected to deliver the only heavy raid of the war on the city of Hildesheim, situated south-east of Hannover and south-west of Braunschweig (Brunswick), where the aiming-point was the marshalling yards. However, any major operation at this stage of the war was essentially an area attack, for which a force of 227 Lancasters and eight Mosquitos was made ready on the 22nd. 1 Group detailed a hundred Lancasters from 13 and 15 Bases, the thirteen belonging to 576 Squadron each receiving a load of a cookie and fourteen SBCs of 4lb incendiaries, before departing Fiskerton between 11.15 and 11.40 with S/L Dutton the senior pilot on duty. They adopted the same course across the North Sea as for the Bremen operation, via Wainfleet and Egmond, and all arrived under clear skies and good visibility, which enabled ground features to be identified. In contrast to the previous operation, defence was non-existent and the 576 Squadron crews delivered their attacks from around 15,000 feet shortly after 14.00 and in accordance with the Master Bomber's instructions. A large column of smoke was rising through 6,000 feet as the last of the bombers turned away, and it was established later that a highly effective raid had laid waste to 70% of the town, including 3,300 apartment blocks containing around ten thousand individual dwelling units. Following this operation, F/L Crowther was declared tour-expired.

A daylight operation was posted on 12 and 14 Base stations on the 23rd, which involved ninety-seven 1 Group Lancasters following on the heels of twenty Tallboy and Grand Slam-carrying Lancasters of 5 Group's 617 Squadron to target a railway bridge in Bremen. On the following day, eighty crews on 13 and 15 Base stations attended briefings to learn of that afternoon's operation against the Harpenerweg benzol plant in Dortmund, for which 576 Squadron detailed ten of its Lancasters, loading each with a cookie and sixteen 500-pounders, before dispatching them from Fiskerton between 12.55 and 13.10 with F/Ls Collins and De-Mille the senior pilots on duty and the new commanding officer, W/C McAllister, flying as second pilot to F/O Button. They headed south to begin the Channel crossing at Hastings and made landfall on the French coast near Berck-sur-Mer in ideal conditions, which persisted all the way to the target. F/L De-Mille's RA514 was hit in both mainplanes and tailplanes while orbiting the target awaiting instructions and also had a burst tyre, but delivered an attack and landed safely on return. The TIs stood out clearly on the aiming point, inviting the bomb loads to fall in accordance with the instructions of the Master Bomber from 17,500 to 19,000 feet between 16.30 and 16.33 in the face of a spirited flak defence. F/O Graham and crew lost their hydraulics and, on landing without flaps, ran off the end of the runway, coming to a halt in a field with no further damage. Returning crews were confident in the quality of their work and reported that they had left behind them a pall of smoke rising through 8,000 feet. After landing safely, F/O Till and crew were declared tour-expired.

Operations on the 25th were directed at urban areas through which enemy reinforcements might pass on their way to the Rhine battle area. 4 Group detailed 131 Halifaxes to act as the main-force for an attack on the marshalling yards at Osnabrück in the Münsterland region of Germany north of the Ruhr, while 151 Halifaxes from 4 and 6 Groups were made ready for Münster, some thirty miles to the south-west, and 251 Lancasters of 1 and 6 Groups for Hannover seventy miles to the east. 1 Group put up 151 Lancasters from all bases for the last-mentioned, with only Fiskerton and Scampton omitted from the order of battle. The attack opened with accurate bombing, although the bright sunlight made it impossible to distinguish the colours of the TIs and eventually smoke obscured the aiming-point, persuading the Master Bomber to call for the bombing to be aimed at the upwind edge. As the last of the bombers turned away, smoke could be seen rising through 14,000 feet, and all were confident that the main weight of bombs had fallen within the built-up area of the city.

The focus remained on the region of Germany to the north of the Ruhr on the 27th, as its encirclement by American ground forces required just the capture of the town of Paderborn, situated some thirty-five miles due east of Hamm. 1 Group provided a main force of 225 Lancasters, including a dozen representing 576 Squadron, while 8 Group contributed forty-four Lancasters and nine Mosquitos. The Fiskerton element took off between 14.41 and 15.19 with S/L Bradbury the senior pilot on duty and each Lancaster carrying a cookie and twelve SBCs of 4lb incendiaries. After climbing out, they headed via Wainfleet for the Dutch coast under fairly clear skies, but the cloud began to build over enemy territory until reaching ten-tenths over the target with tops at around 10,000 feet. This prompted the Master Bomber to call for smoke-puff skymarkers at 17.25, but the first greens did not appear until 17.28, after which, a steady supply maintained the aiming-point for the next ten minutes. The early arrivals had been forced to orbit, but the crews following behind, who had been preparing to bomb by H2S and Gee, were able now to use the skymarkers as a more reliable reference, while confirming their accuracy by means of navigational aids. The 576 Squadron crews carried out their attacks from an average of 16,500 feet between 17.30 and 17.37 and returned home to report a cloud of brown smoke ascending to two thousand feet above the clouds. The operation was an outstanding success, confirmed by a local report, which stated that three thousand separate fires had occurred, and that the town had been virtually destroyed.

The final operation of the hugely busy penultimate month of offensive activity by the Command was to end with a 1, 6 and 8 Group raid on the Blohm & Voss U-Boot yards at Hamburg, where the new Type XXI vessels were being assembled. A force of 361 Lancasters and a hundred Halifaxes was made ready on the 31st, 201 of the former provided by 1 Group, of which seventeen stood ready for departure at Fiskerton. S/L Dutton was the senior pilot on duty as they took off between 06.13 and 06.30 and climbed out through layer cloud on course for Skegness, where they were to rendezvous with the rest of the group and form into a line-astern column. The cloud prevented this, and the force was closing on the Dutch coast at 3° East, before it broke up sufficiently to allow the forming up to take place, only for it to build again from 6° East and remain at ten-tenths for the remainder of the flight to the target. When the leading aircraft of the main force were fifteen minutes out, the Master Bomber warned them to look for smoke-puff markers, and the first of these appeared at 08.43, but only in small numbers. It was a further three minutes before they became plentiful, by which time the bombing was well underway in accordance with the frequent instructions and changing aiming points coming through from the Master Bomber. It caused a degree of jostling for position over the target, but the 576 Squadron crews found red smoke puffs to bomb from 17,000 to 18,000 feet between 08.45 and 08.52. Many crews returned with the impression that the raid had lacked a degree of concentration, but local reports spoke of widespread damage in residential and industrial areas in the south of the city and across the Elbe in Harburg, with energy supplies and communications also hard-hit.

It had been a sobering month for 576 Squadron and Fiskerton, during the course of which it had carried out fifteen operations and dispatched 202 sorties for the loss of six Lancasters and crews.

April 1945

April would be a time to mop up defences, cut off communications and finish off the oil industry, and it began for 1 Group with an operation against what was believed to be a military barracks at Nordhausen, situated in the Harz mountains between Hannover to the north-west and Leipzig to the south-east. The site was actually a pair of enormous parallel tunnels under the Kohnstein Hill, which had been developed originally by the BASF Company to mine gypsum between 1917 and 1934. Following the destruction of Peenemünde, smaller tunnels had been created as a link between them to form a horizontal ladder effect, and the site turned over to the Mittelwerk GmbH (Gesellschaft mit beschrenkter Haftung, or Limited Company) for the manufacture of V-2 rockets and other secret projects. The "barracks" were part of the Mittelwerk-Dora forced workers camp, where inmates existed under the most horrendous conditions and brutal treatment, while they were starved, worked to death or simply executed by an increasingly desperate regime seeking to change the course of the war. 1 Group provided a main force of 210 Lancasters, including seventeen belonging to 576 Squadron, while 8 Group added a further thirty-seven and eight Mosquitos to conduct the marking. At Fiskerton the armourers winched eleven 1,000 and two 500-pounders into each Lancaster and sent them into the air between 13.10 and 13.27 with S/L Bradbury the senior pilot on duty, and Jamaican, F/L William Strachan, undertaking his first sortie with the squadron. Strachan had joined the RAF in the spring of 1940, training as a gunner and serving a tour on Wellingtons with 156 Squadron, before re-training as a pilot and joining 576 Squadron as the captain of his own crew. They flew out over Southwold on course for the Belgian side of the Scheldt estuary, to follow the line of the frontier with France until entering Germany near St Vith, the moderate cloud thickening as the bomber stream progressed eastwards.

By the time that the target drew near, there was ten-tenths cloud, and the Master Bomber issued instructions at 16.02 for the main force crews to descend to the cloud base at 8,500 feet. Four minutes later, as the bombers approached the cloud tops at around 11,000 feet, the Master Bomber rescinded his original order and instructed the crews to climb again. This caused confusion, and all semblance of the previously coherent formation was lost. Some futile attempts were made to reform the stream as the Master Bomber called for smoke-puff markers, but these seem to have burst inside the cloud and were not visible. As a last resort, he ordered the crews to "bomb on best navigational aids", and the main force crews complied, all from 576 Squadron on H2S from an average of 14,000 feet between 16.18 and 16.22. It was impossible to accurately assess the outcome, but a single 1 Group crew dropped beneath the cloud base to 5,500 feet and reported two small fires in the town but no bombing around the aiming point. The target and the nearby town would be attacked again twenty-four hours later by 5 Group and sustain severe damage at the expense of many friendly foreign nationals trapped in the barracks, while those in the tunnels remained safe from bombs, but endured a hellish existence as the evil Nazi regime systematically worked and starved them to death.

The night of the 4/5th brought a return to the oil offensive at three sites, Leuna and Lützkendorf near Leipzig, and Harburg on the South Bank of the Elbe opposite Hamburg. 1 Group detailed 238 Lancasters for Lützkendorf, situated west of Leipzig on the western edge of the Geiseltal Lake. Lützkendorf no longer exists on a map of Germany and is now known as either Mücheln or Krumpa. 576 Squadron made ready eighteen Lancasters, which departed Fiskerton between 21.11 and 21.36 with F/Ls Acheson, Campbell, Collins, Strachan and Woodruff the senior pilots on duty and a cookie and ten 500-pounders in each bomb bay. F/Sgt Abercrombie and crew lost their port-inner engine immediately after take-off and headed directly to the jettison area, while the remainder climbed out through cloud that persisted over England but cleared at the south coast, before building up again between 5° and 11° East. It then dispersed again to leave clear skies and good visibility at the target, which was reached after an outward flight of almost four-and-a-half hours. The first Path Finder ground markers went down at 01.25 and were easily identified by the 576 Squadron crews as they delivered their payloads from 12,000 to 14,000 feet between 01.28 and 01.35. Some crews at the tail end of the main force were instructed by the Master Bomber to aim at the smoke, which had largely concealed the TIs at 01.33. Returning crews reported fewer fires than expected, but several large explosions witnessed at 01.29, 01.31 and 01.40 and accompanied by volumes of thick smoke suggested that the attack had been at least moderately effective. ME671 failed to return with the others, and news was received eventually from the Red Cross that Sgt Hogg and five members of his now rare all-sergeant crew were in enemy hands, the rear gunner having lost his life after sustaining a severe head wound and baling out from 500 feet. Post-raid reconnaissance revealed that the plant had not been decisively damaged, but an attack by 5 Group on the night of the 8/9th would bring an end to all production at the site.

On the 5th, 625 Squadron donated its C Flight to 576 Squadron under the command of S/L Hammond, and on the following day it's A and B Flights moved out of Kelstern to take up residence at Scampton. A major operation against the Blohm & Voss U-Boot yards at Hamburg involved 440 aircraft from 4, 6 and 8 Groups on the night of the 8/9th, while 1 Group enjoyed a night off. The operation cost eleven aircraft, the last double-digit loss of the war to result from a single target.

Preparations were put in hand on 1, 3 and 8 Group stations on the 9th to prepare 591 Lancasters for a raid that night on the harbour area of Kiel, the location of the three major shipyards building U-Boots. 1 Group detailed 256 Lancasters for the main event, including a record twenty-nine representing 576 Squadron, its numbers now bolstered by the addition of a C Flight. The crews were briefed for two aiming points, D and E, before departing Fiskerton between 18.55 and 19.20 with S/Ls Hammond the senior pilot on duty and a cookie and sixteen 500-pounders in each bomb bay. They followed in the wake of a gardening element, beginning the North Sea crossing at Whitby to make landfall at Sankt Peter-Ording on the western coast of Schleswig-Holstein, leaving them with a sixty-mile dash across the peninsula to the target. They encountered a little cloud before the Baltic coast hove into sight, but the target itself lay under clear skies with good visibility, and illuminating flares allowed the Master Bombers to identify the outline of the fjord and inner harbour and the two aiming-points.

Ground marking commenced at aiming-point D at 22.25 and at aiming-point E two minutes later, and both were well-marked with red TIs, backed up by greens, enabling the main force crews to aim at whichever presented the better target. Eventually, all of the TIs became obscured by smoke, and by the end of the attack, the entire area between the aiming-points was on fire, with flames spreading down to the water's edge. A particularly large explosion at 22.35 gave the impression that an ammunition dump had been hit, and strikes on an oil storage depot resulted in thick, black smoke billowing up to a considerable height as the crews turned away. The Fiskerton crews delivered their attacks from an average of 15,000 feet between 22.31 and 22.39, and photo-reconnaissance confirmed the effectiveness of their efforts, revealing the Deutsche Werke U-Boot yards to have sustained severe damage and the other two shipyards also to have been hit. In addition, the pocket battleship, Admiral Scheer, had capsized, the cruisers, Admiral Hipper and Emden were badly damaged and adjacent residential districts had suffered also. After landing safely, F/L de-Mille was declared tour-expired.

The focus of operations on the 10th was upon railway installations in eastern Germany, the Engelsdorf and Mockau marshalling yards in Leipzig for a force of 134 Lancasters, ninety Halifaxes and six Mosquitos by daylight, and a stretch of track linked to the Wahren yards in the same city by seventy-six Lancasters and nineteen Mosquitos of 5 and 8 Groups after dark. A further operation involving 307 Lancasters and eight Mosquitos from 1 and 8 Groups would target the marshalling yards in the town of Plauen, situated close to the frontier with Czechoslovakia thirty miles south-west of Chemnitz. The 1 Group contribution of 253 Lancasters included twenty-four representing 576 Squadron, which each received a bomb load of a cookie and ten 500-pounders, before departing Fiskerton between 17.59 and 18.31 with S/L Bradbury the senior pilot on duty. They began the Channel crossing near Hastings on course for the Boulogne area, before traversing Belgium to enter Germany via the St-Vith region with a further 260 miles and ninety minutes flying time ahead of them, eventually reaching the target area to encounter clear skies and good visibility. The red Oboe TIs went down on time to open proceedings and were backed up by greens in a tight cluster that satisfied the Master Bomber, who then called in the main force crews to deliver their attacks, those from 576 Squadron complying with his instructions from 16,000 to 18,000 feet between 23.09 and 23.16. A large explosion was observed at 23.11, and by 23.20, the town was completely obscured by smoke rising through 12,000 feet. The glow of fires remained visible for a hundred miles into the return journey and post-raid reconnaissance confirmed the accuracy of the attack, which resulted in the destruction of 365 acres, or 51% of the town's built-up area.

The final major attack on a German city was directed at Potsdam on the night of the 14/15th, and this would be the first incursion into the Berlin defence zone by RAF heavy bombers since March 1944. In the twelve months since then, Mosquitos of 8 Group's Light Night Striking Force (LNSF) had maintained a regular presence over the city, acting as a constant menace, dropping cookies to unsettle the populace and robbing the workers of their sleep. So fast was the "Wooden Wonder", that it was not unknown for a single aircraft to make two trips to Berlin in one night after a change of crew. A force of five hundred Lancasters from 1, 3 and 8 Groups was assembled, of which 215 Lancasters were provided by 1 Group, while twenty-four others from 576 Squadron carried out a spoof raid on the port of Cuxhaven at the mouth of the Elbe as a diversion. Their bomb bays were filled with a cookie and sixteen 500-pounders as they departed Fiskerton in poor weather conditions between 19.20 and 19.55 with S/L Dutton the senior pilot on duty and set course for Skegness on course for Heligoland and then the target. They ran into a severe cold front over the North Sea with cloud tops at 19,000 feet and beyond, and this may have contributed to the early returns between 21.45 and 23.52 of the crews of F/L Strachan, F/Sgt Tile and F/O Bury. The two last-mentioned were defeated by technical failures, while F/L Strachan was taken ill and would not take part in the few remaining operations before the end of hostilities. The conditions were probably also responsible for a late and meagre marking performance by the Path Finder element, despite which, sufficient TIs were visible for the aiming point to be bombed. The degree of damage was of secondary importance to the diversionary purpose of the operation, and in this it was deemed to be successful.

Meanwhile, the main event opened with illuminating flares under the watchful eyes of the designated Master Bomber, W/C Le Good, and his Deputy, F/L Douglas, both of 35 (Madras Presidency) Squadron, and the marking commenced six minutes before H-Hour with red TIs, falling initially a little to the west of the aiming-point. These were soon corrected by other reds planted right on the mark and backed up by greens to leave the main force crews with no doubt about where to direct their bombs. The Master Bomber maintained good control throughout the raid, changing the point of focus as required and keeping the attack firmly on the aiming point, returning crews reporting many fires and explosions and an afterglow visible for a hundred miles into the return journey. The raid was confirmed as a success, but some bomb loads were found to have spilled into northern and western districts of Berlin.

There was good news for some main force crews to celebrate on the 17th, when the length of a tour was reduced yet again to thirty sorties, releasing many to contemplate a long future, among which were the 576 Squadron crews of F/Os Battin and Button, F/Ls Bray, Collins and Stephens and S/L Hammond. F/L McPhail, a recent recruit from 625 Squadron, was appointed as the successor to S/L Hammond as the new commander of C Flight.

Early briefings across the Command on the 18th informed 969 crews of an assault on the coastal batteries, naval base, airfield and town on the island of Heligoland. 1 Group assembled a force of 310 Lancasters to be divided equally between aiming points A, at the northern end of the island and B, at the southern end where the harbour and U-Boots pens were situated. A third aiming point, C, was the Luftwaffe aerodrome and would be the first to come under attack by one of the other groups. 576 Squadron made ready thirty Lancasters, loading each with a dozen 1,000 and four 500-pounders and sending them on their way from Fiskerton between 09.38 and 10.10 with S/L Bradbury the senior pilot on duty. They flew out over Mablethorpe and arrived in the target area under clear skies and in good visibility, Heligoland and its smaller neighbour, Düne, appearing as two tiny dots some thirty miles off Germany's north-western coast. The ORB report is scant on detail and focuses mostly on an aircraft corkscrewing violently over the midpoint of the North Sea at 11.50 with its starboard-inner engine in flames. The bombs were seen to be jettisoned, and seven parachutes were observed as the aircraft spiralled down to enter the water, four of the parachutes clearly visible on the surface. Later, two other aircraft were brought down by flak, one a mile-and-a-half south-east of Heligoland and the other off Düne.

We are not told to which of the aiming points the Fiskerton crews had been assigned, but it is believed that they were divided between A and B, and based on the records of other units, those attacking aiming point B delivered their payloads from 17,000 to 19,000 feet between 12.34 and 12.38, and smoke was already rising as the second-phase bomber stream covered the leg between the final turning point and aiming point A. The Master Bomber was first heard there at 12.50 issuing instructions to bomb the yellow TIs, however, these were found to have undershot, and he shifted the point of aim to the upwind edge of the smoke, the bombing taking place from 16,900 to 19,000 feet between 12.45 and 12.56. A very large explosion in the docks area at 12.47 sent a column of black smoke a thousand feet into the air and started an oil fire, and several vessels, believed to be destroyers, were observed to be heading away south-east of the harbour, one of them, it is believed, receiving a direct hit. Post raid reconnaissance revealed the surface of Heligoland to resemble a cratered moonscape, but its ordeal was not yet over, as on the following day it would face an attack by 617 and 9 Squadrons, the former carrying 10-ton Grand Slams and 6-ton Tallboys and the latter Tallboys. If not already totally evacuated, the island certainly was by the end of the 19th. After landing safely, the crews of F/L Stephens and F/O Chalkley were declared tour-expired.

As the British XXX Corps moved in on the city of Bremen, Bomber Command was asked to bomb four enemy strong-points in the south-eastern suburbs, where the attack was due to take place in two days' time. A main force of 691 aircraft was drawn from 1, 3 and 6 Groups, 270 of them provided by 1 Group, while 8 Group put up seventy-six Lancasters and sixteen Mosquitos. 576 Squadron's contribution of twenty-six Lancasters departed Fiskerton between 15.10 and 15.37 with F/Ls Campbell, McCurdy, McPhail and Woodruff the senior pilots on duty and a cookie, six 1,000 and eight 500-pounders in each bomb bay. They flew out over Mablethorpe over cloud that persisted more or less for the entire outward flight, and as the first wave element approached the target at 17.56, the crews could only catch a glimpse of the ground through gaps. The Master Bomber was heard to ask his Deputy whether the aiming point could be marked in those conditions, and a negative response persuaded him to broadcast "Marmalade", the signal to abandon that phase of the operation. The visual marker crews confirmed that they were unable to identify the aiming-points, and the attacks on aiming-points J1, J2 and G were called off at 17.58, 18.13 and 18.49 respectively, and the entire 1 and 6 Group elements returned home with their bombs. 195 aircraft bombed at aiming-point F, before that, too, was abandoned at 19.05. The degree of jettisoning depended upon the experience of the crews, the old hands landing with bomb loads intact, while the freshers dumped part or all of theirs.

The final operations of the bombing war were carried out on the 25th, beginning with what was, perhaps, a symbolic attack by a main force of 335 Lancasters of 1 and 5 Groups and twenty-four Lancasters and eight Mosquitos of 8 Group on Hitler's Eaglesnest retreat and the nearby SS barracks at Berchtesgaden in the Bavarian mountains. 1 Group provided 247 Lancasters, and none of those involved in the preparation and operation of the twenty-three 576 Squadron aircraft had any notion that this would be the final offensive action of 1 Group's war. It required an early start, the Fiskerton crews taking to the air between 05.09 and 05.34 with F/Ls Campbell, Halnan, Lewis, O'Neill and Woodruff the senior pilots on duty and each Lancaster carrying a cookie, four 1,000-pounders and a single 500-pounder as gifts for the Führer. They crossed the coast near Folkestone on course for Cap Gris Nez, and a few patches of high cloud aside, the outward flight benefitted from perfect conditions. However, the attempt by the 1 Group element to form into a line-astern column became somewhat chaotic from 4° East, where two gaggles developed, and the designated leaders found themselves in the rear one. By the time that 6° East was reached, a large proportion of the 1 Group force had managed to form up into a reasonable column, but about eighty remained ahead and made no effort to re-join. Some of these eventually orbited and joined the column as it passed by, but many stragglers remained and the whole 1 Group formation found itself south of track. The attempt to rectify the situation all but eliminated the turning point at 12° East and the final turn to the target was a good ten miles wide. By this time, F/O Pollard and crew were flying on three engines, having lost their port-inner an hour short of the target, but pressed on and would bomb late and be the last to arrive home.

The vanguard of the bomber stream arrived in the target area on time, only to find that all was not proceeding according to plan. The deputy Master Bomber had been unable to mark the target, and, realising this, the leader of the first wave overshot the final turning point by two-and-a-half minutes, before bringing the force back in a wide orbit. This had the effect of splitting up the formation, and aircraft began approaching the aiming-point from a variety of headings. At 09.45 the Master Bomber ordered the crews to bomb visually if they could, but a minute later a red target indicator went down, which appeared to be accurate, and crews selected whatever was best for them, including the upwind edge of the smoke. Based on the records of other units, the 576 Squadron crews carried out their attacks from 15,000 to 18,000 feet between 09.49 and 09.57 and a concentration of bombs was seen to fall across the SS barracks. Despite the lack of cohesion, it seems that most fell within the confines of the general target area, causing a column of smoke to rise to 10,000 feet. The defenders put up a moderate heavy flak barrage to starboard of the approaching force, but this decreased as the attack developed and only two 576 Squadron Lancasters sustained minor damage. When F/O Pollard and crew touched down at Fiskerton at 13.49, they unwittingly brought to an end the offensive wartime career of 576 Squadron. F/L Campbell was declared tour-expired, not knowing that his offensive career was over anyway.

A force of 482 aircraft from 4, 6 and 8 Groups was sent against coastal batteries on the Frisian Island of Wangerooge during the afternoon, tragically losing six aircraft to collisions, and 5 Group attacked an oil refinery at Tonsberg in southern Norway that night to effectively bring an end to the bombing war. Operation Exodus, the repatriation of prisoners of war began on the 26th and would continue on into the summer and Operation Manna, to provide food for the starving Dutch people still under enemy occupation, would run from the 29th to the 8th of May, the day on which the war in Europe ended. 576 Squadron's participation in Operation Manna began on the 29th, and between then and the 8th of May 177 sorties were flown to the Valkenburg, Delft and Rotterdam regions, crews commenting on return on the amazing and emotional sight of Dutch people in the streets and on rooftops waving deliriously in appreciation of their deliverance from starvation. The squadron began Exodus flights on the 11th of May, each Lancaster transporting twenty-four former PoWs back to Dunsfold for processing.

576 Squadron was the proud owner for a time of the highest sortie-scoring Lancaster of them all, ED888, which at the end of its career, having returned to its original owner, 103 Squadron, notched up an estimated 147 sorties in all between April 1943 and December 1944. Other 576 Squadron centurions were ME801, LM227 and LM594. During its short wartime career, 576 Squadron discharged its duties with dedication, professionalism and distinction and contributed immeasurably to Bomber Commands part in the ultimate victory over Nazi Germany.

Roll Of Honour

P/O	Robert William	ABRAMS	06.03.1945.
F/O	Mark Leslie	ABRAMSON	16.05.1944.
Sgt	Clifford Charles	ADDEMS	27.08.1944.
P/O	James William	ALCORN	25.06.1944.
F/O	Arthur James	ALDRIDGE	12.09.1944.
Sgt	Louis Paul Edwin	ALLAIS	20.12.1943.
F/Sgt	Francis	ALLEN	18.08.1944.
Sgt	Harold John	ALLEN	05.04.1945.
Sgt	John William Thompson	ANDERSON	14.01.1944.
F/Sgt	Kenneth	ANGUS	28.12.1944.
F/Sgt	Colin Richard	ANTHONY	02.11.1944.
F/O	Charles	ASHCROFT	16.05.1944.
Sgt	Albert Ernest	BACHELOR	25.05.1944.
F/Sgt	Herman	BACKLER	18.08.1944.
Sgt	Arthur Stanley	BAKER	06.01.1944.
F/O	David	BAKER	25.09.1944.
Sgt	Leonard	BALICH	20.12.1943.
Sgt	Frank	BALL	20.12.1943.
Sgt	Robert Walter	BALL	22.05.1944.
Sgt	Douglas Patrick	BANNISTER	14.02.1945.
Sgt	Arthur	BARCLAY	14.01.1944.
W/O	Eric	BARDSLEY	19.04.1945.
F/Sgt	Donald Arthur	BARNES	27.08.1944.
F/L	Frank Sharpe	BARNSDALE	11.04.1944.
F/Sgt	Stanley James	BARR	04.05.1944.
Sgt	Jack Leslie	BARRETT	16.12.1943.
W/O	Terence Patrick	BARRY	29.07.1944.
F/Sgt	Kenneth Frederick Fisher	BARTON	06.01.1944.
F/O	Richard Stanley	BASTICK	21.02.1945.
P/O	Douglas Frank Jakes	BAXTER	05.07.1944.
P/O	Clarence Herbert	BAYRAM	04.12.1943.
Sgt	Ronald	BEALES	08.03.1945.
Sgt	Donald Jack	BEALEY	04.12.1943.
Sgt	William Walker	BEATTIE	15.07.1944.
Sgt	Joseph	BEESON	02.11.1944.
F/Sgt	Reginald Kenneth	BEGG	25.06.1944.
F/Sgt	Reginald Peter	BELSHAW	08.03.1945.
F/L	Edward	BENNETT	25.09.1944.
F/Sgt	William Victor	BIBBY	21.02.1945.
W/O	Arthur Henry	BILTOFT	07.05.1944.
F/O	Peter Joseph	BIOLLO	29.07.1944.
Sgt	Robert	BLACK	08.03.1945.

Sgt	Donald William	BLACKMAN	04.12.1943.
F/O	Geoffrey Livingstone	BLACKMORE	16.12.1943.
Sgt	Earl Wesley	BOOKHOUT	05.07.1944.
Sgt	Roy James Alfred	BOON	31.03.1944.
Sgt	Wilfred Charles	BOOT	27.01.1944.
F/Sgt	John Milton	BOOTH	03.12.1943.
F/O	Ronald Sydney	BOWDEN	04.12.1943.
Sgt	Herbert Reginald	BOWLES	30.01.1944.
Sgt	Charles John	BRADY	23.09.1944.
Sgt	Clifford Moore	BREWSTER	30.01.1944.
F/O	Peter Upton	BROOKE	24.03.1944.
F/Sgt	John	BROWN	17.06.1944.
F/O	Ronald William	BROWN	29.07.1944.
F/Sgt	Leonard James	BULL	28.12.1944.
Sgt	Noel Vincent	BURGESS	24.03.1944.
F/Sgt	Fred	BURGESS	04.05.1944.
F/Sgt	George Brodie	BURNS	08.03.1945.
F/Sgt	Albert	BURNS	07.03.1945.
Sgt	Harry	BURROWS	21.02.1945.
Sgt	John Hamilton	CALDWELL	16.12.1943.
P/O	Alexander Grant	CAMPBELL	11.04.1944.
F/Sgt	Charles Gerrard	CAMPBELL	28.12.1944.
P/O	Albert Spencer Blair	CAMPTON	07.01.1945.
W/O	James Nelson	CASEY	02.11.1944.
F/Sgt	Keith Leonard	CHALLIS	17.03.1945.
F/Sgt	Cyril	CHAPMAN	16.12.1943.
F/O	Harold Norman	CHEESEMAN	14.02.1945.
P/O	Edward Horace	CHILDS	30.01.1944.
F/Sgt	Maurice	CHURCHMAN	20.02.1944.
Sgt	Clifford	CLAMP	11.04.1944.
Sgt	Brian Edward	CLARKE	14.01.1944.
F/Sgt	Jack	COATES	21.02.1945.
Sgt	John Herbert	CODD	29.07.1944.
Sgt	John Leslie	COLBOURNE	06.01.1944.
F/Sgt	Leslie John	COLLIS	25.03.1944.
F/Sgt	Arthur Wilfred	COOPER	22.05.1944.
Sgt	George James	COOPER	25.05.1944.
Sgt	John Boyle	COWLE	25.06.1944.
Sgt	George Gordon	CRITCHLEY	16.12.1943.
Sgt	Stanley Victor	CULL	16.12.1943.
Sgt	John Rowland	CUTHBERT	29.07.1944.
Sgt	Arthur Henry	DAINES	24.03.1944.
Sgt	Arthur Sydney	DAVIS	06.01.1944.
F/O	Thomas Clough	DAWSON	24.10.1944.
F/Sgt	Walter William	DEWAR	06.03.1945.

Rank	First Names	Surname	Date
Sgt	William	DICKIE	20.12.1943.
Sgt	Raymond Stuart	DICKINSON	25.05.1944.
Sgt	Nelson Alexander	DIXON	06.01.1944.
Sgt	Herbert Horace	DIXON	13.05.1944.
F/L	Frank Edmond	DOTTEN	17.03.1945.
Sgt	Corbett Norman George	DREW	07.05.1944.
F/O	Ernest Augustus	DUERR	18.08.1944.
F/O	Stanley Frederick	DURRANT	23.09.1944.
Sgt	Kenneth George	DURSTON	16.03.1945.
F/Sgt	Edwin William	EBSWORTH	27.01.1944.
F/Sgt	Ernest Charles	EDWARDS	11.04.1944.
Sgt	Alfred	ELAND	13.05.1944.
F/Sgt	Peter Martin Crowle	ELLIS	16.12.1943.
F/O	Eric Charles	ESPLEY	31.03.1944.
Sgt	John	EVE	17.03.1945.
Sgt	Douglas Ernest	FABB	17.06.1944.
Sgt	Ronald Victor	FAIRLEY	29.01.1944.
Sgt	George Alexander	FERGUS	24.10.1944.
F/Sgt	Leslie	FIELDING	29.07.1944.
Sgt	Salvin	FIELDING	02.11.1944.
Sgt	Thomas	FINNERTY	20.02.1944.
F/O	Derrick	FLETCHER	28.12.1944.
F/Sgt	Charles Victor	FOX	07.05.1944.
F/Sgt	William Gordon	FROST	21.02.1945.
F/O	Douglas	FULLER	17.06.1944.
Sgt	Frank Harry	GAGE	20.12.1943.
P/O	Alan William	GARNET	17.03.1945.
Sgt	Ernest	GEDLING	24.10.1944.
P/O	James Stanley Marks	GIBB	17.03.1945.
Sgt	Clive Allen	GIFFARD	30.01.1944.
F/Sgt	Arthur Ronald	GILES	12.09.1944.
F/Sgt	Lloyd William Lewis	GODFREY	03.12.1943.
Sgt	John Phillip	GRAY	24.12.1943.
Sgt	Kenneth George	GREATHEAD	14.02.1945.
Sgt	Arthur Leslie	GREEN	22.05.1944.
Sgt	Noel William	GREEN	25.05.1944.
Sgt	Stanley Stuart	GREENWOOD	23.05.1944.
Sgt	Walter Henry Mills	GREIG	13.07.1944.
P/O	Melvin Douglas	GROUNDWATER	03.02.1945.
F/Sgt	Desmond Hendry	HADLOW	06.03.1945.
F/O	George	HALLOWS	23.05.1944.
F/Sgt	Albert Alfred	HARRIS	16.12.1943.
F/Sgt	Eric Geore	HART	29.01.1944.
P/O	Claude	HART	13.07.1944.
Sgt	Thomas Eric	HAYES	25.06.1944.

P/O	John Romer	HENNINGHAM	06.01.1944.
P/O	William Hendry	HEPBURN	02.11.1944.
F/Sgt	Francis Charles	HICKLING	14.01.1944.
F/Sgt	John Angus	HILDRETH	31.03.1944.
F/L	Farnham	HILL	23.05.1944.
F/O	Raymond Campbell	HILL	21.02.1945.
Sgt	Ralph Frithjaf	HILLMAN	05.07.1944.
Sgt	Kenneth Harold	HODGKINSON	25.05.1944.
Sgt	Alfred Arthur Henry	HODSON	04.05.1944.
Sgt	Robin	HOOD	29.07.1944.
Sgt	Arthur Edward	HOOPER	24.12.1943.
F/O	Francis	HOSIER	29.07.1944.
Sgt	Eric Macpherson	HOWARD	20.02.1944.
F/Sgt	Benjamin Johnson	HUDSON	16.05.1944.
P/O	Richard Lloyd	HUGHES	24.12.1943.
Sgt	Leslie	HULL	21.02.1945.
Sgt	Gordon	HUMPHREYS	06.06.1944.
Sgt	Sidney Walter	IRONS	24.12.1943.
F/Sgt	Ross Alexander	JACK	17.06.1944.
Sgt	Alfred Clifford	JACKSON	14.01.1944.
F/Sgt	Arthur Reginald	JACKSON	07.05.1944.
Sgt	George Reginald	JAMES	14.02.1945.
F/Sgt	Thomas	JEFFERSON	17.06.1944.
F/Sgt	William Edward Arthur	JEFFERY	17.03.1945.
F/Sgt	Murray Noel	JENNINGS	03.12.1943.
Sgt	Harold	JOHNSON	24.12.1943.
F/Sgt	Edward	JOHNSON	13.05.1944.
Sgt	Ronald Mortimer William	JOHNSON	29.07.1944.
F/Sgt	Lloyd	JOHNSTON	18.08.1944.
P/O	Ronald Elliott	JOHNSTONE	30.01.1944.
F/O	James	JOHNSTONE	23.09.1944.
F/Sgt	Maurice William	JONES	03.12.1943.
Sgt	Clifford Leighton	JONES	13.07.1944.
Sgt	George Henry	KAYE	03.12.1943.
Sgt	John Edward	KEARNEY	29.07.1944.
Sgt	James Edward	KENNISON	06.01.1944.
Sgt	Wilfred Owen	KENYON	27.08.1944.
F/Sgt	Andrew Joseph	KIRK	20.02.1944.
F/Sgt	William	KITSON	20.02.1944.
Sgt	Alan Wilfred	KNAPP	16.05.1944.
Sgt	Francis Norman	KNAPP	29.07.1944.
F/Sgt	Henry John	KNIGHTBRIDGE	03.02.1945.
F/Sgt	Stanley John	KOZLOWSKI	15.07.1944.
Sgt	Joseph Willie Conrad	LABELLE	25.05.1944.
F/O	Thomas Charles	LAING	27.01.1944.

P/O	George Albert	LANGFORD	25.05.1944.
W/O	Frederick Albert	LARSEN	06.01.1944.
Sgt	Harold Raymond	LAWRENCE	31.03.1944.
F/Sgt	Robert Edward	LEATHAM	16.05.1944.
Sgt	William Ferguson	LEDINGHAM	29.01.1944.
F/Sgt	Roy	LEE	27.08.1944.
Sgt	Gordon	LESTER	03.02.1945.
Sgt	Alan Richard	LEWENDON	12.09.1944.
F/Sgt	Herbert Edgar	LILLICRAP	17.06.1944.
F/O	Raymond Edwin	LINKLATER	15.07.1944.
F/O	Jack Allan	LINKLATER	27.08.1944.
Sgt	Christopher	LISTER	22.05.1944.
F/L	Charles Henry	LIVING	21.02.1945.
Sgt	Ernest Arthur	LODGE	24.03.1944.
Sgt	James Gordon	MACKEY	23.09.1944.
F/O	Donald McKenzie	MACKINTOSH	15.07.1944.
F/Sgt	Donald Irwin	MacVICAR	29.07.1944.
P/O	James Thomas Joseph	MAGEE	06.03.1945.
Sgt	Leonard	MAIDEN	18.08.1944.
Sgt	Donald George	MANN	14.01.1944.
F/O	Edward James	MANN	29.07.1944.
Sgt	John	MANNION	25.06.1944.
F/O	Jack Purcell	MANSER	25.09.1944.
Sgt	Kenneth Victor	MANT	13.05.1944.
F/O	Bertie James	MARKS	24.12.1943.
F/Sgt	Kenneth Reginald	MARSTON	06.03.1945.
W/OII	Joseph Alphonse Leon	MARTEL	29.01.1944.
Sgt	Frederick George James	MARTIN	21.02.1945.
F/Sgt	Leslie Ronald Bruce	MATTHEWS	04.12.1943.
Sgt	William Ernest	MAY	07.03.1945.
F/O	Ronald Stenhouse	McARA	16.12.1943.
F/Sgt	Wilfred Glenn	McCLELLAND	07.01.1945.
F/Sgt	Edward Jerome	McCLOSKEY	05.07.1944.
F/Sgt	William John	McCOLLUM	15.07.1944.
Sgt	Jeremiah	McCOOL	04.05.1944.
F/O	Reginald Stewart	McGIBBON	29.07.1944.
F/Sgt	John Douglas	McGOWAN	29.09.1944.
Sgt	John Francis	McHUGH	13.07.1944.
F/Sgt	James Robert	McINTYRE	23.09.1944.
F/Sgt	John Wilbert	McLEOD	07.05.1944.
Sgt	Rodney Lewis	McMANUS	14.01.1944.
Sgt	Francis	McWATT	02.11.1944.
Sgt	Leslie Ronald Herbert	MICHELL	27.01.1944.
Sgt	Charles	MILBURN	24.12.1943.
Sgt	Alexander	MILNE	29.07.1944.

Rank	Name	Surname	Date
Sgt	Hubert Stanley (Bert)	MITCHELL	24.12.1943.
Sgt	Edward	MITCHELL	13.07.1944.
Sgt	Peter Ralston	MONTGOMERY	07.03.1945.
Sgt	John Francis Arthur	MOONEY	21.02.1945.
Sgt	Walter	MOORES	20.02.1944.
Sgt	Edward Henry John	MORGAN	17.06.1944.
Sgt	Alan Thompson Tait	MORRELL	25.06.1944.
Sgt	Grenville Malcombe	MORRIS	11.04.1944.
F/O	Clive Watson	MORTAL	02.11.1944.
Sgt	Rupert	MOSLEY	14.01.1944.
Sgt	James Kelly	MOSMAN	14.01.1944.
Sgt	Hector MacDonald	MUNDY	25.05.1944.
F/O	William	MURPHY	23.05.1944.
P/O	Harold Duncan	MURRAY	27.08.1944.
Sgt	Alexander George	MURRAY	24.10.1944.
Sgt	Thomas McKay Arnand	MURRAY	02.11.1944.
F/Sgt	Leslie	MUTTON	29.07.1944.
F/Sgt	Morley Francis	NELSON	12.09.1944.
F/O	William Frederick	NICOL	17.03.1945.
Sgt	James	NORRIS	28.12.1944.
Sgt	Douglas Roland	NORTHCOTE	29.07.1944.
Sgt	John Edward	NOVELL	27.01.1944.
F/O	Henry John	O'CONNOR	03.02.1945.
F/Sgt	Stanley	ORMONDROYD	12.09.1944.
Sgt	Daniel	O'SULLIVAN	07.03.1945.
Sgt	Walter Ronald	OWEN	29.01.1944.
F/O	George Henry	PALEY	08.03.1945.
F/O	Edward	PARKER	02.11.1944.
P/O	Jack	PARKINSON	13.05.1944.
Sgt	James Eric Frederick	PATON	24.12.1943.
W/O	Frederick James Lincoln	PATON	02.11.1944.
Sgt	Harold	PEACH	21.02.1945.
Sgt	Ronald Ernest	PEARCE	23.09.1944.
Sgt	James	PENDER	05.07.1944.
F/Sgt	Charles	PHILP	17.06.1944.
Sgt	Alan James	POLLITT	20.12.1943.
Sgt	George Alfred	PORTER	27.01.1944.
Sgt	Herbert Walter	PORTER	03.02.1945.
F/Sgt	Reginald	POTTER	08.03.1945.
P/O	Edward James	POVERLEY	17.03.1945.
F/L	Ernest James	PRESLAND	16.05.1944.
F/O	Basil Newton John	PRICE	14.01.1944.
Sgt	Vivian Graham	PRICE	25.09.1944.
Sgt	John Wellington Gordon	PRINGLE	15.07.1944.
F/O	Norman Ronald George	PRONGER	24.03.1944.

Rank	Name	Surname	Date
Sgt	Donald William George	PURSE	25.09.1944.
P/O	Alec Lenard	PUTTOCK	17.06.1944.
F/O	Donald Swallow	QUINN	17.03.1945.
Sgt	Anthony Frank	RAYMOND	13.05.1944.
Sgt	Jack Edward	REDMOND	20.12.1943.
P/O	Richard Robert	REED	23.05.1944.
F/Sgt	Norman Parry	REILLY	04.05.1944.
W/OII	Ross Burton	RENNIE	12.09.1944.
F/Sgt	Robert Edward Duncan	RICHARDS	03.12.1943.
F/O	John Henry	RICHARDS	24.12.1943.
F/Sgt	Francis Edgar Arthur	RIVETT	24.12.1943.
Sgt	Frederick David	ROBBINS	14.01.1944.
Sgt	Reginald Alan Wellesley	ROBERTS	29.07.1944.
F/Sgt	Cavan Beadon	ROBINSON	21.02.1945.
Sgt	Thomas Arthur	ROBY	25.06.1944.
Sgt	Joseph William	ROSS	16.12.1943.
Sgt	Arthur Dewhirst	ROULSON	04.12.1943.
F/O	Charles James	ROUSE	06.03.1945.
F/O	John Arnold	RUSSELL	21.02.1945.
Sgt	Eric	RUSSOM	16.12.1943.
F/Sgt	John Francis	RYAN	17.03.1945.
Sgt	Henry Alfred	SARGENT	21.02.1945.
W/OII	Michael Alexander	SARUK	23.05.1944.
F/O	Robert Joseph	SARVIS	24.07.1944.
F/O	Edward Lewis	SASLOVE	07.01.1945.
F/Sgt	Roland James	SAUNDERCOOK	17.03.1945.
F/Sgt	Frederick Roy	SCOTT	16.12.1943.
F/L	James Maxwell	SHEARER	07.05.1944.
F/Sgt	James Sidney	SHEARING	24.10.1944.
Sgt	Donald	SHOOBRIDGE	05.07.1944.
Sgt	Geoffrey	SHUTT	25.05.1944.
F/Sgt	George Robert	SIMS	15.07.1944.
F/Sgt	Rodney Herbert	SINCLAIR	04.12.1943.
P/O	Albert Edward	SLADE	16.05.1944.
F/L	Edwin Donald	SMITH	06.01.1944.
F/Sgt	Royston Laurence	SMITH	20.02.1944.
Sgt	Edward	SMITH	25.03.1944.
Sgt	Robert Eric	SMITH	25.05.1944.
F/L	Howard Arthur Frederick	SMITH	29.07.1944.
F/Sgt	Stephen Allen	SMITH	29.07.1944.
F/O	Richard Christopher	SOWERBUTTS	03.02.1945.
Sgt	David	SPOWART	23.09.1944.
F/Sgt	Leslie Howard	STEVENSON	27.12.1944.
F/O	Donald Winterburn	STEWART	17.06.1944.
Sgt	Alexander	STEWART	24.10.1944.

F/L	George Edward	STOCKDALE	17.06.1944.
Sgt	William John	STOCKWELL	24.10.1944.
Sgt	Ronald Ernest	STREATFIELD	03.02.1945.
Sgt	Robert Leslie	SWAFFER	21.02.1945.
Sgt	David Walter Edward	SWIFT	17.03.1945.
Sgt	John	SYMONDS	17.03.1945.
F/Sgt	Geoffrey Leonard Vyvyan	TABOR	21.02.1945.
F/Sgt	Douglas Richard Gordon	TASKIS	03.12.1943.
Sgt	Arthur	TAYLOR	23.05.1944.
Sgt	John Edward	TAYLOR	17.03.1945.
Sgt	Patrick Joseph	TAYLOR	27.08.1944.
Sgt	Frank	THACKERAY	27.08.1944.
Sgt	Alan	THOMPSON	29.01.1944.
Sgt	George Thomas	THORLEY	07.03.1945.
F/Sgt	Derrick Gordon Cobley	THORPE	25.05.1944.
Sgt	James	TORODE	11.04.1944.
Sgt	Arthur Henry	TREADWELL	05.07.1944.
W/OII	Alfred Arthur Joseph	TREMBLAY	25.05.1944.
Sgt	Victor Frederick Thomas	TRUMPER	29.07.1944.
Sgt	Ronald Harold	TWIN	06.03.1945.
F/Sgt	Alfred Edmund	UNWIN	14.01.1944.
F/Sgt	Henry William	VINE	21 02.1945.
F/O	Francis Peter	WALKER	25.09.1944.
Sgt	Walter	WALKER	16.03.1945.
Sgt	Harold Edward	WARD	14.02.1945.
P/O	Gordon	WARREN	28.12.1944.
Sgt	Leonard George	WASHER	31.03.1944.
F/O	Frederick Herbert	WATTS	18.08.1944.
Sgt	Ernest William	WEBB	14.02.1945.
F/Sgt	Richard	WEEKES	29.07.1944.
Sgt	George	WEST	27.01.1944.
F/Sgt	Malcolm George	WESTERN	16.12.1943.
P/O	Roy	WHALLEY	04.05.1944.
Sgt	David	WHITE	25.05.1944.
F/Sgt	Brian Price	WICKS	16.12.1943.
F/O	Kenneth Hubert Dearden	WILDE	06.01.1944.
Sgt	Joseph	WILKINSON	12.09.1944.
Sgt	Kevin Joseph	WILLETT	11.04.1944.
Sgt	George William	WILSON	13.05.1944.
Sgt	Donald Frederick	WOOD	16.03.1945.
Sgt	Frederick John	WRIGHT	06.01.1944.
Sgt	Arthur George	WRIGHT	16.05.1944.
F/O	Roland Robert John	YOUNG	14.02.1945.

576 Squadron

MOTTO **Carpe Diem** (Sieze the day) Code **UL**

Stations

ELSHAM WOLDS	25.11.43. to 31.10.44.
FISKERTON	31.10.44. to 13.09.45

Commanding Officers

WING COMMANDER G T B CLAYTON	25.11.43. to 23.06.44.
WING COMMANDER B D SELLICK	23.06.44. to 28.02.45.
WING COMMANDER F R MCALLISTER	01.03.45. to 06.45.

Aircraft

LANCASTER 25.11.42. to 13.09.45

Operational Record

OPERATIONS	SORTIES	AIRCRAFT LOSSES	% LOSSES
197	2788	66	2.4

CATEGORY OF OPERATIONS

BOMBING	MINING
189	8

A further 9 Lancasters were destroyed in crashes.

Aircraft Histories

R5853	From 1660 Conversion Unit. To 1 Lancaster Finishing School.
W4123 UL-R^2	From 83 Squadron via Navigation Training Unit. FTR Berlin 2/3.12.43.
W4245 UL-S^2	From 156 Squadron via Navigation Training Unit. FTR Berlin 30/31.1.44.
DV333 UL-K^2	From 103 Squadron. FTR Stettin 5/6.1.44.
DV342 UL-G^2	From 103 Squadron. FTR Berlin 16/17.12.43.
DV365 UL-Z^2	From 166 Squadron. FTR Duisburg 21/22.5.44.
DV386 UL-E^2	From 166 Squadron. FTR Leipzig 19/20.2.44.
ED562	From 100 Squadron. To 550 Squadron.
ED713 UL-W^2	From 103 Squadron. FTR Berlin 23/24.12.43.
ED767 UL-T^2	From 103 Squadron. To 1651 Conversion Unit.
ED888 UL-V^2	From 103 Squadron. Returned to 103 Squadron. Completed 135 operations, eleven to Berlin.
ED913 UL-U^2	From 103 Squadron. FTR Berlin 23/24.12.43.
ED994	From 57 Squadron. To 467 Squadron RAAF.
JA715 UL-W^2	From 97 (Straits Settlements) Squadron. To 101 Squadron.
JA857	From 635 Squadron. To 103 Squadron.
JA868 UL-J^2	From 103 Squadron. To 1656 Conversion Unit.
JA957 UL-X^2	From 103 Squadron. To 9 Squadron.
JA968 UL-Y^2	From 7 Squadron. FTR Montdidier 4.5.44.
JB410 UL-H^2	From 405 (Vancouver) Squadron RCAF.
JB460 UL-V^2	From 103 Squadron. FTR Flers 24/25.6.44.
JB555 UL-R^2	From 103 Squadron. To 1668 Conversion Unit.
JB744 UL-K^2	From 103 Squadron. Returned to 103 Squadron.
HK759 UL-G^2	
LL748 UL-A^2	To 550 Squadron.
LL794 UL-D^2	To 1651 Conversion Unit.
LL796 UL-T^2	To 550 Squadron.
LL799 UL-N^2	FTR Stuttgart 27/28.7.44.
LL800 UL-S^2	To 550 Squadron.
LL830 UL-R^2	FTR Aulnoye 10/11.4.44.
LL838 UL-K^2	To 550 Squadron.
LL905 UL-H^2	FTR Stuttgart 28/29.7.44.
LM120 UL-T^2	To 405 (Vancouver) Squadron RCAF.
LM122 UL-X^2	FTR Düsseldorf 2/3.11.44.
LM133 UL-H^2	FTR Stettin 16/17.8.44.
LM227 UL-I	Completed more than one hundred operations.
LM294 UL-G^2	
LM332 UL-Z^2	From 103 Squadron. Collided with JB670 (103 Squadron) over Lincolnshire when bound for Berlin 16/17.12.43.
LM381 UL-E^2	From 103 Squadron. FTR Braunschweig (Brunswick) 14/15.1.44.
LM438 UL-C^2	To 3 Lancaster Finishing School.
LM439 UL-T2	FTR Aachen 24/25.5.44.
LM469 UL-J^2	FTR Berlin 24/25.3.44.
LM470 UL-U^2	FTR Nuremberg 30/31.3.44.

LM471 UL-J^2	FTR Berlin 24/25.3.44.
LM492 UL-J	
LM527 UL-U^2	Damaged during take-off and abandoned to crash at sea 30.4.44.
LM532 UL-A^2	FTR Orleans 4.7.44.
LM594 UL-A	Completed more than one hundred operations.
LM651 UL-Z^2	
LM679	
ME317 UL-C^2	FTR Nuremberg 16/17.3.45.
ME492 UL-J^2	
ME583 UL-F^2	To 550 Squadron.
ME585 UL-H^2	FTR Braunschweig 14/15.1.44.
ME586 UL-B^2	FTR Mailly-le-Camp 3/4.5.44.
ME593 UL-T^2	FTR Berlin 27/28.1.44.
ME671 UL-V^2	From 300 (Masovian) Squadron. FTR Lützkendorf 4/5.4.45.
ME687 UL-S^2	From 550 Squadron. FTR Dortmund 22/23.5.44.
ME703 UL-N^2/S^2	Damaged beyond repair during operation to Mailly-le-Camp 3/4.5.44.
ME726 UL-X^2	FTR from a mining sortie 15/16.5.44.
ME735 UL-B^2/P^2	FTR Duisburg 21/22.2.45.
ME792 UL-Q^2	FTR from a mining sortie 26/27.8.44.
ME800 UL-W^2	FTR Stettin 29/30.8.44.
ME801 UL-W^2	Completed more than one hundred operations.
ME810 UL-K^2	FTR Sterkrade-Holten 16/17.6.44.
ME811 UL-S^2	FTR Vire 6/7.6.44.
ME854 UL-D^2	FTR Frankfurt 12/13.9.44.
ME862 UL-J^2	From 625 Squadron.
ND362 UL-Q^2	To 103 Squadron.
ND385 UL-N^2/W^2	To 170 Squadron.
ND386 UL-P^2	FTR Berlin 28/29.1.44.
ND402 UL-R^2	To 103 Squadron.
ND403 UL-G^2	From 550 Squadron. Damaged beyond repair 12.5.44.
ND405	From 550 Squadron.
ND416 UL-G^2	FTR Stettin 5/6.1.44.
ND521 UL-L^2	From 460 Squadron RAAF.
ND783 UL-C^2	FTR Aubigne-Racan 6/7.5.44.
ND859 UL-L^2	FTR Revigny 12/13.7.44.
ND903 UL-R^2	To 103 Squadron.
ND994 UL-F^2	FTR Revigny 14/15.7.44.
NE115 UL-B^2	FTR Düsseldorf 1/2.11.44.
NE171 UL-Y^2	FTR Aachen 24/25.5.44.
NF975 UL-J^2	FTR Dortmund 20/21.2.45.
NF976 UL-Q^2	
NG119 UL-D^2	FTR Wiesbaden 2/3.2.45.
NG183	To 166 Squadron.
NG273 UL-I^2/Y^2	From 150 Squadron.
NG464 UL-O^2	FTR Duisburg 22.2.45.
NN711 UL-L^2	FTR Neuss 23/24.9.44.

NN749 UL-G^2
NN750 UL-M^2 Crashed at Manston on return from Bonn 27/28.12.44.
NN806 UL-M   Crashed on take-off from Fiskerton during Operation Manna 8.5.45.
NX562 UL-F
NX563   To 153 Squadron.
NX576 UL-K
PA173 UL-Q^2 FTR Munich 7/8.1.45.
PA175 UL-K^2 From 625 Squadron.
PA176 UL-H^2 From 625 Squadron.
PA265 UL-O^2/V^2 FTR Nuremberg 16/17.3.45.
PA282 UL-C
PA307 UL-W
PA318 UL-E
PA997 UL-D^2 From 103 Squadron. FTR Sterkrade 16/17.6.44.
PB128 UL-S^2 FTR Stuttgart 28/29.7.44.
PB253 UL-A^2 FTR Stuttgart 28/29.7.44.
PB265 UL-W^2 FTR Stuttgart 24/25.7.44.
PB400 UL-J^2 FTR Kiel 26/27.8.44.
PB472   To 153 Squadron.
PB574 UL-A^2 From 625 Squadron.
PB635 UL-C^2 To 166 Squadron.
PB753 UL-X   From 170 Squadron.
PB785 UL-L^2 FTR Nuremberg 16/17.3.45.
PD232 UL-F^2 FTR Dresden 13/14.2.45.
PD235 UL-N^2 FTR Calais 24.9.44.
PD271 UL-T
PD309 UL-W^2 FTR Zeitz 16/17.2.45.
PD312 UL-R^2 FTR Wiesbaden 2/3.2.45.
PD363 UL-K^2 FTR Dessau 7/8.3.45.
PD376 UL-C^2 From 625 Squadron.
PD403 UL-F^2 FTR Chemnitz 5/6.3.45.
RA514 UL-R^2
RA516 UL-Q^2 FTR Duisburg 21/22.2.45.
RA562 UL-B
RA563 UL-Q^2
RA587
RA594 UL-V
RE127 UL-L
RF120 UL-D^2 FTR Dessau 7/8.3.45.
RF197 UL-F^2 From 630 Squadron.
RF200 UL-D
RF213 UL-B^2 From 625 Squadron.
SW270 UL-K
SW276 UL-G^2/G   From 170 Squadron

www.ingramcontent.com/pod-product-compliance
Lightning Source LLC
Chambersburg PA
CBHW081841230426
43669CB00018B/2775